THE
STRUGGLE
^AND ^THE PROMISE

Praise for *The Struggle and The Promise*

'Shri Naushad Forbes is a visionary leader of Indian industry who has produced a thought-provoking book that gives meaning and content to his deep belief in India's promise and potential for great achievement.

He rightly believes that meaningful solutions to India's economic problems can be found in the framework of a rapidly expanding economy, and, in this context, he lays emphasis on the achievement of a growth rate of 9-10 per cent of GDP year on year on a long-term basis.

He also lays emphasis on the need for creation of jobs for a more inclusive growth process and on more quality jobs, where productivity growth can be robust, where both employee and employer have an incentive to invest in skills and training. Of equal importance is the pursuit of sound educational policies, a viable national agenda for research and labour reforms.

Shri Naushad Forbes also stresses on the great importance of industrial development, more ethical and better corporate citizens, more innovative and internationally competitive economy. These and many other ideas add to the richness of the book as a guide to the formulation of public policies.'
—Dr Manmohan Singh, former Prime Minister of India

'Naushad Forbes is a successful businessman, an accomplished engineer and an insightful writer. *The Struggle and the Promise* is a distillation of his decades of experience. Through both research and personal reflection, he shares what government, industry and institutions can do to accelerate India's development. Like Naushad Forbes, I too believe that India can do more to fulfil its immense potential. He spells out how India can fulfil its promise and contribute to a peaceful and prosperous Asia. This thought-provoking book is a valuable addition to the literature on understanding India's economic past, present and future.'
—Goh Chok Tong, former Prime Minister of Singapore

'Naushad Forbes is an unusual combination of an academic and a businessman. In *The Struggle and the Promise*, he offers a rich discussion of what ails India and what it must do to achieve its promise, informed both by his extensive learning as well as his ringside experiences as president of one of India's foremost business associations. This refreshingly frank analysis should be read by all those who care about where India is heading.'

—Dr Raghuram G. Rajan, former Governor, Reserve Bank of India

'Among Indian entrepreneurs, Naushad Forbes has had the most rigorous intellectual training. Among Indian intellectuals, he is unique in his experience of running a successful high-tech company. In this deeply researched and compellingly relevant book, Forbes brings both his scholarship and his practical experience to bear on understanding how India got to where it is. Ranging widely over economics, design, institutions and culture, *The Struggle and the Promise* provides sharp insights into the challenges we face as well as wise suggestions on how we can overcome them. Regardless of profession or political affiliation, every Indian who cares for our country would benefit from reading this book.'

—Ramachandra Guha, author of *India After Gandhi: The History of the World's Largest Democracy*

'This book is an absolute must-read for the importance of its message, its considered analysis and (not least) reader enjoyment. Naushad Forbes has used his lightly worn scholarship, clarity of thought and real-world experiences as a forward-looking business leader to make a passionate case for his agenda for action. This refreshingly easy read, leavened by a steady flow of witty asides, is particularly important for what Forbes has to say on why and how India must fundamentally change its approach to technological development, scientific research and industrial design. It is hard to praise this book too highly.'

—T.N. Ninan, former chairman, *Business Standard*

'*The Struggle and the Promise* by Dr Naushad Forbes ties together the cultural and economic outlook of India. It will serve as a good guide for students, economists and anyone interested in the future of Indian industry and ways to navigate it.'
—**Ratan N. Tata, chairman emeritus, Tata Sons**

'Naushad Forbes provides a clear-eyed narrative of our nation's standing in the current global economic pecking order based on an innovation-led growth trajectory. He argues convincingly for the need to leverage our nation's diverse culture, the energy of our young and aspirational population, and the spirit of our diverse and entrepreneurial private sector to pursue global leadership in a post-Covid world. His prescription for large-scale investments in innovation, education and research is key for India to strategically evolve a global brand position as a "value adding" partner rather than just a "low cost" vendor. This book will appeal to a wide variety of readers spanning industry leaders, policymakers, academicians and the layperson interested in India's future role in a world transitioning to a new normal.'
—**Kiran Mazumder-Shaw, chairperson, Biocon**

'A leading industrialist of India, Naushad Forbes reads widely, thinks deeply and writes brilliantly. In *The Struggle and the Promise*, he draws on this unusual mix of strengths to paint a memorable portrait of what India has been in the last seventy years, what it can be in the coming decades and how it can get there.'
—**Arvind Panagariya, former vice chairman, NITI Aayog**

'At a time when pessimism seems ever-more tempting, *The Struggle and the Promise* makes a strongly articulated and thoughtful case for India's future. In this data-rich and incisively argued book, Naushad Forbes uses his decades of experience to set out a clear analysis of India's problems and offers concise ideas for overcoming these challenges. His is a proposition worth listening to.'
—**Dr Shashi Tharoor, Member of Parliament, Lok Sabha**

THE
STRUGGLE
AND PROMISE
THE

Restoring India's
Potential

NAUSHAD FORBES

HARPER
BUSINESS

An Imprint of HarperCollins *Publishers*

First published in India by Harper Business
An imprint of HarperCollins *Publishers* 2022
4th Floor, Tower A, Building No. 10, Phase II, DLF Cyber City,
Gurugram, Haryana – 122002
www.harpercollins.co.in

2 4 6 8 10 9 7 5 3 1

Text copyright © Naushad Forbes 2022

P-ISBN: 978-93-5489-395-7
E-ISBN: 978-93-5489-396-4

Cover design: HarperCollins *Publishers* India
Author photo: Courtesy of CII

Typeset in 11.5/15.4 Baskerville
Manipal Technologies Limited, Manipal

Printed and bound at
Thomson Press (India) Ltd

❋ⓘⓞ◯ HarperCollinsIn

For my family,
Darius, Maharookh, Farhad and Rati,
and especially Riah, Darius and Aaron, who are only promise

Contents

Just Rambling

Prologue
The Struggle and the Promise

India lives in all centuries at once.

—Manmohan Singh

'Do you know Sir Roderick Glossop?'
'Only to the extent of having sat next to him at a public dinner not long ago.'
'A talented man, I believe.'
'So he told me. He spoke very highly of himself.'

—*Uncle Fred in the Springtime*, P.G. Wodehouse

What is India's future?

I deeply believe in India's promise, in our potential for great achievement. I am also old enough to appreciate our ability to snatch failure from the jaws of success. We long followed policies—particularly in the 1970s—that kept India poor. From 1991 onwards, reforms opened India to the world, reduced controls and unleashed entrepreneurship. The dominance of one political party waned. As politics fragmented, space was created for institutions to become more independent and strengthen. From 1991 to 2017, every year saw India in better shape than the previous one. There were bumps along the way, but there was consistent improvement. The return to a politics with one dominant party was accompanied by increased bureaucratic control, protectionism and more state intrusiveness. Stronger political control also affected the independence of institutions.

As I write this prologue, Covid-19 prompts particularly sharp doubt about India's future. The second wave of infection was so sweeping, and its impact so graphic, that it deeply affected both the reality and perception of life in India. This was a once-in-a-century event; it was epochal. Domestic and international press coverage was damning, the worst in my memory, but it merely sensationalised the grim reality. This recent experience led to a mix of emotions— sadness at loss of life, anger at incompetent leadership and the gusto with which people embraced unsafe practices, frustration at how unnecessary all this was. What is the future of a country which struggled to provide enough oxygen to keep the severely ill alive? Which disregarded Covid-19 protocols in organising massive election rallies and religious gatherings in the same month that saw dramatic increases in infection? Where the government seemed more concerned about managing the optics than the dismal reality?

How do we square this experience with India's long-term future?

I continue to believe in India's great potential, but we will struggle to fulfil it. Clearly much must change to deliver on our promise.

A diverse culture, a young and aspirational population, and a varied and entrepreneurial private sector are the foundation of our promise. Equally, India's future does not and cannot rest on a suddenly wise and competent state: low state capacity is so obviously in evidence in our miserable public health response to the Covid-19 pandemic. This means the role of the government will be essential but limited, and must be focused on only a few things, public health among them. When the government does less, citizens and firms must do more. How can this, done right, become a strategy for leadership? How can we fix things by learning from best practice elsewhere? How can we ensure openness, inclusivity and innovation? What is the right balance of industry, institutions and policy? How can our culture deliver leadership?

This book is my answer to these questions. As we will see, by being open to the world; by investing in innovation, education and research; by building independent institutions step by step that set the rules under which we all operate; by policies that unleash the enterprise that fixes the problems; and by constantly acting in consonance with our culture.

By doing all this, we can deliver leadership.

But why leadership? This book is about India's promise. To achieve it, we must set our sights high, high enough for India to provide leadership far beyond our borders. If we aspire to lead the world, as I think we can and must, that means we must be judged by a higher standard than anyone else. We cannot accept excuses—of our past, of poor leadership, of democracy, of complexity, of size. There is much we must change as we struggle to lead. And to change, we must first learn.

I have thought about these issues all my life. I bring to these pages a hybrid background—as an industrialist, an academic interested in innovation policy, a past president of the Confederation of Indian Industry, and someone who enjoys participating in public debate in our newspapers. These pages also reflect my special ('warped' is the word my friends use) sense of humour. I do not like to take anything too seriously, myself included. I include several cartoons by the great R.K. Laxman, who so perfectly captured the essence of the India we lived in in the 1970s—and, in many respects, still live in.

I have been fortunate to be inspired by conversations, courses and books from some great teachers. You will find many of them in these pages—the historians David Landes, Gordon Wright and Ramachandra Guha, the sociologists Alex Inkeles and Ronald Dore, the engineers Jim Adams, Malcolm McWhorter and Stephen Kline, the political scientists Devesh Kapur and Pratap Bhanu Mehta, and the university leaders Gerhard Casper and Pankaj Chandra. Many economists have framed my world view: Abhijit Banerjee, Albert Hirschman, Anne Krueger, Arvind Panagariya, Arvind Subramanian, Ashok Desai, Dave Wield, Gary Becker, Harry Rowen, Keith Pavitt, Ken Arrow, Moe Abramovitz, Nate Rosenberg, T.N. Ninan, Raghuram G. Rajan, Rakesh Mohan, Richard Nelson and T.N. Srinivasan.

My experience with the Confederation of Indian Industry is also something I constantly draw on. I have many wonderful friends in the secretariat and membership; my many references to Tarun Das and Chandrajit Banerjee stand for them all. Many industrialists have set paths of ethical, innovative and public-spirited business that are models for the rest of us. They are represented by Darius, Farhad and Rati Forbes; Jamshyd, Adi and Nadir Godrej; Kiran Mazumdar-Shaw; Kris Gopalakrishnan and Nandan Nilekani; Meher Pudumjee; Rahul, Rajiv and Sanjiv Bajaj; and Ratan Tata.

This book has benefited greatly from the expert assistance of Madhurjya Deka at the Centre for Technology Innovation and Economic Research in Pune, and Tanya Gill and Chhaya Gogate at Forbes Marshall. The comments from many on drafts of this book are greatly appreciated—Ramachandra Guha, Riah Forbes, Dave Wield, Abhay Puri and Ashok Desai in particular provided a mix of broader and detailed comments that greatly sharpened and improved what I was trying to say. They will recognise some of their words in revised sentences. My friends Bharat Puri, Denzil de Souza, Mehul Vaidya, Raj Dugar, Salman Noorani, Satyadeo Purohit and Virendra Gill provided constant encouragement, as did Sachin Sharma, my publisher at HarperCollins. All books reflect the preferences of their

authors; in this book, I wear my values on my sleeve. My family—
Darius, Maharookh, Farhad, Rati, Riah, Darius J. and Aaron—have
been and are the source of my values. They are my moral compass.
This book is the result.

Pune, 4 December 2021
Naushad Forbes

1

Can India Really Aspire to Lead?

Charlie Brown: 'There are a lot of smart people in the world.'
Snoopy: 'Yes, but most of them are asymptomatic.'

The world's largest event devoted to family business is the annual Family Business Summit. The 2019 summit took place in Udaipur, hosted jointly by Family Business Network International (FBN) and the Confederation of Indian Industry (CII). All feedback says it was the best one yet, combining wonderful sessions full of content with the outstanding organisation of CII and the spectacular backdrop of Udaipur. This is not merely an advertisement for Udaipur, FBN and CII. Great opportunity lies in India's soft power, but we need hard action to realise it.

The closing dinner was held on the shores of Lake Pichola, looking across at a magnificently lit City Palace. There is an FBN tradition that the closing dinner requires national dress or ethnic wear. Two-thirds

1

of the participants were from overseas. Without exception, they all chose Indian attire. Earlier that evening, CII–FBN arranged an hour of Bollywood dance classes. Looking at hundreds of people from forty countries dressed in sherwanis or salwar-kameez or saris, dancing to Bollywood songs, with the lake and the City Palace as a backdrop, my niece and I agreed that this was India at its most beautiful. Indian clothes have a variety of design, fabric, pattern, texture and colour that cannot be matched. This is cultural diversity on display. Bollywood songs illustrate Indian culture at its most inclusive. The instruments, rhythm and tunes draw in the best of every culture and produce something uniquely Indian.

Three days later, the FBN WhatsApp group was still live with pictures of Austrians in kurtas saying they would wear only this from now on. An FBN member from Japan, along with her daughter, visited us in Pune after the summit. They too said this was the best summit ever. On their first visit to India, they were travelling around, enjoying their trip greatly. But, talking to them, we were also clear how much we must fix. Over fifty countries have an e-visa arrangement with India, where one applies for the visa at least three days ahead of arrival. Japan was the first country in the world to have a visa-on-arrival facility with India.[1] Japan is meant to be special. The mother arrived with a pre-issued visa on a separate flight and took around an hour to get through immigration in Mumbai. Not great, but on par with a typical immigration experience at Heathrow or most American airports. The daughter, arriving separately, wished to take advantage of the visa-on-arrival facility. She ended up taking four hours to go through immigration. Why? Because no one knew how to handle her—she was pointed at several wrong lines before she got through. So a special dispensation, formulated in Delhi with

---

1   There are now a total of eleven countries with visa on arrival into India, including Singapore, New Zealand and Finland.

the best of intentions, gets implemented in so shabby a way at our second-largest airport.

That story illustrates our promise and our struggle as we try to lead. So does the second wave of Covid that showed the Indian state struggling to provide oxygen, fumbling with the vaccination programme, and largely missing in action as states and cities grappled with the crisis as best they could. Meanwhile, a fragmented but widespread volunteer effort saw private companies financing oxygen plants and ventilators for public and private hospitals, coordinating with the Air Force for special planes to fly them in, and civic groups launching ambulance services. This combination of simultaneous struggle and promise is so often evident in India. How do we unleash the promise and minimise the struggle?

Our promise comes from our culture—things that only we have and that others cannot match. Our struggle comes from how policy is implemented. As we will see in this book, we must get the balance right between industry, institutions and policy in anything we do, whether small (getting a Japanese visitor through Mumbai immigration efficiently) or big (building a world-leading Indian industry). When we don't get the balance right, we struggle. When we do, we can lead.

But why should anyone lead the world?

Our Covid times tell us why. Global crises need international coordination. As Covid-19 spread around the world in 2020, the lack of leadership and coordination meant that each country devised its own rules without regard to others. Countries hoarded masks, personal protective equipment kits and life-saving drugs. There was no coordination on any matter, whether economic assistance or norms for travel and transit. Multilateral institutions such as the World Health Organization, the World Trade Organization and the International Air Transport Association get their heft from enough big countries following their lead. With the world's largest economy unwilling to subscribe to multilateral norms in 2020, why should anyone else? The vaccine nationalism of 2021 is, equally, a plea for leadership, coordination and a sense of shared human destiny. The same applies to climate change. There is no point in one country becoming carbon neutral if its neighbours pollute like mad. One country of adequate power or a group of countries, which between them have adequate power, can make all the difference. We can at least aspire to be part of a like-minded group—countries like Germany, Japan, South Korea, Australia, Canada, Indonesia and Singapore—all subscribing to international rules and giving multilateral institutions their credibility. And perhaps, over time, India could aspire to lead more on its own.

Why us?

Leadership comes in three spheres: economy, institutions and culture. Let's start with the first. India has been one of the world's ten best performing economies in the last thirty years. Until recently, almost every projection said we would be one of the world's ten best performing economies in the next thirty years. A falling growth rate since 2018, dramatically depressed by Covid, has called this destiny into question and means we can no longer take high growth for granted. Our immediate task, then, is to restore long-term growth to its thirty-year trajectory of 6 to 7 per cent.

That said, by simple dint of population, we are one of the world's top economies, by current estimates fifth (after the US,[2] China, Japan and Germany) in terms of aggregate gross domestic product (GDP) at current prices. Regardless of how well it performs, a country like Singapore or Norway can never aspire for world-leadership.

---

2   I use US or USA for the United State of America.

Table 1.1: Top Twenty Countries by Population and Absolute GDP (nominal and purchasing power parity [PPP]), with Corresponding GDP Per Capita (2019)[3]

Top 20 countries by population, 2019			Top 20 countries by GDP (nominal), 2019				Top 20 countries by GDP (PPP), 2019			
Rank	Country	Population (million)	Rank	Country	GDP US$ billion	GDP per capita (US$)	Rank	Country	GDP US$ billion PPP	GDP per capita PPP (US$)
1	China	1,398	1	USA	21,374	65,118	1	China	23,460	16,785
2	India	1,366	2	China	14,343	10,262	2	USA	21,374	65,118
3	USA	328	3	Japan	5,082	40,247	3	India	9,612	7,034
4	Indonesia	271	4	Germany	3,846	46,259	4	Japan	5,459	43,236
5	Pakistan	217	5	India	2,875	2,104	5	Germany	4,660	56,052
6	Brazil	211	6	UK	2,827	42,300	6	Russia	4,282	29,181
7	Nigeria	201	7	France	2,716	40,494	7	Indonesia	3,329	12,302
8	Bangladesh	163	8	Italy	2,001	33,190	8	France	3,315	49,435
9	Russia	144	9	Brazil	1,840	8,717	9	UK	3,255	48,710
10	Mexico	128	10	Canada	1,736	46,195	10	Brazil	3,220	15,259
11	Japan	126	11	Russia	1,700	11,585	11	Italy	2,665	44,197
12	Ethiopia	112	12	South Korea	1,642	31,762	12	Mexico	2,604	20,411
13	Philippines	108	13	Spain	1,394	29,614	13	Turkey	2,326	27,875
14	Egypt	100	14	Australia	1,393	54,907	14	South Korea	2,225	43,029
15	Vietnam	96	15	Mexico	1,258	9,863	15	Spain	1,987	42,214
16	Congo	87	16	Indonesia	1,119	4,136	16	Canada	1,930	51,342
17	Turkey	83	17	Netherlands	909	52,448	17	Saudi Arabia	1,676	48,908
18	Germany	83	18	Saudi Arabia	793	23,140	18	Australia	1,352	53,320
19	Iran	83	19	Turkey	754	9,042	19	Thailand	1,339	19,228
20	Thailand	70	20	Switzerland	703	81,994	20	Poland	1,299	34,218

Source: World Development Indicators (2019), indicators available at: https://databank.worldbank.org/source/world-development-indicators

---

3   While 2020 data is available, it was such an unusual year that it is best to use 2019 data.

But can we lead the world? We have serious competition. Britain led the world as the first industrial nation from the mid-eighteenth to the late nineteenth century. The US then took its place, a position it held through the twentieth century. As the US steps back from global leadership, we know that China aspires to take its place. Starting at much the same level as India in 1980, the Chinese economy is today five times the size of the Indian economy (and the US economy is eight times our size).[4]

I believe we are better placed for this leadership role in India. We are a noisy democracy—you just need to watch the nightly entertainment shows that we pass off as The News for confirmation. (TV's Arnab Goswami once asked Finance Minister Arun Jaitley what advice he had to improve his show. He replied, 'I'd suggest that no more than two people speak at once.') But, harnessed well and wisely, our democratic traditions can be an unalloyed strength for us and our country. When President Xi Jinping made a claim for global leadership at his speech in Davos in 2017, much was made of the fact that he quoted Charles Dickens and Abraham Lincoln. This would not be remarkable in India. Along with Ambedkar, Gandhi and Tagore, Dickens and Lincoln are also a part of our heritage. Every time I watch a new Bollywood song, I am struck by how inclusive our culture is. We take the best that the world has to offer and seamlessly integrate it all into something that is distinctly Indian. Our ability to make sense of various strands, to integrate and include, to thrive on diversity of ethnicity, community and language—this is what makes us unique.[5] We Indians come in all shapes, sizes and colours—and we are all Indian.

On almost any CII mission to the US, we hear an India–China comparison.[6] There is a typical complaint about India—contradictory

---

4   This is not an economics book, but a note on GDP is important. Unless otherwise specified, I use nominal GDP (that is, at current prices and exchange rates). Purchasing power parity has merit but some comparisons can be misleading.

5   I like to describe myself as a Parsi from Pune, who struggles to speak Hindi, eats beef and reads P.G. Wodehouse.

6   As the US attempts to reset its own relationship with China, I think we will hear this less on post-Covid visits.

policies being pursued by the Union government and states (Delhi plans the National Population Register, some states say they won't implement it), or a newly formed government threatens reversal of a previous policy (Amaravati, the bullet train), or outlandish or shameful words and phrases used by politicians ('termites', 'chowkidar chor hai', 'pappu', 'tukde tukde gang'). The contrast is always China—where no one contradicts anyone, the provinces (at least officially) toe Beijing's line, and policy is consistent to the point of boredom. My response is that the US should not expect India to be like China, but expect it to be like, well, the US. The administration in Washington took the US out of the Paris Accord on Climate Change in 2016 and California passed a resolution saying it would pursue it. It withdrew from the Iran nuclear deal and other supposedly binding agreements. And the forty-fifth US President was surely a world champion of political invective!

The point is that China is an authoritarian state; debate ends when the boss says so, and action follows his words. India and the US are cacophonous democracies. We do not work in a coordinated, planned manner, following the dictates of any one leader, however strong, however popular. The protests against the Citizenship Amendment Act of early 2020 must be seen in this light. So fundamental a change requires widespread support across the population, and not only a parliamentary majority.

So, how do noisy democracies progress? By checks and balances from autonomous and independent institutions such as universities, election commissions, courts, a free media, an effective opposition—and, in both India and the US, a federal structure where power is shared with the states. Instead of a strong leader determining what's right, independent institutions frame the rules. And these rules are built on a foundation of distinctive and balanced values. Our leaders must be able to listen, tolerate, include, compromise and balance as much (or even more) as they are strong, decisive, visionary and courageous. Leaders who wish to leave a permanent positive legacy on vibrant democracies must set aside things that divide and make people fearful, and focus on things that unify and inspire. So, while economic leadership is essential, it is not sufficient. We need those independent institutions that balance incentives with protection, economic freedom with social responsibility. And underlying it all are cultural attributes of openness, generosity and tolerance. When democracies progress, they do so because millions of animal spirits are liberated, and not just the spirit of one state animal. The process may be messier and less efficient than in an authoritarian state, but it is much more powerful as well as more enduring.

It is this power that provides our potential. But what must we *change* to lead the world? The chapters in this book explore this question. Some chapters are grounded in empirical research and observation. Some are more in the nature of personal reflections.

Between them, I hope to first make the case that we have an opportunity, indeed the *unique* opportunity, of leading the world. And second, that we have much to do to achieve this aspiration—in economic policy, in the role of industry, in building and nurturing great institutions, all this acting in consonance with our unique culture. And, especially, in getting the role of the state right. There are essential things the state must do—in public health, say, as the second Covid wave so loudly and graphically shouts. But there are many other areas where the state must retreat, enabling instead of trying to do itself.

Some underlying principles provide the foundation for leadership.

An economy that leads the world has to be inclusive—a larger share of the population has to become prosperous than in its peers. Economic historians who have studied Britain and the US over the last three centuries differ on why each country moved ahead when it did. However, they agree that Britain in the eighteenth century was a more equal place than the much more aristocratic, even feudal, societies across the channel, and that the benefits of growth and progress flowed down through society in however imperfect a manner.[7] The same for

---

7   Eighteenth-century Britain was *not* an equal place. Privilege determined opportunity to a great extent. The difference I am talking of here is relative

the US from the nineteenth century onwards, which gave the world its first definition of a good life for all; indeed, American society perceived itself as being predominantly middle class. India must similarly be inclusive in progress. This means a focus on enhancing skills and education, both by industry and government, at a much greater pace than at present. As firms, we need to have in place strong affirmative action policies. Recruiting from a country of 1.4 billion skilled and educated people will make our firms champions. Selling to a country of 1.4 billion consumers will create wealth for all of Indian industry and for the world.

Whoever has led the world in history has tended to be open. Open— to trade. Openness to trade shows in high levels of exports *and* high levels of imports. Britain emerged as the world's first industrial power, accounting for a colossal share of world-manufactured output and trade. In 1870, Britain accounted for one-half of the world's output of coal and pig iron, one-third of its total manufacturing output, a quarter of its steam power, two-thirds of its cotton production, and over half of all imports into, for example, Brazil.[8]

Open also to immigration, as the world's talent seeks to make the country its home. Britain in the nineteenth century saw many continental entrepreneurs and technicians make their home there as immigrants. The US, until Donald Trump, defined itself as a nation of immigrants. Silicon Valley, it is said, rose to technological dominance through the IC—integrated circuits, for you Luddites out there—but, many say, IC should stand for Indians and Chinese.

---

to continental Europe, it is one of degree, and as the historian David Landes once said, degree is everything; see Landes—(i) *The Wealth and Poverty of Nations: Why Some Are So Rich and Some So Poor* (New York, NY: Norton, 1998); and (ii) *The Unbound Prometheus: Technological Change and Industrial Development in Western Europe from 1750 to the Present* (Cambridge: Cambridge University Press, second edition, 2003)—and T.S. Ashton, *The Industrial Revolution, 1760–1830* (Oxford: Oxford University Press, 1948).

8   Landes, *The Unbound Prometheus.*

These policies of openness went with cultural-leadership and a liberal intellect.[9] Britain's policy of free trade from the 1850s and the US' policy of free trade from the 1950s until Trump were advanced not just as economically superior but ethically superior—for all people. Both countries were willing to use force to achieve market access. Two examples that give the name to gunboat diplomacy: when Palmerston as Britain's Foreign Secretary had Canton shelled by gunboats in 1843, he did so because China had tried to close itself to imports (the imports they tried to block were of opium exported from India). A nice bonus to market access was the territory of Hong Kong, ceded to Britain in perpetuity.[10] When the Japanese tried to resist being opened to the world in 1852, Commodore Perry from the US Navy said he'd be back the next year to receive their answer on market access. Gunboat diplomacy of the day was justified not on the grounds of economic self-interest, but on the grounds of free trade being ethically superior and economically advantageous to *both* sides. Britain, in the eighteenth and nineteenth centuries, and the US in the twentieth century, were the key advocates of ideas of openness—to trade, to immigration, to technology.[11] They were also advocates of individual freedoms—of

9   I know this argument might grate for many, but leaders in Britain and the US at the time truly thought the world would be better off with the culture and ideas they were bringing to it. Some of them still do.

10   There is an impression that Britain had to hand Hong Kong back to China in 1997 because its ninety-nine-year lease expired then. That isn't true. The colony of Hong Kong consisted of three territories: Hong Kong Island, a bit of mainland directly across the bay called Kowloon, and a larger interior on the mainland called the New Territories. Hong Kong (in 1842, after the First Opium War) and Kowloon (in 1860, after the Second Opium War) were ceded to Britain by China in perpetuity. It was the New Territories that were leased for ninety-nine years in 1898. Such nuance was somewhat inconvenient for a strong leader like Margaret Thatcher to have to explain to the public, so she generally didn't, and simply said Britain had no choice as the lease for Hong Kong was running out.

11   One of my favourite facts in economic history is that Britain was a net importer of technology from the 1750s through to the 1850s—precisely the period when it most dominated the world economically. It was only after

speech, of the media, of public dissent (at least at home; the colonies were another matter). And they were generous—the Marshall Plan being a great example. These ideas of openness, generosity and immigration were never practised in a manner that was pure or undiluted. They were often compromised, but they were powerful, compelling and advocated enough to be part of the national ethos. And what was earlier a national culture became more and more an international culture.

All this went with each society becoming a magnet for the best and the brightest as immigrants sought to make it their new home. I recall a conversation at lunch just near the Stanford campus a few years ago between three leading economists (Ken Arrow, Moe Abramovitz and Harry Rowen), a leading sociologist (Alex Inkeles), a leading engineer (Jim Adams) and the editor of *Die Zeit* (Josef Joffe). The conversation turned to how American universities had achieved world-leadership since World War II, and Joe Joffe suggested that the man who should take greatest credit was Adolf Hitler. After the initial shock, each of the professors (four in their eighties at the time, three of whom were Jewish) started listing their older colleagues at Stanford, Harvard, Columbia and Princeton who had helped build the intellectual-leadership of these institutions. The number of leading scientists, social scientists, humanists and artists who were driven out of a hostile Europe and made homes in the US was striking—typically three to five of the top ten in the field, worldwide. My point is not the obvious one that we should seek to hang on to our intellectuals. It is that we should count on history throwing up enough tyrants as leaders of various countries, who will drive some of their most talented countrymen to seek homes elsewhere—and a country that seeks leadership should welcome all comers. Note that we have to welcome *all* comers, and not try to

1850 that Britain became a net exporter of technology, at the same time as relative industrial decline set in. Joel Mokyr, *The Lever of Riches: Technological Creativity and Economic Progress* (Oxford: Oxford University Press, 1992), 263–64.

pick the best and brightest. Today's unimpressive Russian or Iranian or Burmese or Turkish student might tomorrow create a Google or BioNTech or win a Nobel or write a best-seller.

Finally, a country that leads the world has to be driven by its private sector. It is not that government does not matter or doesn't have *a* key role to play, but it is the private sector that must play *the* key role in national development. My major concern with criticism of the Indian government, now and in the past, on what it is doing or not doing, is that this criticism misses the point. Economic historians have argued that the state needs to play a bigger role in development in countries that come later to development.[12] The state certainly played a bigger role in national development in Germany and Japan as they took off in the 1870s, than it did in Britain or the Netherlands (in the early 1800s). It played an even bigger role in the development of South Korea and Taiwan in the 1960s and 1970s, and, of course, China in the 1990s and 2000s. But in India, this book argues, a good government is not one which leads itself. It is one which enables the private sector to do the right things. India today requires policies to be framed such that independent institutions—and not the government—set the rules under which citizens and the private sector operate.

I can think of no other large country better placed than we are to provide the inclusion, openness, liberal resilience, and private sector primacy that would lead to global leadership. A country that leads the world must do so economically (in growth and wealth and inclusion), in institutions (independent balancing mechanisms that provide an edge) and morally (in ideas and social inclusiveness). Our diversity and tolerance, and our private-sector-led economy, can help us lead the world in a manner which is distinctly liberal and distinctly Indian at the same time. We are not there yet by any means, as this book makes

---

12 The case was made persuasively by the economic historian Alexander Gerschenkron, in 1951, in one of the great essays in economic history– 'Economic Backwardness in Historical Perspective', later reprinted in his book of the same title (Cambridge, MA: Belknap Press, 1962).

clear. But we have many attributes—culture, a diverse and vibrant private industry, distinguished private and public institutions, a large and committed non-government organisation (NGO) sector, inspiring norms of behaviour—that make for a unique foundation. A relatively small state is also a strength, provided it facilitates those same attributes to perform, while focusing its limited capacity on getting a few essential things broadly right.

This is India's promise.

Leading the World Economically

The Chinese sage Confucius is supposed to have said, 'May you live in interesting times'. Confucius meant this as a curse. We live in very interesting times. If Brexit and Trump (and his pal Kim Jong Un) did not divert us enough internationally,[13] we ensured we all remained awake at home by withdrawing 86 per cent of the currency in circulation overnight. And to truly capture the interest of every person on the planet, there's the health crisis. Covid-19 is unprecedented—in international spread (200+ countries), in economic impact (pushing most major economies into sharply negative annual growth) and in changing how the world lives (in April 2020, 60 per cent of the world's population was under some form of lockdown, a word most of us had never used before). In April-May 2021, India was the country hardest hit by Covid, setting new records for daily infections and deaths, while a hapless government appeared to have vanished from the scene at our time of greatest need. But we should not let our interesting times divert us from our fundamental long-term potential.

The Economist did a survey of the Indian economy in June 1991 in which it said 'nowhere in the world ... is the gap between what might have been achieved and what has been achieved as great as it is in India'. Thirty years later, so much has changed that today no

---

13 With Trump out, Brexit done, and vaccines flowing, we can only hope 2022 augurs a less interesting era.

one could make that same statement. We have become one of the world's ten best performing economies. So, in the midst of whatever monthly scandal our media demands the Nation Must Know, I think it is good to remind ourselves of an India that was uncaged in the years following 1991 and an India that had very much been moving in the right direction.

I say 'had', with deliberation, and sorrow. From 1991 to 2017, every year saw India in better shape than in the previous year, with prospects constantly improving. Yes, the road was occasionally bumpy, but the upward trajectory was solid. Every forecast used to also say that in the next thirty years we would continue to be one of the world's ten best performing economies. But as I write this book in 2020–21, our prospects no longer seem as sure. Some of this is temporary, a reflection of the severe hit that Covid has had on our health, our psyche and our economy. But some of it is more long-lasting. We already had a severely slowing economy before Covid hit in March 2020, with seven straight quarters of decline in GDP growth, from 8 per cent to 3 per cent. A government re-elected with an absolute majority seemed to be using its political and financial strength against the independence of institutions—the media, the courts, the Central Bureau of Investigation and the Election Commission of India (ECI). And politicians appeared to be fanning enthusiasm for what divides (religion, Kashmir, language) instead of what unifies (our economic prospects). While Covid came as a huge shock, it also brought an opportunity for a huge reset, one that could set us back on the more positive path of reform that we embarked on in 1991—if we choose to take it.

It is not as if we have seen no forward action under the current government. With the goods and services tax (GST) in place, the Insolvency and Bankruptcy Code progressively implemented, the Apprenticeship Act finally notified by the states, liberalisation of foreign investment in various sectors, and legislation reforming labour laws and agricultural markets, there are significant economic reforms to show. But much remains to be done in the immediate term.

Does the average Indian company find it easier to do business today than in 2014? No. Are Indian companies prepared to invest today (even before Covid), when they weren't in 2014? Again, no. Is GST needlessly complex and in crying need of simplification? Absolutely so. Instead of delivering on a promise of cooperative federalism, relations between the Union and the states have repeatedly hit new lows, voiding prospects for an effective implementation of the new labour and agricultural laws and delivering a politicised and fumbling response to the pandemic, paid for in thousands of lives. From our outward orientation, we have turned decisively protectionist, repeatedly raising tariffs, stymieing trade negotiations, and seeing a stronger rupee as somehow automatically good. These short-term issues need addressing and will determine our growth rate over the next half-decade.

There are also longer-term issues.

First, the GDP growth we need is not the 6–7 per cent we have been averaging since 1991, but 9–10 per cent, year on year, for decades. Only a few countries, mostly in East Asia, have bridged much of the gap with the rich world in one generation. They grew at 8–10 per cent annually for thirty to forty years. Our best growth episode was between 2003 and 2011 when we grew at 8 per cent. Achieving high rates of economic growth requires a proper understanding of where growth comes from—the combination of investment, human capital, productivity growth, trade and labour mobility that powers economic development.

Second, we must create jobs for a more inclusive growth process. The problem is not that we are not creating jobs. If we had not been creating jobs, there would have been incessant social strife, if not a revolution. The problem is job quality. We are creating millions of jobs in informal services and contract labour. We need more quality jobs, jobs where productivity growth can be robust, jobs where both the employee and employer have an incentive to invest in skills and training. Our jobs challenge is one for both policy and industry, as we will see later in this book. Answers must be sought in education policy, skills provision and labour reform.

Third, manufacturing. Economic history says that only labour-intensive manufacturing has been able to move millions of unskilled people to higher-productivity occupations in a single generation. Across two governments and fifteen years, we have had the goal of raising manufacturing to 25 per cent of GDP but it has been stubbornly stuck at 15 per cent. Again, this is a challenge for both government policy and industry. Government policy must be focused on making it easy and cheap to do business and manufacture in India, efficient logistics, and forcing industry to compete with the best in the world through low tariffs. Industry must be focused on building international competitiveness and investing in technology to move up the value-chain.

Those are three of our most critical long-term economic challenges, and they must shape the national economic agenda in the years ahead. Chapter 2 deals with these priorities. The important message is not only that these are the three priorities, but that nothing else is remotely as important. So the state should stop doing many, many things—owning the public-sector banks and insurance companies, fixing pharmaceutical and stent prices, telling colleges what fees they should charge, determining if we should stand for the National Anthem and when it should be played, and dictating whether we can eat beef or not. I say this not as an ideological choice, but as a practical proposition. If there is one thing I have learnt to appreciate of the workings of our government, it is that the commitment and knowledge of the highest levels of government (secretaries, say, or additional or joint secretaries) is matched only by the paucity of talent further down the system. This means the state has very limited implementation capacity and if we wish to see progress we had better focus on just a few things and get the state out of the way for everything else, leaving the rest to India's entrepreneurial energy, private enterprise and the market. This has been the Modi government's big mistake—each announcement of a worthy scheme has been followed not by focusing bandwidth on implementing the first scheme effectively, but by the formulation and announcement of another worthy scheme. Governing by announcement adds up to little. So, let ease of doing business and Make in India receive the exclusive attention (I stress *exclusive*, nothing else should be undertaken) of the industry department. Let the Ministry of Education focus *only* on improving outcomes in primary and secondary schools, and get out of the way in higher education. Let the Prime Minister's Office (PMO) worry about the skilling missions, using the National Skills Development Corporation and other institutions set up for this purpose, and partnering fully with industry. And let the ministries of finance and commerce focus on all those things that would enhance ease of doing business and give us equal access to foreign markets through free trade agreements.

But this book is not only about what the government should do. I have limited faith in the capacity of government (any government) to do good, in the economic sphere at any rate. I am not a subscriber to the inscription on Vidhana Soudha[14] which reads, 'Government's work is God's work'. I have more faith in the ability of industry to do good, if we choose to. And our institutions—of higher education, the media, CII, the judiciary, the ECI and the Constitution—have a critical role to play. In this book, I spend most of my time on those subjects (Indian industry, CII, higher education, research and development, design and public research) where I can claim some direct expertise. I should add, too, that my many references to CII, the valuable role it plays and could play as a leading development institution reflects my personal experience with it in various roles over decades. I do not imply that other industry bodies are incapable of good work, but the institution I know and admire is CII.

I stray some in chapter 2 on economic priorities, and more in chapter 9 on the wider institutions a country as diverse as ours needs. Chapters

---

14   The Karnataka Legislative Assembly's building in Bengaluru.

10 and 11 (on culture, and politics and political economy) reflect in equal parts my own impressions and conversations with friends who know more about these subjects than I do. Putting this together, the government and policy environment is one of the three pillars of leadership. An inclusive, international, innovative and independent industry is the second. Independent and effective institutions make up the third.

The Future of Indian Industry: Inclusive, International, Innovative, Independent

I begin with industry. For India to lead the world, Indian industry must in the future be more of four things:

1. We must be **more ethical and better corporate citizens**: Ethical practices build our credibility as industry with the government, but especially with society at large. Nirav Modi and Vijay Mallya are less typical of Indian industry than Tata, Bajaj, Infosys, Forbes Marshall and the great bulk of Indian industry, and the world (as well as our own compatriots) must see that. This job—of changing public perceptions about industry—is a combination of communication and changing the reality of industry itself. The Chief Economic Advisor between 2014 and 2018, Arvind Subramanian, has argued passionately that stigmatised capital is one of our great national challenges, hampering everything from privatisation to the resolution of bad debts. Indian industry has to take the lead in dispelling that stigma.

For much of the 1990s and 2000s, the Indian consumer goods industry grew at a rate faster than GDP, but has more recently grown slower than GDP. This, to me, is a failure of inclusion. We have millions more who are eager to become first-time buyers of restaurant meals, refrigerators, hospital services, holidays, motorcycles, ready-made clothes and even toothpaste. In his insightful book *The Turn of the Tortoise,* T.N. Ninan estimates that roughly one-quarter of India's population would consume a wide variety of consumer goods and a further quarter some basic consumer goods.[15] But that means half the population is either poor or lives too marginal an existence to be consistent consumers. If we can bring 700 million more people into the consuming class, we can create wealth for thirty years for all of industry. This will take a focus on skills and education by both government and industry—it really is in our direct interest. This is the Indian opportunity. Many cite inclusive growth as a caveat to our economic progress. I am going further and saying that being inclusive *is* the way to lead the world. Indian industry must see it as our direct responsibility to drive an agenda of inclusive growth. Improving education outcomes, skilling, affirmative action, increasing female participation in the labour force and a new social contract to cover most of our 1.4 billion is in our direct long-term interest. Chapter 3 considers these issues.

2. We must be **more international**: Indian firms must increasingly operate around the world, investing in brands and markets. The industry delegations that CII has taken in recent years to Iran, Myanmar, Sri Lanka, Indonesia, Vietnam, Malaysia, Egypt and Bhutan kept giving us the strong message that India is seen as a benign force in the world. We were told again and again how welcome Indian industry is, as suppliers and as investors. This opportunity awaits us across South East Asia, Africa, the Middle East and Latin America. Where other countries seek to develop twenty or thirty national champion firms, CII and Indian industry must develop a thousand multinationals with Indian roots, reflecting the diverse strengths of our industry across sectors. We must all develop the capacity to build global brands, and to operate around the world. CII has offices in Egypt, South Africa, Singapore, Indonesia and on the way in Vietnam, all facilitating market access and easing the establishment of local subsidiaries of

---

15 T.N. Ninan, *The Turn of the Tortoise: The Challenge and Promise of India's Future* (New Delhi: Penguin Random House India, 2016).

Indian firms. Chapter 4 discusses how Indian industry can become more international.

3. We must become **more innovative**: For various historical reasons, Indian industry is more scale- and skill-intensive than in other countries at our level of development. Industrial success thus requires significant investment in R&D, otherwise manufacturing will remain stuck at 15 per cent of GDP. Indian industry's investment in R&D is about 0.3 per cent of GDP. We need to expand our investment in R&D fivefold to match the global average of 1.5 per cent. Design can play the key role in enabling a firm to move up the value-chain of global production. Together with more investment by Indian industry in R&D and design, the state needs to scale up investment in public research in the higher education sector. Chapter 5 explores investment in technology and chapter 6 looks at design.

4. We must be **more independent**: Decades of the licence raj bred a private sector that looked to the government for protection and favours. A private sector dependent on the government cannot speak with an independent voice. Post 1991, the licence raj retreated, but the deference that industry accords to government continues as a hangover. Some industrialists have found an independent voice; it must become the norm. I return to this point in chapters 9, 10 and 11. For industry to be one of the three pillars of leadership, independence is essential.

Building Independent Institutions for Inclusive Economics and Politics

The economic historian Douglass North, who won the Nobel Prize in 1993, has remarked:

> Institutions are the humanly devised constraints that structure human interaction. They are made up of formal constraints (rules, laws, constitutions), informal constraints (norms of behaviour,

conventions, and self-imposed codes of conduct), and their enforcement characteristics. Together they define the incentive structure of societies and specifically economies. Institutions and the technology employed determine the transaction and transformation costs that add up to the costs of production.[16]

This broad definition of institutions—covering physical institutions (such as universities and schools, courts, industry associations, the civil service, constitutional bodies), rules (such as laws, law enforcement, property rights) and social norms (such as trust and social capital)—forms the fabric of development. Another great economist, Moses Abramovitz, wrote a seminal paper on economic catch-up thirty-five years ago.[17] Abramovitz argues that coming late to development provides the potential for rapid economic growth, but that social capital (overall education levels plus social norms such as trust) determines how fast one can grow. Leading the world requires that we have world-leading institutions. It is not that every institution needs to be world-leading—just that enough are, and that the way they interplay with each other and society at large leads to positive outcomes.

I deal with two specific institutions—our higher education system and public research system. It is over fifty years since the publication of Gary Becker's *Human Capital* brought analysis of higher education into the mainstream of economic analysis.[18] Independent India invested early and strongly in both higher education and public research, with the explicit objective of economic development. Recent years have seen a boom in higher education, with massive

---

16 Douglass C. North, 'Economic Performance through Time' (Nobel Prize Lecture, Oslo, 9 December 1993), https://www.nobelprize.org/prizes/economic-sciences/1993/north/lecture/

17 Moses Abramovitz, 'Catching Up, Forging Ahead, and Falling Behind', *Journal of Economic History* (June 1986).

18 Gary Becker, *Human Capital: A Theoretical and Empirical Analysis, with Special Reference to Education* (New York: National Bureau of Economic Research, 1964).

growth concentrated in professional fields (engineering, management, pharmacy) that open up employment opportunities. The private education sector has proved itself to be highly entrepreneurial, but issues of quality, access and equity all need to be addressed. So, too, does higher education in non-professional fields (the humanities, social sciences and physical sciences).

India's first Prime Minister, Jawaharlal Nehru, was a great believer in higher education and science and their importance for development. This belief led to the creation of many wonderful institutions of higher education—including the Indian Institutes of Technology and of Management, and the National Institute of Design. It led also to the state being a generous funder of scientific research, ahead of many countries much richer than India at the time. But we went wrong in locating publicly funded research in autonomous public sector laboratories rather than in universities, where teaching and research go hand in hand. Almost every other country does most of its public research in the higher education system. Over seventy years after Independence, and thirty years after economic reform began, we have not yet begun to correct this problem—or even to recognise that it is one. Until we do, our higher education system and public research effort will remain a shadow of what they could be. And we can make this correction at no extra cost. Moving our investment in public research to the higher education sector will grow it eightfold, from 0.05 per cent of GDP to the international average of 0.4 per cent. Chapters 7 and 8 look at the reform needed in higher education and public research. We have the potential to build world leadership in both, but much change is needed, particularly in the role of the state and its interaction with private institutions and firms.

I take this argument on the appropriate role of the state in India much further in chapter 9, where I address institutions as a whole. Limited capacity says that the Indian state must focus its energy on a very limited set of things that only it can do, and rely on the private sector and NGOs to fill in the gaps. We struggle when the state either overplays or underplays its role. By controlling things in an attempt to determine outcomes, we achieve less than if we relied on the private sector to deliver. We have seen this consistently in how we have handled both the spread of Covid and vaccinations. Neglecting what only the state can do is just as damaging. An effective police and judicial system—where adequate capacity and institutional autonomy deliver equality for all—is an essential state role. And we must design our institutions so that we include an ever higher proportion of our population in our growth and development, and include more people and firms both economically and politically. I provide some examples of how this can be done for intellectual property and competition policy.

Indian Culture and the Norms of Politics and Political Economy

The two final chapters are the most personal. As a teacher of courses on development to university students, I long struggled with explanations of what worked and did not work in development. As I studied the successes and failures of South Korea, Taiwan, Brazil, Mexico, Malaysia, Thailand, Indonesia and China (with the Indian experience constantly in my head), it appeared that the same development policies had very different results in different countries.

I came to the conclusion that it was the interplay of policy with local culture that delivered success or failure. I certainly don't believe that culture determines success, but I do believe that culture can shape which policies will work and which do not. I also believe that India's culture can provide the foundation on which leadership would rest. This means we must be clear about how our culture can be a great strength and help us achieve world-leadership, instead of formulating policy that depends for its success on Indian firms and Indians behaving like Japanese, Chinese or Koreans. Fostering a will to develop across the world's most diverse country is not easy. It means we must focus on the things that unify to foster a shared will to develop. It requires that we hear, and respond to, voices of criticism instead of trying to suppress them. As we give voice to all, treating all equally, we can build social capital and trust in government, in industry, and in institutions. We can then unleash the entrepreneurship that is so much a part of our culture, and build off the great strength that lies in our soft power. That is the subject of chapter 10. I hope it will be read in the spirit in which it was written, with whisky on the breath.

My term as president of CII provided the chance to see government at first hand—the central government, state governments, foreign governments, as well as the domestic and international institutions that between them make development policy. Seeing our government up close left me both impressed and depressed. I was impressed by the intelligence, commitment and hard work of many of our past and present ministers and senior bureaucrats. I was depressed by how unprepared, unmindful of international best practice, diverted by optics over content, and petty some of these same great minds were. I kept a daily journal through my year as president, trying to capture not only what I did but what was notable, and how it made me feel. India starts with the huge advantage of being liked; people around the world want us to succeed. We must not squander this advantage. It means having shoulders broad enough to be held to a higher standard than our peers. It means dealing with the world, and each other, with authenticity and humility. And it means adhering to those norms of behaviour that make living in a vibrant and noisy democracy constantly stimulating. When we behave in a manner that is petty, or hypocritical, or dismissive, or intolerant of criticism, we struggle. There were days when, in the words of P.G. Wodehouse, I felt 'like Noah listening to someone make a fuss about a drizzle'.[19] The final chapter reflects some of the most positive and negative emotions of viewing government up close.

An epilogue then pulls it all together. Each of policy (chapters 2 and 11), industry (chapters 3, 4, 5 and 6) and institutions (chapters 7, 8 and

---

19 P.G. Wodehouse, *Uncle Fred in the Springtime* (London: Herbert Jenkins Ltd, first edition, 1939).

9) must perform. Each does not need to operate perfectly, but if the state leaves a gap, industry must fill it. If a public institution is lacking, a private one must make up for it. As this book shows, the private sector can often make up for the state underplaying its role. A massive public health crisis like Covid demands that the state play the lead role. But when the state overplays its role, controlling instead of enabling, we struggle. We must get the balance between government, industry and institutions right. By harnessing our culture for development (chapter 10), and with policy, industry and institutions operating in consonance with it and each other, we can deliver on our promise.

2

Economic Policy: Do Less to Achieve More

To say that a country is rich, is to say it has experienced economic growth in the past.

—Joel Mokyr

Economics afflicts us all.

—Ashok Desai

The 1970s were a terrible decade for the economy (as well as fashion and haircuts).

—Diane Coyle

A Historical Overview

Five hundred years ago, the world was a pretty equal place. Every country was poor, and the richest country had around twice the per capita GDP of the poorest. By 1800, the richest country was around five times as rich as the poorest. By 2020, the richest countries (Switzerland, Norway) were three hundred times richer than the poorest (Niger, Malawi).[1] When some of our present-day nationalists talk of reclaiming some bygone golden age of Indian history, they are mistaken. There was glory if you were the ruler, or near him (almost always 'him', and not 'her'). For an ordinary person, in every country, life was 'solitary, poor, nasty, brutish, and short'.[2] There is only one reason India accounted for a much larger share of world GDP five hundred years ago than now—every country was poor, and we had many more poor people.

A few countries started to grow consistently over long periods of time, first Britain in the 1700s, then much of continental Europe, the US and Canada (1820 onwards), Japan (1870 onwards), Australia, New Zealand, a few countries in Latin America and South Africa (1900 onwards), South Korea, Taiwan, Hong Kong and Singapore (1960 onwards), and China (1980 onwards). The countries that grew in the 1700s and 1800s grew at low rates (1.5 per cent per capita was typical), but over long periods—a century or more. After becoming the world's richest country in the mid-eighteenth century, Britain held that position for a century and a half. The US overtook Britain in 1913 by growing its per capita GDP at 1.5 per cent per year for a hundred years. The countries that have caught up with the West since 1950 (Japan, South Korea, Taiwan, Hong Kong, Singapore) grew much faster, at 8 per cent or more per year, bridging the gap with the rich world in one generation. Coming late to development provides the potential for more rapid catch-up, but only a few countries actually do so.

---

1   The economist Angus Maddison worked throughout his career at the Organisation of Economic Co-operation and Development (OECD) and the University of Groningen, constructing national accounts and estimating GDP for countries going back two millennia. The work was indeed heroic; consider the challenges of estimating GDP today, and then think of doing it for all countries in 1 AD and 1000 AD. Anyone interested in long-run economic growth depends on Maddison's work. Even those who argue with his estimates must begin with them.

2   Thomas Hobbes's famous quote from *Leviathan.*

It is only since 1991 that India grew at rates that allowed for some convergence with the richer world. We can congratulate ourselves on overtaking France and the UK in 2019, to become the world's fifth-largest economy at $2.9 trillion. But we should remind ourselves that this is largely because we have 1.4 billion people; per person, we are still among the poorest one-third of countries in the world.

Catching-up comes from decades of sustained growth: In 1960, South Korea and India had much the same per capita GDP. In 1980, China and India had much the same per capita GDP. South Korea ($32,000) is now fifteen times richer than we are and China ($10,300) is five times richer. It's all a matter of growth rates. Between 1960 and 1990, South Korea grew at 9 per cent each year, to India's 4 per cent. Between 1980 and 2019 China grew 9 per cent each year, to our 6 per cent.[3] In the three years before the Covid-19 pandemic, India and China both grew at around 6 per cent.

Figure 2.1: Sustained Periods of High Growth in East Asian Countries Narrow the Gap with Rich Countries

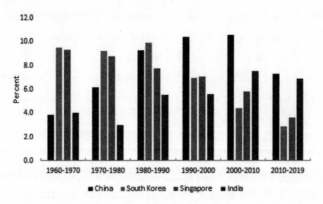

Note: The chart presents the average GDP growth rate in each decade for the selected countries starting from 1960.

Sources: World Development Indicators (World Bank); World Economic Outlook Database, October 2019 (International Monetary Fund); CTIER.

---

3   Our best growth episode was the eight years between 2003 and 2011 when we grew at 8 per cent.

Our national priority, then, must be to catch up, through long-run economic growth. Table 2.1 tells us the rates of economic growth that we need to catch up with where China, Malaysia and South Korea are today.

Table 2.1: Required Growth Rate for India to Match Current Nominal GDP Per Capita in China, Malaysia and South Korea

Country	GDP per capita in 2019 (US$)	India's GDP per capita in 2019 (US$)	CAGR* required over 25 years (%)	CAGR required over 30 years (%)
China	10,262	2,104	6.5	5.4
Malaysia	11,415	2,104	7.0	5.8
South Korea	31,762	2,104	11.5	9.5

CAGR*: Compound annual growth rate

Sources: World Development Indicators (2019), indicators available at: https://databank.worldbank.org/source/world-development-indicators; author's own calculations.

We must grow 9 per cent anually for four years to achieve the $5 trillion by 2024 goal set by the Modi government. Thanks to the pandemic and associated lockdowns, March 2022 will see us where we were in absolute terms in March 2020. These two lost years are something we can ill-afford, so our $5 trillion goal must now be set back to 2026. With a $5 trillion economy, we will be as rich in 2026 as Indonesia is today ($4,000). But to be as rich as China is today, we must sustain 9 per cent growth per year for twenty years. That, surely, must be our minimum aspiration—to be as rich *in twenty years* as China is *today*.

What must we do to sustain growth of 9 per cent for a generation?

Achieving high rates of economic growth requires understanding where it comes from. The first attempts to estimate GDP, in the

1930s, were by Simon Kuznets in the US and Colin Clark in the UK. These efforts were followed by the first growth accounting exercises by Robert Solow and Moses Abramovitz in the 1950s. They concluded that a proportion of growth could be explained by capital investment and labour supply. Giving each worker more capital to work with made her more productive. Increasing labour supply—for example, when women entered the workforce by the million during the world wars—grew per capita output dramatically. More sophisticated studies from Gary Becker onwards looked at investment in human capital—increases in average years of schooling, and higher education. But even after accounting for all this there was a residual, 'a measure of our ignorance' in Solow's words,[4] which economists call Total Factor Productivity (TFP) and is attributed to technical change. This residual of technical change generally accounted for between a half and two-thirds of rapid long-run economic growth. These factors are also not independent. Higher TFP growth often rides on higher levels of human capital. Investment in new capital goods (such as a new machine) often incorporates technical change in itself.

Economic development, then, is a messy combination of investment, education and human capital, technical change, labour mobility, and trade. I will deal with technical change in chapters 5, 6 and 8, and education in chapter 7. But the biggest growth driver as a country develops is the movement of people from low-productivity occupations to those with higher productivity. A poor country has many people employed in marginal occupations. As the country develops, more and more move to more productive occupations. The archetype is someone in subsistence farming moving to manufacturing. That is the subject of this chapter—placing employment, jobs and manufacturing at the heart of our economic agenda.

---

4   Robert M. Solow, 'A contribution to the theory of economic growth', *Quarterly Journal of Economics* 70, no. 1 (1956): 65–94. https://doi.org/10.2307/1884513

What Leads to Rapid Economic Growth?

Ever since Adam Smith, economists have worried about this question
and have come up with varying answers. Abhijit Banerjee and Esther
Duflo, in an extended chapter ('The End of Growth?') in their 2019
book, *Good Economics for Hard Times*, conclude that we can draw few
policy lessons from growth economists.

> What does this leave us with? It seems relatively clear that there
> are things to avoid: hyperinflation; extremely over-valued fixed
> exchange rates; communism in its Soviet, Maoist, or North Korean
> varieties; or even the kind of total government chokehold on
> private enterprise India had in the 1970s with State ownership
> of everything from ships to shoes. This does not help us with the
> kinds of questions most countries have today, given that no one,
> except perhaps the Venezuelan madmen, seem to be very keen on
> any of these extreme options. What Vietnam or Myanmar want to
> know, for example, is whether they should aim to emulate China's
> economic model, given its stunning success, not whether to follow
> North Korea ... The bottom line is that, much as in rich countries,
> we have no accepted recipe for how to make growth happen in
> poor countries.[5]

Turning to India, they argue that the reason India grew more rapidly
in the 1990s and 2000s is because we misallocated resources less badly.
Reading that sentence came as something of an affront to me, as a
great fan of our 1991 reforms. Surely we did something more heroic
than 'misallocate less badly'? Banerjee and Duflo then deal at length
with many opportunities for misallocating less badly:

---

5   Abhijit Banerjee and Esther Duflo, *Good Economics for Hard Times: Better
    Answers to Our Biggest Problems* (New Delhi: Juggernaut Books, 2019), 184,
    186.

- Simply reallocating capital across firms (from 'bad' firms to 'good' firms) would eliminate most of the gap in productivity between Indian firms and US firms.
- 'Owners perhaps do not care enough about growth to put all they have behind that agenda. If no one else is growing fast, they are not at risk of being pushed out.'[6] The learning from this is the role of high-quality competition in weeding out under performing firms. If firms aren't producing international-quality products at globally competitive prices, they do not deserve to exist.
- Banerjee and Duflo point out that young educated Indians wait for years to get a job they deem worthwhile:[7]

… 26 percent of all Indian males between the ages of twenty and thirty with at least ten years of education were not working. This is not because there were no jobs: the fraction of those under thirty with less than eight years of education who were not working was 1.3 percent. And, in fact, the fraction of those with ten years of education *above thirty* who were not working was about 2 percent … There are plenty of jobs, just not jobs these young men want. They will eventually accept jobs they refused to take when they were younger....

Part of the problem is a mismatch of expectations …

---

6 I found exactly the same thing when I did my doctoral fieldwork studying entrepreneurs in Pune, well before liberalisation in 1991. The entrepreneurs were content with running a modestly successful business—they did not wish to risk all in making it big. When I presented my thesis to my committee at Stanford, Hank Riggs—one of my advisors, who had himself been a part of successful start-ups, and was a pioneer in the study of technical entrepreneurship—found this really difficult to accept. As my committee chair Jim Adams pointed out, a finding that an entrepreneur was not a maximiser ran directly against Hank's religion.

7 Abhijit Banerjee and Esther Duflo, *Good Economics for Hard Times: Better Answers to Our Biggest Problems* (New Delhi: Juggernaut Books, 2019), 195, 198, 199, 204, 207.

Labor markets frozen by this kind of radical mismatch are wasting resources. These young people are waiting for jobs they will not get....

At the risk of over simplifying their broader argument into two quotes, they point to:

... one very real danger is that in trying to hold on to fast growth, India ... will veer toward policies that hurt the poor now in the name of future growth. The need to be 'business-friendly' to preserve growth may be interpreted ... as open season for all kinds of anti-poor, pro-rich policies (such as bail-outs for over-indebted corporations and wealthy individuals) that enrich the top earners at the expense of everyone else, and do nothing for growth.... The best bet, therefore, for a country like India is to attempt to do things that can make the quality of life better for its citizens with the resources it already has: improving education, health, and the functioning of courts and the banks, and building better infrastructure (better roads and more liveable cities, for example).

But these kinds of interventions are exactly what the more thoughtful growth economists advocate. Having a growth target—10 per cent for India—supported by precisely the kinds of investments in education and health that Banerjee and Duflo advocate, and an industrial policy that delivers long-run productivity improvement, are mutually reinforcing.

Let us consider East Asia.

To sustain growth, sequence policy: There has been an ongoing debate about the sources of East Asian growth, in particular on the relative role of markets and government. But there is wide acceptance of a few contributing factors.[8] First, all East Asian countries

---

8   I say this mindful of Banerjee and Duflo's comment that 'those who herald the experience of the East Asian countries to prove the virtue of one approach or the other are dreaming; there is no way to prove any such thing'.

grew as exporters of manufactured goods, beginning with the export of simple items like garments, footwear and toys. As wages rose, they moved to more sophisticated items such as electronics, appliances and cars. Second, all began with relatively high levels of human capital, with literacy levels ahead of their peers. They then invested sequentially in expanding their education systems, from primary to secondary to higher. The rise in average levels of schooling supported the move to higher-value-added products. Third, as wages rose and firms moved up the value-chain to more sophisticated products, they substantially increased investments in technology. As we will see in chapter 5, investments in R&D by South Korea and China grew dramatically, especially in-house R&D in firms. South Korean firms grew investment in in-house R&D a thousandfold in twenty years.[9] In both countries, all this was accompanied by a massive change in occupation as millions moved from rural to urban areas and were employed in factories.

An Industrial Policy for Productivity Growth in the Long Run

My first contact with economic history was reading about the Industrial Revolution in Britain in the late eighteenth century. Countries since then have assumed that rapid development requires industrialisation.

After more than a century of leadership as the world's richest country, the largest occupation in Britain in 1900 was domestic service (servants),[10] indicating the potential that still existed for productivity growth from occupational change. When people migrate to cities, even for informal occupations such as delivery agents and security guards,

---

9   See chapter 5 for further discussion on technology and Indian industry. The South Korean and Chinese growth multiples were a result of more rapid growth in GDP, a growing share of industry in national R&D, and growing R&D investment as a percentage of sales, all working together.

10   The great economic historian Moe Abramovitz pointed this out at a seminar at Stanford in the late 1990s.

they add to GDP by being employed more productively. When they move to cities and are employed in manufacturing, we get the jump in output that this more productive occupation entails *and* the potential for further productivity growth over time. The most dramatic growth driver is the movement of people from low-productivity agriculture to much higher-productivity manufacturing. India's inability to participate in large-scale, labour-intensive export manufacturing has been our biggest missed development opportunity.

Inclusive growth and the jobs challenge: If rapid growth is our first priority, the quality of growth matters. Putting more and more people into productive employment boosts growth in itself, and creates new consumers, who in turn spread the growth around. This is the growth multiplier at the heart of Keynesian economics. In his fine book on the Indian economy, T.N. Ninan estimated four classes of Indians:

Table 2.2: T.N. Ninan's Possible Class Break-up in India, 2014–15

Category	People (million)	Expenditure cut-off (Rs per month/per family)
Middle-class rich	340	> 28,500
Aspiring neo-middle class	285	15,000–28,500
Vulnerable non-poor	285	7,000–15,000
Poor	340	< 7,000

Source: 'Table 12.2', Ninan, *The Turn of the Tortoise.*

The top 27 per cent live a relatively comfortable life and provide the bulk of discretionary purchases. This 'top 27 per cent' is no homogenous group. It ranges from Asia's richest person, Mukesh Ambani, to someone owning a small shop to an engineer at a good company. The next 23 per cent, that Ninan calls the aspiring neo-middle class, would typically be 'the owners of commuter two-wheelers, especially in urban areas'.[11] The 23 per cent after that are the vulnerable non-poor, 'who have emerged out of poverty but are not yet high enough above the water level to be free from the fear of falling back in, if the fates are unkind—think a poor harvest, a recession that leads to lack of work, or a medical episode'. (The lockdown of March–April 2020 during the pandemic was a perfect storm for this group.) The fourth group of 27 per cent are the poor, who live on a family income of less than Rs 7,000 per month. In the absence of robust national income data, Ninan emphasises that his estimates are just that; they are the most plausible for the entire population that I have come across.

A favourite story concerns a security guard at our factory in Pune. A few years ago he said to us with great pride that his son had graduated as an engineer and gone to work for GE, and his daughter had qualified as a doctor and started work in a hospital. So within a year, this family had gone from a monthly income of Rs 15,000 or so to Rs 1,50,000. Such increases in consumption potential have been our driver of GDP growth. This dynamic is real, widespread, and could run for thirty years. This security guard is not unique as there are hundreds of thousands like him. But he is also not typical; there are many millions of Indians who aspire to go through the same process but cannot. This is our development challenge—how do we create opportunity for all 1.4 billion of our population? Note also the crucial role of education—it was the key to progress for our security guard's family as they climbed the ladder from borderline vulnerable to a comfortable middle-class life.

The key is inclusive growth. That has long been a political objective in India, including for our two most recent governments. The inclusion

---

11 T.N. Ninan, *The Turn of the Tortoise: The Challenge and Promise of India's Future* (New Delhi: Penguin Random House India, 2016).

of broader sections of the population in national development not only enables social objectives of widespread health and well-being, but also directly boosts the growth process. Since 1991, around two-thirds of Indian growth has come from consumption. Including more people in the growth process directly impacts the rate of growth, as more and more people become first-time consumers of processed foods, textiles and garments, and consumer durables (with smart phones demonstrating the greatest elasticity of consumption). They educate their children in private schools and colleges, paying far higher fees than they would for public education. The demand for better healthcare means we can grow our healthcare system at double the rate of GDP for decades.

Our key national priority is creating jobs for a more inclusive growth process. The problem is job quality. We are creating millions of jobs in informal services and contract labour. We need to create millions of high-quality jobs—those that can grow productivity in the long run. We know how to do so in manufacturing and we are learning for services. If our entire workforce had the productivity of our factory sector, we would be fifteen times wealthier with an average per capita GDP matching that of South Korea ($32,000).[12] Our economy struggles with less than 20 per cent employment in the formal sector (larger factories; public services such as government, the armed forces and government schools; and private services such as banks, airlines, airports, organised retail, and hotels). The bulk (over 80 per cent) is informal—50 per cent of the workforce in agriculture, a further 30 per cent in microenterprises and informal services (including domestic staff, security staff, drivers, delivery agents, and those at smaller

---

12 Organisation for Economic Co-operation and Development, *OECD Economic Survey of India: Strong Reforms Are Boosting Inclusive Growth* (Paris: OECD Publishing, 2017).

restaurants).[13] These jobs suffer from limited potential for productivity growth, thus limiting the worker's own growth prospects.

How do we grow millions of high-quality jobs? We need to address both supply (improving the quality and flow of talent) and demand (ensuring high-quality talent gets absorbed).

Jobs—addressing the quantity and quality of supply: India leads the world in the potential flow of quality talent—a young population, with a growing proportion in the working-age group, constitutes the most spectacular *potential* demographic dividend in world history. We need to urgently address how effectively we skill our population, improve the quality of school education and how we can get the bulk of our working-age population to participate in the workforce. I will discuss school education and workforce participation in the next chapter.

Skilling: In 2006, CII launched the India@75 initiative. A centrepiece of this initiative was skilling—CII's India@75 initiative targeted skilling 500 million people. In response, the government of the day set up the National Skills Development Corporation, with an ambitious target of skilling 150 million by 2022. This ambition has since diminished. In 2016, the government's primary skill development programme, the Pradhan Mantri Kaushal Vikas Yojana (PMKVY),[14] set a highly scaled-down target of skilling 10 million people by 2020. As of mid 2020, 5.5 million have been certified as skilled under this leading government scheme, a little over 1 per cent of our workforce. All this leaves India one of the least skilled countries in the world. Under 5 per cent of our workforce is formally skilled, as compared

---

13   This informal labour force was most seriously affected in the April 2020 lockdown, which deprived them of their livelihood, with many living day to day. A lockdown, declared with four hours' notice, was followed with no support by Union or state governments.

14   PMKVY—the Prime Minister's skill development scheme.

to 96 per cent in South Korea, 75 per cent in Germany, and 52 per cent in the US. The NSDC has put in place a great foundation, with detailed skill levels covering hundreds of skills in dozens of sectors. We need to see these efforts bear fruit.

Done right, skilling enhances productivity. Jobs in manufacturing are high-quality jobs precisely because they have the potential for long-run productivity growth. Skilling can also help transform regions. On a visit to Assam and Meghalaya in 2017, when Chandrajit Banerjee and I met the chief ministers, the request was for CII to help with skilling specifically in the conventional Northeast skills of hospitality and parlour services. This would enable people to get jobs, but they would be in other parts of the country. Everywhere we looked, there was construction under way—in Guwahati, in Shillong, and all along the road in-between. The construction was almost uniformly awful, shabby in design and finish, leaving scars across a spectacular countryside. The tourism potential of the Northeast is great. Could a skilling programme focused on construction improve the quality of life of those who used the buildings and also preserve the natural beauty of the place? And create many thousands of jobs at home?

Addressing supply issues can fundamentally improve the quality and flow of human capital into our workforce each year. That creates the potential for a massive growth miracle.

Jobs—addressing demand through labour-intensive industry: Fixing the demand for this talent will realise the potential by growing employment massively in industry (particularly labour-intensive industry), and through mass employment in formal services. Most emerging markets have put millions of people to work in low-skilled manufacturing. China employs over 100 million people in export-oriented labour-intensive manufacturing. As a middle-income country (with a per capita GDP of $10,000), low-wage jobs have been moving out of China. This exit has been further encouraged by uncertainty over trading relationships, widespread distrust of China as a result of deceit over Covid and its active bullying of everyone from Australia to Hong Kong to Taiwan. Countries like Vietnam and Bangladesh are picking up millions of such jobs in the thriving garment, footwear and assembly industries. Why aren't these jobs coming to India?

We occasionally make the argument that while large Indian manufacturing firms have not created millions of jobs, our small firms have. A 2019 CII survey of micro, small and medium enterprises (the largest ever undertaken) surveyed more than 100,000 small firms on job-creation between 2014 and 2018.[15] The great bulk of firms were micro-firms, employing three people on average. Small enterprises live a tenuous existence, constantly starting up and vanishing.[16] Think of the churn in your neighbourhood, the street vendors, barbers, restaurants and shops. Once we factor in firm mortality—which the CII study did not do—it would seem no net jobs were created in this period.

What is true of small industry is also true of large industry. Between 1991 and 2017, according to the Annual Survey of Industries (ASI), industrial output increased five times in real terms.[17] Labour employed in ASI firms increased 1.8 times. This made firms roughly three times more productive. This is decent progress for industry, but not for industrial employment, which went up by a little over a quarter million people a year on average. With fifteen million people employed in the firms surveyed by ASI (i.e. those employing over ten people), India is missing mass-scale industrial employment. In particular, we are missing the huge firms in export-oriented, labour-intensive sectors that employ millions in China, Vietnam

---

15 'Survey on Jobs Creation and Outlook in MSME Sector', March 2019.

16 There is no good Indian data on firm mortality. The best we can do is look at typical mortality rates for enterprises in other countries. The OECD reports firm mortality for most of its member economies. It ranges between 2 per cent and 15 per cent annually, with a median of 7.7 per cent.

17 ASI findings, as cited by the *Economic Survey 2017–18* (New Delhi: Ministry of Finance, Government of India, 2018).

and Bangladesh. This matches anecdotal observation too. Foxconn's largest factory in China, making iPhones among other products, reportedly employs 400,000 people. It employs over a million people in the country overall. Samsung employs 100,000 people in its largest phone assembly plant in Vietnam. These giant factories are simply missing in India.

Consider the most labour-intensive sectors. A large garment factory in India employs 3,000–5,000 people, while a large garment factory in Bangladesh employs 30,000–50,000 people. A company we came across on a recent visit to Vietnam manufactures agarbattis.[18] They learnt how to make agarbattis by sending ten workers to a factory near Chennai for training. They today employ 10,000 people to make agarbattis, which they mainly export to India. What does it say when the technology is Indian and the market is India—but the economics of it says mass manufacturing is more efficient 4,000 kilometres away from India?

Labour reform: The mention of labour reform prompts the reaction that this is in the interests of industry and capitalists. That is incorrect. Labour reform is in the interests of labour. Labour regulations protect incumbents—those already in permanent jobs in large factories. Easy entry and easy exit are two sides of the same coin: making it easier to fire people makes it easier to hire them. We must ensure adequate social safety nets so that those displaced are protected, but a flexible labour market could transform our job market.

We otherwise prompt behaviour contrary to the broader national interest—with firms first avoiding labour-intensive manufacturing, and then relying on contract labour instead of direct employment. The result is that at present our fastest-growing large private-sector employer in the country is Teamlease, a provider of temporary and contract manpower, which employs over 100,000 people. There is

---

18   Agarbattis are incense sticks found in most Indian homes.

nothing wrong with contract labour for certain roles. But companies have little incentive to invest in their training and productivity tends to stagnate. In recent years, we reportedly added 7 million jobs in security services and one million jobs as private drivers in the National Capital Region alone. These contractual jobs are welcome to those who get them in the absence of alternatives, but they are not the high-quality jobs we need.

This government came to power in 2014 promising to reform our outdated labour policies. This key area was then treated in a half-hearted manner. In September 2020, forty-four labour laws were finally consolidated into four simpler laws. A move was made to provide greater flexibility to formal-sector labour and some minimal protection to informal-sector labour. These moves are welcome, and must be taken further—with consultation across labour representatives, industry and state governments. If we wish to attract millions of jobs in garments, footwear and assembly moving out of China, an environment where one can cheaply increase and reduce hiring as needed is essential. We may rightly express concern about the 'sweatshops' making garments in Bangladesh, but given the choice, workers have chosen in millions to move off the rice field and into the sweatshop. Indian workers should have the same choice. I will return to this subject in the next chapter when I discuss the new social contract that we need between industry, labour and government—and the need to use the Covid-triggered economic crisis to make real change happen.

High-quality jobs raise productivity and make people modern: The great Stanford sociologist Alex Inkeles was a seminal contributor to modernisation theory. It starts with the premise that the development of a country is built on the development of its people. In particular, as a society modernises, people adopt more modern attitudes. These include 'a sense of personal efficacy; openness to new experience; respect for science and technology; acceptance of the need for strict scheduling of time; and a positive orientation toward planning ahead'.[19] These modern attitudes are the essential building blocks of an advanced society and indeed an advanced economy. Not only do they make the individual modern, but they also make for participant citizens, who have an interest in the news and a sense of national identity that rises above religious and local ties.

So how does an individual become modern?

Alex Inkeles's classic book *Becoming Modern* reported the results of a major multi-year, six-country (that included India) research project.[20] Its major contribution was to provide an empirical scale of modernity that applied universally, and to identify where it came from. The two key sources of modernity were the school and the factory, one year in school being worth roughly two in a factory. Nothing else came close—not family background, the friends one had, what one read, mass media or the speeches of political or religious leaders. One can understand the school, as developing the individual is what schooling does. But a factory employs people not to develop them, but to produce things. Why was it such a powerful moderniser, in Inkeles's words, 'a school for modernity'?

A factory is about production, but the way it is organised inherently develops the individual. People work to a manufacturing schedule; this teaches planning. One sees a direct connection between work and output, so it isn't luck that delivers results but learning and using skills. That fosters efficacy. Any decent factory has a focus on efficiency,

---

19 Alex Inkeles and David H. Smith, *Becoming Modern: Individual Change in Six Developing Countries* (Cambridge, MA: Harvard University Press, 1974); and Alex Inkeles, *Exploring Individual Modernity* (New York City, NY: Columbia University Press, 1983).

20 The fieldwork was done in the late 1960s and early 1970s. Modernisation theory in general was criticised for being ethnocentric and prescribing a single path for development of all countries. Alex Inkeles himself was always subtle, sensitive and precise in his analysis and did not push his theories beyond the data.

which directly connects productive use of time to output.[21] Change is the norm in factories, so new experience is valued. Technology is all around, making the individual more productive. And decision-making requires data, valuing science over superstition.

It is for these reasons that manufacturing jobs matter. But why not service jobs? Formal service jobs can be powerful modernisers. Our challenge is, first, that most formal service occupations require high levels of education, and, second, there aren't that many jobs. Take our most successful industry—the IT sector. An industry that has boomed for over thirty years directly employs four million people today. And some of those directly employed, and most of those indirectly employed, are in informal occupations—drivers, security services, and domestic staff—that are not 'schools for modernity'. A country of 1.4 billion, with a workforce of 400 million growing at twelve million a year, needs a lot more.

Tourism as a moderniser: There is one big exception—tourism.[22] Tourism can be as effective a school for modernity as the factory. Done right, it can be even better. One of my favourite resorts anywhere in the world is the Shillim resort. Shillim is in the middle of a thoroughly rural area, 30 kilometres from the nearest town, Lonavla. Lonavla is itself no metropolis, sitting off the highway between Mumbai and Pune. Shillim today directly employs around 450 people. A policy of recruiting locally has created 200 jobs for young men and women from the nearby villages that have a population of around 1,000. These young people are taught all those things that make people modern. An intensive training programme teaches everything from hospitality domain skills to the soft skills essential to success in a luxury resort. In the ten years since Shillim opened, hundreds of lives have been

---

21 Efficacy is doing the right thing. Efficiency is doing that thing with minimum input.

22 At least pre Covid-19. Ah, nostalgia, even for the sweetness of delayed flights and endless immigration lines!

transformed, and with it, the fortunes of their families in the next generation.

India needs to become Shillim writ large. Tourism is our greatest untapped opportunity. No country can match us in the combination of architectural diversity (with everything from Mughal forts and tombs to Hindu temples and the colonial grandeur of New Delhi), unmatched natural beauty (from the backwaters of Kerala to the beauty of the Kashmir Valley), and a richer diversity of culture than in any other country (there is no such thing as Indian dress or Indian food—we have dozens of distinct dress styles and even more cuisines). With all this to offer, why are we country #25 in the world tourism rankings? Why can't we match country #1, France, with eighty-three million annual tourist arrivals instead of our current fifteen million (half of whom are non-resident Indians)? A first step would be to match Thailand's thirty-three million.

The alternative to hundreds of millions of formal high-quality jobs—in manufacturing or tourism—is one of millions of informal marginally employed drivers and cleaners and delivery boys. A thought-provoking edit by T.N. Ninan in the *Business Standard* many years ago on the horrendous Nirbhaya rape has always haunted me. He pointed out how different the victim and rapists were in their paths of modernity. The victim and her friend were educated, with good job prospects in formal occupations. The rapists were all in informal, unstable occupations with nothing that either taught them modern attitudes or gave them a stake in the existing system. The difference was not where the victims and rapists had come from, but in the education, exposure and employment of their families.

A modern future for India requires that we do all that is necessary—labour reform to unleash labour-intensive manufacturing, policies to promote garments and footwear and foodprocessing, and a tourism czar with the power to work across ministries and state governments to attract eighty million tourists annually to India in the term of this government.

India's Elusive Manufacturing Miracle

Across two governments we have had the goal of raising manufacturing from 15 to 25 per cent of GDP. To do so in five years requires a 20 per cent annual rate of growth. Only a few countries have ever managed to do this over an extended period. This is a challenge for both government policy and industry. Government policy must be focused on making it easy and cheap to do business and manufacture in India, providing access to world markets through free-trade agreements with our major trading partners and forcing industry to compete with the best in the world through low tariffs. Industry must be focused on building competitiveness and investing in technology to move up the value-chain.

From time to time, we have sought to adopt an industrial policy aimed at picking winners. In the last six years, CII has been involved in three successive attempts to foster the development of high-potential sectors, under three industry ministers. Most of these attempts aimed to develop the industries of the future. A close reading of the experience of Taiwan and South Korea, and perhaps also China, says that their governments played a useful and even decisive role in getting industry to move up the value-chain of global manufacturing. But, as I will argue later in this chapter and further in chapter 11, we should seek a better outcome without the state attempting to pick winners. In chapter 4, I argue for an outward-looking confident industry as the foundation for an outward-looking confident trade regime that forces firms to be competitive. The key way for the state to help manufacturing prosper is to make it easy and cheap to do business.

The ease of doing business: For over a decade the World Bank has ranked countries on their ease of doing business. India used to figure very poorly in the rankings. In 2014, we ranked #134 of 190 countries. Since then we have progressively improved our position, and in 2020 ranked #63. Yet, if one goes around and asks the average

Indian firm if they think it is easier for them to do business today than seven years ago, the answer would be 'No'. How come? The World Bank ranks countries on ten sub-indices as Table 2.3 shows.

Table 2.3: World Bank Scores on Ease of Doing Business in India in 2015 and 2020

S. No.	Indices	Score	
		2015	2020
1	Starting a business	62	82
2	Dealing with construction permits	36	79
3	Getting electricity	70	89
4	Registering property	54	48
5	Getting credit	65	80
6	Protecting minority investors	76	80
7	Paying taxes	54	68
8	Trading across borders	57	83
9	Enforcing contracts	29	41
10	Resolving insolvency	33	62
Overall EODB score		**53**	**71**

EODB: Ease of doing business

Source: Doing Business 2015 & 2020, World Bank, available at https://www.doingbusiness.org/en/custom-query

In all countries, the World Bank's approach is to collect data in a limited manner. In India, for example, data is collected only in Mumbai and Delhi. This means that a focused effort to improve even one aspect—for instance, getting an electricity connection or construction permit in Mumbai and Delhi—can substantially improve our ranking. And that, by the way, is exactly what we did. We are of course not alone in this manipulative ability, but a focus on the ranking instead of actually easing how business is done dilutes the purpose of the exercise. Quite discouragingly, for every improvement driven by one government department, two new requirements or items of discretion come up from some other department, regulator, or state government. More encouragingly, when Amitabh Kant was secretary of the then Department of Industrial Policy and Promotion (since renamed Department for Promotion of Industry and Internal Trade [DPIIT]), he initiated an annual ranking of India's states on the ease of doing business. This prompted some healthy competition between states for a few years, but like all such initiatives, unless there is ongoing ownership at higher levels, the objective becomes number-gathering instead of improving outcomes.

A much more granular approach is needed. I would suggest an effort, based in CII, that identifies a shortlist of twenty doable improvements at a time. A joint group comprising the PMO, DPIIT and CII, meeting monthly, should be tasked with seeing that this list shrinks between meetings. As items are resolved (hopefully each month), new ones should be added. The source of all improvements should be the actual issues faced by firms as they go about daily operations. Once every quarter, a Net Promoter Score survey should ask firms if they now find it easier to do business than they did three months and one year earlier. By anchoring the exercise in CII, it can actually happen.[23] I have my own favourites that should be worked on, ranging from the mundane (in this supposedly digital age, why do annual accounts in India need five signatures—up from three signatures a few years ago—of at least two directors on every copy?) to the frustrating (why does the government effective October 2020 want tax collected at source for sales to companies, with no revenue gain, and many thousands of hours of extra work for each company?) to the substantive (why should it be the buyer's responsibility to ensure that her suppliers file GST returns?). I believe a focused and industry-driven effort could

---

23 Other industry associations should, of course, also be engaged in this task. As I said in chapter 1, I have confidence in CII because that is the institution I know.

truly transform the ease of doing business, and firms could experience it for themselves within two years.

In many interactions across the country with the CII membership (most of which are small and medium enterprises), the key issue was the ease of doing business. Large firms cope with a difficult business environment by hiring liaison people and tax consultants, and setting up whole departments to cope with the regulatory environment. This adds cost, but doesn't kill them. Small firms cannot afford to. Regulations stymie their growth and keep them from prospering. I am convinced that the very best policy to promote small industry is to make it easier for them to do business.

Picking winners is a policy of exclusion. Making it easier and cheaper for all to do business is a policy of inclusion.

Infrastructure and logistics: An increasing share of world trade in goods now happens within what are called global value-chains, where firms in different countries specialise in a small piece of the chain that builds the final product. Margins are razor thin, efficiency is paramount, and time of the essence. This demands world-class infrastructure and logistics.

Today, a power plant in western India finds it cheaper to import coal from Australia than to transport it across India from Bihar. A paper manufacturer selling in Mumbai finds it cheaper to ship paper in from a plant in Thailand than to truck it in from its own plant outside Delhi. Firms in India's largest garment cluster in Tiruppur in Tamil Nadu find it cheaper to ship goods for export from the port at Tuticorin (a ten-hour drive from Tiruppur), rather than from Chennai (a seven-hour drive, but they claim the port is rife with delays), or from the port at Cochin (just a four-hour drive away, but that involves crossing the state border into Kerala). The Indian High Commissioner to our neighbour Bangladesh perceptively pointed out that it is cheaper for both countries to ship goods to Germany then to each other. These are fixable problems, but they should not need fixing in the first place.

Priorities and Government Bandwidth: Less is More

I have long held the view that we should not seek better government, we should seek less government. That is my reading of the 1991 reforms—the state retreated from industrial licensing, control of foreign investment, public-sector monopolies in everything from airlines to steel, and opened up to imports. Perhaps Abhijit Banerjee and Esther Duflo are right that this led 'merely' to misallocating resources less badly, but the resulting jump in growth multiplied our GDP eight times from $340 billion in 1991 to $2,650 billion in 2017. It is only in the last four years that we have seen growth sag; it is no coincidence that these years have also seen a substantive return of state control in many areas of the economy. Since 2017, the discretionary power of officials across ministries and regulators has increased. How they dealt with the Covid-19 pandemic reflects this impulse. The draconian Disaster Management Act of 2005 was invoked, together with the colonial Epidemic Diseases Act of 1897, which gave the home ministry complete power over economic activity and movement. To what effect? As I wrote in an article in *Business Standard* in May 2020, on our own organisation's experience over the previous weeks:

> We need passes for everything. We need a pass to bring people to work. A pass to source packing material. A pass to get the logistics providers in. Another pass to get a truck in and on its way to the customer. Each takes time, and is variably interpreted by each individual policeman.[24]

My point was not that the end district official or policeman was doing the wrong thing. A dynamic economy demands that no official should have the discretion to stop legal activity. In our zeal to control, we rediscovered what Abhijit Banerjee and Esther Duflo call 'the kind

---

24 'The Stanford Prison Experiment', *Business Standard*, 21 May 2020.

of total government chokehold on private enterprise India had in the 1970s'.

We may argue that a worldwide pandemic is an unprecedented event, requiring unprecedented power for officials to act. Yes, provided those powers improve matters and not make things worse. With each state, city and policeman interpreting the rules as they chose, clarification after clarification followed. In the three months after the first lockdown in March 2020, the Union government issued 270 separate notifications, clarifications and advisories. Some of these directives were even well meaning, many just to undo the confusion caused by a previous directive. Most ended with a statement of the punishment and penalties that would follow a breach. The result was an economy tied up in knots. We shut the economy down in four hours. We took two months to restart it.

The Union government's response to the second wave was equally erratic, in the opposite direction. In the first wave, the government declared a lockdown with four-hours notice, ranking 100 per cent on the Oxford University stringency index. The same government advocated avoiding lockdowns and highly local containment in the (much worse) second wave. Many states ignored the advice and locked down anyway. The state where I live, Maharashtra, approached matters in a balanced way in the second wave. The local police implemented restrictions on movement that were much less capricious and targeted only at safe social distancing.

There is a better way. We have to start with the reality of India and recognise that we have low state capacity. A state with low capacity should seek to do less and should greatly limit its actions to very few areas (such as public health) where it tries to do well. Vijay Kelkar and Ajay Shah wrote a marvellous book in 2019, *In Service of the Republic: The Art and Science of Economic Policy,* that tells us how to approach things. Their book should be required reading for anyone in any public policy role whatsoever. The book even has a fine chapter on public health. Implementing the suggestions in it could have saved many, many thousands of lives during the pandemic.

Kelkar and Shah argue that state power has to be used with great caution. The state should increase coercion (in the form of taxes or penalties) only when a lower level of coercion has been proven to work well. 'Keep the stakes low while one learns.' A weak and cogitating state is better than one that is strong, decisive and immediate. 'Crises offer aspiring authoritarians an escape from constitutional shackles.'[25]

So, what must we do? This chapter has argued that three principles will enable us to lead the world economically. First, we need to achieve higher rates of economic growth than any other country and sustain these for decades. Our task is to bridge much of the gap with the developed world in a generation. Growing at 9–10 per cent year on year has to be our national target. Growth in employment is at the heart of economic growth. The easy movement of people to cities and higher-productivity occupations drive growth, as does job quality. So, second, we need an industrial policy aimed only at long-run productivity growth. This focus on productivity brings with it a need for manufacturing, inclusive growth, jobs, and investing in human capital.[26] And third, in designing sound economic policy for India, less is more. We must operate with the understanding that the Indian state has limited capacity to deliver, and therefore good government is not better government, it is less government. Or, with more nuance, as we will see in chapters 9, 10 and 11, a good government would seek to do fewer things, but do them better.

So, what are the policy priorities the government must have, and what must it not do? It should exit Air India,[27] Centaur hotels, and banking,

---

25 Vijay Kelkar and Ajay Shah, *In Service of the Republic: The Art and Science of Economic Policy* (New Delhi: Penguin Random House, 2019), 388.

26 It also brings with it a need to invest in technology and design, which is the subject of chapters 5 and 6 respectively.

27 As this book goes to press, it is wonderful to finally have Air India privatised.

and stop fixing pharmaceutical prices and the prices of stents. Let ease of doing business receive the complete (I stress *complete—nothing* else should be undertaken) attention of the DPIIT. Let the PMO worry about the skilling missions, financing the effort but using the NSDC (it was set up for this purpose) and relying on institutions like CII to deliver. And let the ministries of finance and commerce focus on all those things that would enhance the ease of doing business and give us equal access to foreign markets. The national economic agenda in the years ahead must be: getting to 10 per cent annual growth; putting the third and then the fourth quartile to productive work, thus ensuring that they participate in the growth process; and using manufacturing and tourism as our growth dynamo. The important message is that these are the priorities—and nothing else must come close.

THE FUTURE OF INDIAN
INDUSTRY

3

Citizenship: Doing More for Wider Development Goals

Government's work is God's work.
> —Inscription on Vidhana Soudha, Bengaluru

The nine scariest words in the English language are 'I'm from the government, and I'm here to help.'
> —Ronald Reagan

Every policy folly has a precedent in a good country.
> —Ashok Desai

I ended the previous chapter by saying that I expect the government to do less in an India that aspires to lead. More precisely, limited capacity says the state should do fewer things but do them far better. What those things are and how state and institutional capacity should be built is a theme I will return to, especially in chapter 9 on institutions. Limited state capacity leaves space for others to contribute

57

to wider development goals. For India to lead, Indian industry must do much more. Working together with the state and NGOs, we can jointly deliver on wider development objectives in a unique manner. Industry must start by being more ethical, complying with all applicable laws. But Indian industry should go much further, and be good citizens, collaborating with one another and with NGOs, to deliver the inclusive growth that makes for a thriving economy and society. Indeed, in the absence of a capable state, the lead must come from private industry and its associations.

This takes Indian industry much beyond the normal role of business. There are some things within industry's control, such as behaving ethically, that it must do without qualification. There are others that are partially controllable by industry, where we must do more, such as fostering inclusive growth. And then there are things that are quite hard to do, but nevertheless important to try, such as contributing to broader development objectives. We will address all three, starting with 'must do's' and moving onto 'tries'.

An Ethical Industry

As industry, ethical practices build our credibility—with the government, but especially with society at large. As I have said, Nirav Modi and Vijay Mallya are less typical of Indian industry than Tata, Bajaj, Infosys and most other Indian firms. The world must see that. This job—changing public perceptions about industry—is a combination of communication and changing the reality of industry itself. A voluntary code of conduct for full compliance with all applicable laws can help.

Table 3.1: CII Model Code of Conduct

Ethical Business Practices: Ethical Business Practices are a Journey. All Member companies should adopt policies and procedures intended to achieve the following in its business practices:

Accurate Books and Records: The Company will maintain accurate accounts and records which reflect the true and fair picture of the company's affairs in compliance with accepted accounting principles and standards for financial reporting.

Bribery and Corruption: The Company will prohibit bribery in any form in all its business dealings and will maintain strong controls to prevent and detect improper payments. The Company shall comply with anti-money laundering and terrorist financing laws and report unaccounted cash or suspicious transactions.

Fair and Equitable Treatment: The Company shall not unfairly discriminate on the basis of race, caste, religion, colour, ancestry, marital status, gender, sexual orientation, age, nationality, ethnic origin or disability. The Company shall not tolerate harassment, whether sexual, verbal, physical or psychological against any employee.

Health and Safety: The Company shall provide a safe, clean and healthy work environment.

Quality of Goods and Services: The Company shall strive to ensure that its products and services meet the legally required safety and quality standards.

Environment and Society: The Company shall strive to be a good corporate citizen by promoting social welfare activities, promoting sustainability and minimising the adverse impact of company operations on the environment.

Source: CII

This code is designed to be simple—it is less than a page long, covering seven straightforward clauses. CII emphasises that the code is a process and not a destination: the first two sentences say 'Ethical Business Practices are a Journey. All Member companies should adopt policies and procedures intended to achieve the following in its business practices.' The most contentious clause, in all internal discussion within the CII membership, was the one on bribery and corruption: 'The Company will prohibit bribery in any form in all its business dealings and will maintain strong controls to prevent and detect improper payments.' As we discussed this clause, companies fell into three groups. There were those that saw this clause as essential—indeed, there was no point in a code of conduct without such a clause. These firms were already there, and didn't really need the code of conduct. There were those who thought such a clause completely impractical in the Indian context and didn't see much point in any such code beyond window-dressing. And a very large number of firms took the middle ground, they wanted to be compliant but were constantly drawn into making small payments as bribes to get a routine job done. It is for these firms that the code is intended, with the emphasis on ethical practices as a journey and statement of intention. The more that compliance becomes the norm, the easier it is for an honest firm to function easily, as the expectation of bribery declines. As of 2021, around 700 CII members had signed the code, out of a membership strength of 9,000. That is much too few.

CII has also launched codes for the healthcare, real estate and higher education sectors—all sectors with widespread public connect and where self-governance can be powerful. Providers should thrive on quality and transparency to prosper. Again, the goal is to progressively move these vital people-facing sectors of industry forward.

Has corruption increased? If you ask the average person whether there is more or less corruption today than in 1991, they will say it has increased. But has it? Corruption requires two things—scope and opportunity. Scope arises when choices are made by politicians or bureaucrats instead of the market. The opportunity stems from some market distortion that raises prices. For example, raising steel tariffs results in a price and profit increase, which can be shared. If one raises tariffs on a case-by-case basis, then the opportunities for gaming the system increase. The February 2021 budget, for example, raised the tariff from 0 to 10 per cent for cotton fabric, 15 per cent for solar lanterns and 20 per cent for solar arrays. The logic behind the variation is unknown. Other opportunities come from the state awarding large infrastructure projects with conditions that limit bidders; or a contract to buy defence equipment, with transparency hidden behind the label 'national security'; or one may need to apply for a telecom or airline licence to operate (or even to fly to a particular destination overseas), and these licences are in the gift of ministers or bureaucrats instead of being either freely available or transparently auctioned; or FSI (Floor-space Index) regulations in real estate, where a higher limit is within the discretion of the state government, instead of freely available to all. The examples I've given are all in those areas where state discretion still applies—land, defence purchases, telecom, infrastructure contracts, mining and tariffs. It is no coincidence that these are the areas where rumours of corruption still circulate. Before 1991, when almost anything required a licence, the scope for corruption was much greater. So, while a few sensational cases capture our attention and tell us that corruption has increased (which economists call salience), the reality is that the scope for corruption was dramatically reduced post 1991. We must not go back to a control and tariff economy: corruption will accompany its return.

We should go further. For too many years Indian industry has looked to the government for help—for protection from imports, tax relief to help boost demand, concessions and incentives for investment, and to put in a word with a bank to extend a loan. Corruption feeds on this culture of supplication, deference and vassaldom. We must deal with the government as independent equals—praising when praise is due, but criticising when criticising is called for. In return, the government should trust industry to do right. Arvind Subramanian, Chief Economic Advisor between 2014 and 2018, argued passionately in his *Economic Surveys* that stigmatised capital is one of our great national challenges, hampering everything from privatisation to the resolution of bad debts. Indian industry has to take the lead in dispelling that stigma.

Being more ethical and independent of the government is the 'must-do' category for Indian industry. But it is also in our long-term interest to be good citizens and promote a wider development agenda.

Good Citizenship

Corporate Social Responsibility (CSR): In 2012, a new company law mandated companies to spend 2 per cent of net profits on CSR, and if they did not, to explain why in their annual report. The initial message was one of trust, the expectation one of responsibility. Over time, this became more coercive and in August 2019 the law was amended to make officers of a company culpable for not meeting the 2 per cent norm.[1] When the law first came into force, I was against it. I felt that companies should undertake CSR work because they saw it as their responsibility as good citizens, not because it was mandated by company law. Over time, I've changed my mind and believe the law to be broadly a good thing. The better companies around the country have set up active CSR committees. NGOs submit many proposals to them and companies bring clear assessment criteria for both awarding funds and reviewing impact. The net effect is a flow of better development projects that are better funded—an overall significant impact. The data on compliance for the larger companies shows a substantive contribution. For instance, KPMG reports that 76 per cent of India's 100 largest companies in 2018–19 spent the mandated 2 per cent, up from 36 per cent in

---

1   Initially, violations were made a criminal offence, with penal provisions for the officers of a company. This absurd provision was later dropped, but the culpability of company officers remains.

2014–15, the first year that the law applied. Even more encouraging was the fact that India's top 100 companies spent Rs 8,700 crore on CSR in 2018–19, against the prescribed Rs 8,500 crore (some companies spent more than the prescribed 2 per cent). This amount only covers the corporate CSR spend—it does not include spending by associated trusts. To take just two examples, the Tata Group spent Rs 940 crore as corporate CSR and another Rs 1,560 crore from the two main Tata Trusts—a total of Rs 2,500 crore on a profit of Rs 40,000 crore. The Bajaj Group spent Rs 223 crore from its corporate CSR and another Rs 43 crore from trusts. During the pandemic, where firms in the West looked to the government for massive support, companies in India have themselves been generous. In the second year (2021), Tata provided Rs 2,000 crore and Bajaj Rs 200 crore towards Covid relief.

Table 3.2: India's Top Twelve CSR Spenders, 2018–19 (Rs crore)

		Profit	CSR spend
1.	**Tata Group**	40,000	940 + 1,560
2.	**Reliance**	41,000	850
3.	**HDFC Group**	30,300	617
4.	**ONGC**	24,000	615
5.	**IOCL**	24,500	491
6.	**Infosys**	17,000	340
7.	**ITC**	15,300	307
8.	**NTPC**	11,900	285
9.	**Bajaj Group**	11,100	223 + 43
10.	**Powergrid**	9,300	187
11.	**Wipro**	8,800	185
12.	**BPCL**	10,200	178

Source: CTIER and author's analysis from individual annual reports of India's most profitable companies

I would still argue for a return to CSR spending being an expectation of responsibility, with compliance resting on trust, as being more consistent with an India that wants to lead. While CSR is the most obvious—and direct—area where industry contributes to wider development goals, it is not the most powerful. Industry can have a dramatic impact on national development by making growth more inclusive, which would in turn feed into more rapid growth itself.

Fostering inclusive growth: For much of the 1990s and 2000s, the Indian FMCG industry grew much faster (1.8 times) than GDP. In the last eight years, it has grown slower (0.8 times) than GDP. This, to me, is a failure of inclusion. We have millions more who are eager to become first-time buyers of restaurant meals, refrigerators, hospital services, holidays, motorcycles, ready-made clothes and even toothpaste. Let us continue the discussion we began in the previous chapter on inclusive growth. As we saw there, T.N. Ninan estimates that roughly a quarter of the population would consume a wide variety of consumer goods, and a further quarter some basic consumer goods.[2] That means half the population are either poor or live too marginal an existence to be consistent consumers. If we can bring 700 million more people into the consuming class, we can create wealth for thirty years for all of Indian industry, and for much of the world's industry. This will take a focus on skills and education by both government and industry. It really is in our direct interest. *This is the Indian Opportunity.* Speaking to a CII gathering in his last months as President of India, Pranab Mukherjee said that 'An inclusive growth process requires Indian industry to assume the mantle of responsibility and corporate citizenship'. Many cite inclusive growth as a *caveat* to our economic progress. I am going further and saying that being inclusive *is* the way to lead the world.

---

2   T.N. Ninan, *The Turn of the Tortoise: The Challenge and Promise of India's Future* (New Delhi: Penguin Random House India, 2016).

Primary education is key: What will it take? The key is to enable inclusion through education. The NGO Pratham provides us with an *Annual State of Education Report* (ASER) that measures learning outcomes for schoolchildren. The 2018 report illustrates how poorly we fare in giving our children the basic tools needed to function in a modern economy. In 2018, only 44 per cent of children in class five could read a text meant for class two. Just 23 per cent of children in class five could do division. The spread between states is sobering—in the bottom four states (Jharkhand, Assam, Madhya Pradesh and Uttar Pradesh), only a third of children in class five can read a text meant for class two, and under a fifth can do division. In the 'top-performing' states (Himachal Pradesh, Kerala, Punjab and Maharashtra), around two-thirds of children in class five can read a class-two text, and a third to a half can do division. ASER sums up that 'we are far from becoming an educated nation'.[3] Children do, eventually, learn to read and to do division: by class eight, the great bulk can. But if it takes all of primary and middle school to learn to read and do arithmetic, most of the learning that should happen in school simply goes missing and the child struggles to ever catch up.

The solution is to ensure they do not fall behind at the start. Karthik Muralidharan, a specialist in the economics of education, has a clear prescription: 'The single most important outcome that education policy needs to deliver on for the future of the country is to ensure, by 2022, universal functional literacy and numeracy for all schoolchildren by the end of grade three.' He then discusses how: by investing in 'universal preschool education ... supplemental instructional support to children who are falling behind ... and independent measurement and monitoring of the achievement of these goals'.[4]

---

3   *ASER 2018*, published in 2019, is the latest comprehensive report. The 2019 report that came out in 2020 focuses on early learning. The 2020 report is focused on responses to Covid-19 instead of being comprehensive.

4   Karthik Muralidharan, 'Fixing Schools: Reforming the Indian School Education System', in *What the Economy Needs Now,* edited by Abhijit Banerjee, Gita Gopinath, Raghuram Rajan, and Mihir Sharma (New Delhi: Juggernaut Books, 2019).

The ASER report has become the primary source of assessing outcomes for school education in India. Many countries rely on an international comparison—the Programme for International Student Assessment (PISA)—to assess how their school system performs. It is conducted by the OECD every three years. In the last round, eighty-eight countries participated in this assessment of science, reading and mathematics for fifteen- and sixteen-year-olds. In 2009, India tentatively participated with two states, Himachal Pradesh and Tamil Nadu; we ranked 72 out of 74. We then blamed the test, and dropped out. The current government, to its credit, has said we will participate from the next round in 2022. The intention is to have some of our best public schools (the Kendriya Vidyalayas, Jawahar Navodaya Vidyalayas and those from Chandigarh) participate the first time, with greater coverage following in the future.

Primary education is a key state role. In every country, it is one of the state's primary responsibilities, but industry can help. As a part of CSR, many CII companies work actively with schools around the country. Education is already the largest single area for CSR spending, accounting for one-third of the Rs 8,700 crore spent by the top 100 companies. My estimate is that the top 1,000 firms in the CII membership work with around 30,000 schools in the country. Assuming an average of fifty children in class two per school, if every CII company worked on this one goal of ensuring that a child entering class three could read and do arithmetic at class-two level, we could improve education outcomes for 1,500,000 children a year. Just our own firm, Forbes Marshall, works with eighty schools in Pune district and could influence outcomes for 9,000 primary school children.

Education in the English language: A close college friend is a bilingual schoolteacher in California. Over the years, she convinced me that teaching young Hispanic children in a mix of English and Spanish delivered better learning outcomes. The key, though, was *bilingual* instruction—teaching content in a language of familiarity while simultaneously teaching the child to be fully comfortable in English. We do not, officially, have bilingual schools in India. Unofficially, that's just what we have in abundance. Given a choice, parents opt for their children to be schooled in English, which is seen as the language of upward mobility. It is. But if you walk into a typical English-medium school, you will find much of the instruction—and most of the supplementary explanations—happening in the regional language, while the texts and tests are in English. That's not what is supposed to happen, but in my view, it is an effective combination. Our principles may baulk at this elevation of English, that colonial hangover, but let's leave the choice to parents. In an April 2020 survey of the parents of 1.8 million children in Andhra Pradesh, 96 per cent opted for English as the medium of instruction to 3 per cent Telugu.[5] The wonderful R.K. Laxman, as always, caught it best.

Oh, I delivered the speech in English, did I? I forgot!

<hr />

5   *The New Indian Express*, 'Whopping 96.17 per cent parents prefer English medium: Government survey', Vijayawada, 1 May 2020.

In Gujarat and West Bengal, the state government stopped teaching English at the primary level in government schools in 1961 and 1983 respectively. Ever wonder why these two states, otherwise culturally advanced, lag the country in the presence of the information technology and IT services industries? Look no further.[6] If we let ideology come in the way of common sense and parental choice, we directly affect the subsequent economic choices and prospects of our young people. In West Bengal, English was restarted in primary schools in 2004 and in Gujarat in 2007, but these states remain years behind Tamil Nadu, Maharashtra, Andhra Pradesh, Telangana and Kerala in the presence of the IT industry.

The choice of English-medium instruction by parents might offend the sensibilities of activists, but it demonstrates a deep understanding of economics. A study done in 2013 compared average hourly wages for English and non-English speakers.[7] The study corrected for age, gender, social group, educational attainment, secondary school leaving certificate test performance, and district of residence (urban or rural). On average, men fluent in English earn 34 per cent and women 22 per cent more per hour.

What can Indian industry do? In 1991, an NGO called Akanksha was set up in Mumbai to provide English-conversation skills to socially disadvantaged children. Companies were encouraged to set up Akanksha Centres. At its height, in 2007, there were sixty Akanksha Centres run by several different companies in Mumbai and Pune, with 3,000 children. In the process of learning English, children also discovered that learning could be fun. Akanksha has since morphed into an enterprise where schools are adopted by and run by corporates.

---

6   Gujarat is also one of our richest states. West Bengal was our richest state at Independence and is now around the median.

7   Mehtabul Azam, Aimee Chin and Nishith Prakash, 'Does it pay to speak English in India?' in *Ideas for India*, 20 September 2013. The degree concerned is the minimum graduate degree of a three-year bachelor of arts or commerce. https://www.ideasforindia.in/topics/macroeconomics/does-it-pay-to-speak-english-in-india.html

The impact might be greater on the children covered, but years after the change, I cannot help thinking that the original Akanksha model of a low-cost supplement to the existing public-school system had much to offer in impacting thousands of children each year.

Table 3.3: Effect of English-language Skills on Wage Rates

Age	Qualification	For men		For women	
		Returns to fluent English (%)	Returns to little English (%)	Returns to fluent English (%)	Returns to little English (%)
—	Average	34	13	22	10
36–65 years	No degree	53	34	49	44
	With degree	28	14	15	23
18–35 years	No degree	13	-6	-11	-9
	With degree	40	17	55	29

Source: Adapted from Azam, Chin and Prakash, 'Does it pay to speak English in India?'

Workforce participation: India has among the lowest female participation rates in the labour force worldwide and the lowest among the top twenty world economies.[8] This has been getting worse. Since 2005, female participation in the labour force has declined from 35 per cent to 21 per cent. The International Monetary Fund (IMF) estimates that if female participation in India matched the world average of 50 per cent, we would be 27 per cent richer as a country. And if we equalise female to male participation (76 per cent), we would be 60

---

8   See World Bank, Labour force participation rate (data.worldbank.org). When I wrote the first draft of this chapter, India had the second-lowest female labour force participation of the top twenty economies—only Saudi Arabia was lower. As I write this last draft, at 21 per cent we have now fallen below even Saudi Arabia's 22 per cent.

per cent richer as a country. Clearly, we have to educate girls better. We especially need to change cultural attitudes that keep women away from the workforce. Families should encourage women to work and enterprises should actively seek to employ more women. This must be a key national priority, which industry can substantially contribute to.

Let me narrate an experience from the company I work with, Forbes Marshall. One of our most satisfying CSR projects is aimed at enabling girls to finish high school. This project runs in forty hamlets in and around Chakan, a prime industrial area on the outskirts of Pune. These hamlets are within a few kilometres of some of the leading companies in India; their residents have a tribal background, speaking a dialect of Thakari which has very little to do with the state language of Marathi. The larger hamlets have a primary school within them and most children go to them. But once the girls turn twelve or fourteen and need to go to a secondary school, things become difficult. The secondary school is around 8 kilometres away, through hilly terrain. The bus service is erratic and not coordinated with school timings, so the girls walk to and from school taking two to three hours a day. They do so in groups of three or four for safety, but if there is only one girl from the hamlet, she often drops out.

The Forbes Marshall intervention has been very simple. We provide the transport, track the girls' performance in school and help the school with any facilities it needs. In all, 300 girls come from 40 hamlets within a radius of 15 kilometres of the secondary school. The cost is negligible—a full cost of around Rs 8,000 per girl per year. But it is quite management-intensive (including the personal involvement of our gifted CSR manager), as each girl's needs are different. We are now being joined by Tata Motors and some other Chakan companies in scaling up the programme to all 188 villages and 80 schools in Khed Taluka. As things currently stand, around 1,000 girls in the taluka (one-third) drop out of school between classes six and ten.

The impact is on one girl at a time. In one family in Koregaon village, two sisters have very different prospects. One, aged sixteen, is going to a secondary school under this scheme 10 kilometres away. Her sister, aged seventeen, has dropped out. The parents live a tenuous existence as landless labourers, working for a few months a year to bring in a harvest, for which they are paid in grain. Within 200 metres of their home on the side of a hill is an auto component factory of India's largest industrial house. They are happy to hire local girls and boys for various services, but they require that they complete class ten. The younger sister can hope for such a job, and in turn, a life with better prospects; for the older sister, her next step is getting a job in domestic service in Mumbai through some connection and/or marriage.

I am providing all this detail because including hundreds of millions of the youth in our growth process is both a macro and micro challenge. Yes, we need the right policies, for education, infrastructure, public transport and the like. But we also need an on-the-ground connect that meets the needs of one village, even one person, at a time. As a result of such an intervention, if those 1,000 girls in the taluka who drop out instead of completing school each get a good job it transforms the prospects of their families. Maybe some can go on to college and repeat, for each of their families, the story of our security guard (discussed in chapter 2) whose children became engineers and doctors. Do this with enough families and one builds the community at the level of the whole village. Over time, the village can become self-sustaining. At very low cost, but with high management involvement, company CSR can help provide that village-by-village connect. This is an area where industry can do much more.

I learnt this from watching my father, Darius, at work. I saw him spending hours helping individuals in all walks of life perform better— our social worker, a carpenter, a mason. I kept thinking that he should spend his time on 'bigger things', but today if I consider the hundreds of individuals whose lives are simply better thanks to him, I can't think of anything better to do. A few years ago, one of our product designers was scouting around for a plastic moulding, not a typical thing we buy. He visited a company that was one of the leading local suppliers. The sales team said our requirement was too small for them to be interested. At some point, the owner came in and joined the conversation. When he found out that the designer was from our company, he said he'd do it and asked the designer to specify the price at which he wanted it, to the surprise of both our designer and his own sales team. The owner explained that some twenty-five years earlier, he had got his start in business thanks to my father. Development happens one individual at a time.

A Broader Development Agenda

In 2007, when independent India turned sixty, the management thinker C.K. Prahalad gave a speech in New York for CII where he called for some ambitious goals to be achieved by the time we turned seventy-five. The CII India@75 trust that resulted has provided thought leadership for some important initiatives, which have evolved into official government policy. The ambition to skill 500 million Indians led to the creation of the NSDC in 2008, with industry leadership of skills development councils for forty different skills. The NSDC is 51 per cent private sector owned and 49 per cent government owned. Another initiative aims to improve traffic flow, civic amenities, public transport and urban planning in several Indian cities.

The Pune model: In the mid-2000s, as India's growth far outstripped its ability to commission new power plants, power shortages were rife across the country. State governments coped by load-shedding, where different cities in the state fixed weekly holidays on different days. When this was not adequate, states adopted compulsory shutdowns of power for a few hours each day for all commercial and domestic consumption. The leading industrial city of Pune had an average daily shortage of 100 megawatts (MW), on a total baseload of 650 MW. The then head of CII's Pune Zone, Pradeep Bhargava, came up with an innovative idea. Larger industrial units had their own generators as backup power for power outages. They would run their generators through the day, making up the 100 MW shortfall. In turn, they would be paid the difference between what they paid the state electricity board for power and the variable cost of running their own generators. This total cost would be recovered by a cess on the electricity bills of more affluent consumers of power in Pune, who were guaranteed 100 per cent availability of power. Pradeep and the CII secretariat steered the whole project to success, convincing the thirty-two firms concerned and interacting with the electricity companies, civil society organisations and the state government. For three or four years, Pune was able to avoid load-shedding when it was common across the country—until capacity caught up with demand and, with it, the need for the scheme.

The Pune Platform for Covid-19 Response (PPCR): As I write this paragraph in September 2020, the fifth WhatsApp message of the day has come in from PPCR. This group was formed by Sudhir Mehta (currently president of the Mahratta Chamber) to coordinate voluntary response to the pandemic. In its first three months, the group raised resources for a range of the essential medical supplies needed—PPE kits, N95 masks and ventilators—largely for public hospitals. This was not simply a matter of funding. One member of the group arranged for PPEs to be imported from China in a special plane, at a time when international flights had ceased. Another located a source of ventilators, imported them and funded them from corporate CSR. The group was even more active in the second wave—funding, finding, buying and transporting in several thousand oxygen generators, concentrators and ventilators on special aircraft and getting private hospitals to expand Covid-bed capacity. Indeed, PPCR put in over 35 per cent of the ventilator capacity in Pune district. It was a remarkable voluntary effort, all paid for and organised by private industry.

One could argue that the government is responsible for ensuring smooth traffic flow, a 24/7 supply of electricity and adequate medical supplies for government hospitals. It is, but in a country like ours, it is not resources that are in short supply. It is management and implementation capacity. Only industry has the capacity for such initiatives that make for better cities and a healthier society. We need many more such initiatives.

Can Covid prompt a new social contract? The Prime Minister, while addressing an industry function in June 2020, urged those present to think big and partner with the government in putting India on the path to growth. This is an important call. There is much that we can achieve if government and industry work towards the same objective and in a spirit of mutual trust.

Employment is one such area. Over 85 per cent of employment in India is in the informal sector. We saw terrible scenes as the Covid-19 health challenge prompted a zero-notice, uncoordinated lockdown which led to an economic crisis. Uniquely in the world, the lockdown stopped logistics and most manufacturing. Smaller firms struggled to stay afloat and pay wages as sales went to zero in April 2020. Airlines, hotels and malls shut down with no prospect of normalcy. Shops and restaurants closed. Construction, our biggest job creator, halted affecting millions. The net effect was a shutdown economy, with dramatic consequences on employment, especially for informal workers. The Centre for Monitoring Indian Economy (CMIE) estimates that between mid-March and mid-April, 120 million people lost their jobs. The labour force participation ratio, amongst the world's lowest, dropped further—from 42 per cent to 35 per cent in a month—and unemployment rose from 7 per cent to 26 per cent in the same period.[9] This was particularly devastating for an economy where most employment is informal. Over two-thirds (seventy million) of our hundred million urban households rely on informal employment—casual labour, construction, petty traders,

---

9   Data from CMIE from an article by Mahesh Vyas in *Business Standard* and personal interview notes.

delivery boys, drivers and domestic service.[10] Most live from day to day, with little cushion. The collapse of these jobs led to a migrant labour tragedy we saw unfold on our TV screens as millions in Delhi, Bandra, Surat and Bengaluru who were left with nothing, returned home to their villages.

For a while, our media was full of discussion of the need to address some of our most chronic social problems. As things improved, CMIE reported that employment bounced back by June 2020, partly by an increase in agricultural jobs. As economic activity restarted in cities, workers returned from villages. As things returned to normal, the priority for addressing our most chronic social problems retreated. We must use this crisis to address labour regulation and living conditions for migrant labour in our cities.

Labour regulation must start with a clear-eyed recognition of facts. We have stringent labour laws to protect workers, but these laws cover only the formal sector (under 15 per cent of employment). This 'labour aristocracy' has almost complete protection and employers almost no flexibility. The informally employed make up 85 per cent of our workforce and have almost no protection, while their employers have almost complete flexibility. The net effect has been that almost no employment has been created in formal employment, while the informal employment market has been vibrant, creating tens of millions of jobs. We must address both ends of the labour spectrum to get the balance right between flexibility and protection for all labour. We need a new employment contract, which retains flexibility for temporary work, part-time work, self-employment and some combination of all three. The flexibility should come with some protection for labour—insurance premiums, say, payable in lieu of contributions to the Employees' State Insurance Corporation that provide support in case of loss of earnings or health emergencies for self or family.

---

10   Rama Bijapurkar and Rajesh Shukla, 'Experts explain: Loss of income—ground-up assessment of recovery support to households', *Indian Express*, 12 April 2020.

This huge project of a new social contract demands good faith and strong leadership by industry, labour and government. Pradeep Bhargava has often involved himself with schemes that help bring out the best in industry. He long chaired the CII Industrial Relations Committee and worked to get eleven core firms (that grew to sixty later) to sign a voluntary code on good practices in dealing with contract labour. Together with Unnikrishnan, the CEO of another firm, he worked for many years in bringing industry, unions and government together at the national level to bring about new labour regulations that increase flexibility for formal labour and increase protection for informal labour. It was these new labour laws that were passed in September 2020. They are a significant step in the right direction, but there is more to do. It will take years to get it right, but if we don't fix our employment system when this issue has achieved such prominence, we will always regret the missed opportunity.

Living conditions in our cities are the second challenge. For too long, we have been content to drive by slums where some of the people who clean our homes, deliver our goods and repair our equipment live in squalor. How do we set in force a massive private home-building programme? It probably needs much more liberal land-use regulations—our cities have among the least generous FSI in the world. New York, Hong Kong and Tokyo have an FSI five times Mumbai's. If five times as many people can live in the same area, this would dramatically reduce rents for quality housing in our cities. Again, this is a multi-year project, and involves state and city governments partnering with private developers. India is unique in having 70 per cent of its population still residing in rural areas. Three-quarters of a century after Independence, this is a statement of failed development. We must encourage the migration of people to higher-productivity occupations in our cities. And we must ensure that clean, affordable and accessible housing is available for all in our cities. A massive project again, with the scale that can prompt a new economic future, post-Covid.

This ties in with our discussion in the previous chapter of the potential for productivity growth by moving occupations. Our lockdown-induced crisis prompted the return of ten million migrants to their villages. An average monthly fall of even Rs 10,000 in each worker's earnings would subtract around a half per cent from GDP. The fact that people moved back to villages out of sheer necessity is a damning development failure.

This must be our programme of work: to fundamentally reform our labour market and to attract migration to our cities where we ensure healthy living conditions. The task is huge, and only a collaboration between all levels of government (Union, state and city) and our dynamic private sector can hope to make substantial progress. If we use the unprecedented health and economic crisis triggered by the Covid-19 pandemic to truly build a new social contract, we will emerge a better nation.

What Role for Policy?

Foreign Contribution Regulation Act (FCRA): September 2020 was a busy month on the policy front. The Union government reconvened Parliament for the first time in six months to push through several laws. The labour reforms I spoke of earlier were passed after great deliberation over many years, and could be implemented well as a result of the groundwork done. The agricultural reforms were also a good idea and in the right direction, but were passed using a brute majority on a Sunday, on a voice vote, with no debate permitted. This caused the Shiromani Akali Dal from Punjab to leave the Union government and prompted massive farmer protests. Agriculture is a state subject under the Indian Constitution, and how the new laws are implemented will depend almost entirely on the states. Time will show how these work out.[11]

---

11   It did. The agricultural reforms were reversed.

We have also seen an amendment to the FCRA. This law was originally introduced by Indira Gandhi during the emergency in 1976. The law was made worse by the UPA Government in 2010. And the NDA Government, in September 2020, perfected the bad law.[12] Individual trustees of social organisations are criminally liable for any violations, even those of a technical nature. Every five years a new application has to be made to the home ministry, which in the past year has approved only a handful of new applications. Instead, 19,000 NGOs have had their FCRA approvals cancelled. Any organisation that receives funds in India from a foreign source now cannot pass these funds on to another social organisation, including another organisation that is FCRA-approved. So, the Gates Foundation or Ford Foundation in India cannot now fund any other organisation in India, unless they get a specific exemption. If an NGO loses, or even gives up, its FCRA status, any assets it has created from the foreign funds are confiscated by the Union government. The entire objective, in a straight line from the government of Indira Gandhi to Narendra Modi, is one of control. Many of our large NGOs get the vast majority of their operating funding (i.e. non-programmatic funds) from foreign contributors. This is partially because foreign funders have deeper pockets, but also because Indian donors tend to not be as open to funding overheads. Ideally, Indian donors will step in and make up for the shortfall from the new FCRA rules, but that's going to take a while to happen. So, this change in law cripples many of our best NGOs, forcing them to try to do more with less infrastructure and skilled talent—ironically at a time when we really need them to be at their highest performance. This is all so contrary to what India needs.

12　The journalist Shekhar Gupta has often pointed out, correctly, that a bad idea only worsens over time. Indira Gandhi was the source of many bad ideas that were perfected by subsequent Congress and BJP (Bharatiya Janata Party) governments alike.

Non-government organisations: We have hundreds of thousands of NGOs in the country (an article some years ago said we had over three million, which must include everyone's socially committed grandmother). Having more NGOs than any other country reflects limited state capacity. If we were Sweden or Singapore, we would not need so much NGO activity. We are India, so we do. These NGOs work in varied fields, including education, health, community development, the arts, and in helping particular disadvantaged groups. Some are small—depending on the voluntary effort of a few committed individuals who have come together. Some have scale—offices in different cities, run by professionals recruited from good universities. In a country like ours, with limited state capacity, NGOs often fill the gap. Some help provide basic needs of education or health. Some play a key role in holding the state to account—providing poorer citizens with the voice to demand that a scheme be implemented or law applied. Most NGOs need access to funds. We should welcome contributions from everywhere, domestic and foreign. Not all this will be to fund work that is equally worthy. The NGO sector, like every other, has its deviants. But should we make law to suit the honest or the criminal?

Make it easy to be good citizens: I've argued in this chapter that industry has a critical role to play in achieving our broader national development goals. At the base level, we need to be ethical and comply with all applicable laws. But India demands much more. The state's low capacity to implement leaves gaps everywhere. These gaps are opportunities to contribute. Only industry has the widespread management and implementation capacity that is needed. Our CSR work can fundamentally improve the education outcomes of a large proportion of the population. We can actively improve women's participation in the workforce. We can work in our cities meeting specific needs of the day—whether these be traffic flow, power supply or dealing with a health crisis. Working with government and city authorities can address some of our most intractable problems, such as getting the balance of flexibility and protection right for the full workforce, or ensuring they have decent housing in our cities. All this may sound much beyond what companies should be expected to do, but when we improve education outcomes, we make the entire country more productive and richer. When we increase workforce participation, we directly increase GDP. Improving the health and quality of life in our cities makes it better for us all. If Covid has taught us anything, it is how interconnected we all are—informal labour with formal, slum with skyscraper, city with village, poor with rich. Development is a long-haul project. We need to think of the India we would like to live in thirty years from now and do our part to get there. Government policy must make it easy to be philanthropic and to be a good citizen in general. It must also trust its citizens to broadly operate in the national interest. The keyword is 'broadly': let the government encourage the 90-plus per cent who are honest, and not penalise us all for the venality of a few. Companies, NGOs and individuals must repay that trust by being good citizens.

4

International: Leading the World by Being in the World

Manmohan Singh has a terrible vice: he actually reads the stuff his friends give him. Worse still, he remembers it.

—Ashok Desai

Miss Prism: 'Cecily, you will read your Political Economy in my absence. The chapter on the Fall of the Rupee you may omit. It is somewhat too sensational. Even these metallic problems have their melodramatic side.'

—*The Importance of Being Earnest,* Oscar Wilde

I have been a reader of *The Economist* for over forty years. In June 1991, it published a survey of the Indian economy, titled 'Caged Tiger', which began with a damning statement: 'Nowhere in the world, not even in the Soviet Union, is the gap between what might have been achieved and what has been achieved as great as it is in India.' As a description of the past, the statement was depressingly accurate. As a forecast of the future, it could not have been more wrong. The survey and statement coincided with the formation of a new government under Narasimha Rao, with Manmohan Singh as finance minister. Dr Singh heralded a new India in a brilliant budget speech one month later on 24 July. He said:

> The thrust of the reform process would be to increase the efficiency and international competitiveness of industrial production ... It is essential to increase the degree of competition between firms in the domestic market ...
>
> The time has come to expose Indian industry to competition from abroad in a phased manner ... We should welcome, rather than fear, foreign investment ...
>
> ... we must restore to the creation of wealth its proper place in the development system. For, without it, we cannot remove the stigma of abject poverty, ignorance, and disease ... We have also to remove the stumbling blocks from the path of those who are creating wealth ... At the same time, we have to develop a new attitude towards wealth ... the philosophy of trusteeship.[1]

Dr Singh's budget speech of 1991 must rank amongst the greatest speeches in Indian history, but it didn't stop at rhetoric. Fully supported and encouraged by Prime Minister Narasimha Rao, major structural policy changes followed. Industrial licensing, Monopolies and Restrictive Trade Practices (MRTP), and the Directorate General of Technical Development (DGTD) were all scrapped, freeing large industry to perform. The rupee was devalued by over 30 per cent, triggering an export boom. Import duty was slashed, with a promise of more to come until we reached global levels.

---

1   Manmohan Singh, 'Budget 1991–92', Speech, Minister of Finance (New Delhi: Government of India, 24 July 1991), https://www.indiabudget.gov.in/doc/bspeech/bs199192.pdf

Dr Singh ended his speech by quoting Victor Hugo, 'No power on earth can stop an idea whose time has come.' He went on to say, 'The emergence of India as a major economic power in the world happens to be one such idea. Let the whole world hear it loud and clear. India is now wide awake.'

That budget speech had so great an impact on my brother Farhad and me that within two weeks the senior management of our company, Forbes Marshall, had completed a detailed analysis. We presented our full product portfolio, and asked what we would still make competitively if it could be imported free of duty (and assuming of course that we could also import any raw materials or components free of duty). We identified half of our manufactured product range as uncompetitive in this scenario and took two calls. First, that investment in R&D would be quadrupled and work only on developing products that we could sell internationally; no more import-substitution projects from then on (which used to be the bulk of what our R&D did, as was the case then for almost all Indian firms). Second, that we would enter international markets in a big way. In 1991, less than 1 per cent of our turnover came from exports. We set a goal of 10 per cent in five years, which we met in six, and then set a goal of 20 per cent, which took us another ten years (we are today at 25 per cent with a goal of crossing 50 per cent in five to seven years). We did so because the world's best would be coming to India, and the best test of whether or not we could compete with them at home was if we could compete with them overseas. Both objectives were a struggle, involving a great deal of learning—R&D took three years of investment before we got our first products out, and five or six years before it became a routine flow. It all started within two weeks of that speech. We look back at that speech as the turning point for our company.

In 1991, Farhad and I did not know Tarun Das or CII, but he had a great deal to do with India's decisive turn to openness and reforms.

In 1963, a twenty-four-year-old Tarun Das was deputed to a small industry body, the Indian Engineering Association in Calcutta. Two mergers and a shift to Delhi later, the institution he built, CII, had become the country's leading industry association. Tarun retired as Director-General in 2004. CII's strength derives from a faithful and strong membership of some of India's leading firms, but even more from a large, independent and professional secretariat. Tarun ensured that office-bearers would be the public face of the institution, but the place would actually be run by the secretariat. My brother Farhad and I have played various roles at CII over three decades. We have been attracted by fine fellow-members, many of whom have become close personal friends. But we have been particularly attracted by the commitment and dedication of the wider CII secretariat to building a great development institution, one which in our view has no parallel in the world.

As CII's reputation grew in the 1980s, Tarun found a receptive ear in the reformers who were increasingly being given voice in government. Never more so than in 1991 when Manmohan Singh, with A.N. Verma in the PMO, Montek Ahluwalia, Ashok Desai and N.K. Singh in the finance ministry, and Rakesh Mohan in the industry department, put through the reforms that transformed India. Opening Indian industry to much greater competition, both domestic and international, was an essential plank of the reform process. We forget how much opposition those reforms triggered at the time—from both the Opposition and within the Congress Party. I remember reading a report of a visit that Manmohan Singh and Ashok Desai made to Kolkata, where they had to leave a public function from the back door because the police feared for their safety. They were attacked for selling out the nation, not least by some prominent industrialists. Tarun Das and CII's support and encouragement of the reform process was, in my view, decisive in making the reforms stick. Montek Ahluwalia says in his memoirs, 'Tarun Das, director-general of the Confederation of Indian Industry (CII), was regarded by many of us as the moving force behind Indian industries' push for bold liberalisation.'[2] Tarun has always had great confidence in Indian industry's ability to compete.

Although I met Tarun often over the years as I played various roles at CII, it was only after my year as president that I have had the pleasure of working closely with him—in the Ananta Aspen Centre, in various Track II Strategic Dialogues, and as a friend and mentor whose guidance I often seek. The consistent freshness of his mind and his ability to push everyone around him to do the right thing for India each time is a constant inspiration. I typically introduce him as the country's second greatest builder of institutions (after our first Prime Minister). His legacy includes the Ananta and Ananta Aspen Centres, the Centre for Energy Environment and Water (CEEW), the Bharatiya Yuva Shakti Trust, the Sasakawa Leprosy Foundation, and Track II dialogues with a dozen countries, but more than any other, the unique institution that is CII.

Exports and the Indian Economy

Forbes Marshall was not alone in the impact of the 1991 reforms. It is worth reminding ourselves just how much of a watershed it was for India, on several counts. In 1991, trade accounted for a smaller share of GDP than in the US or China. Today, after almost a decade of a declining share of trade in our GDP, we are still above the US and China. In 1991, we were the sixteenth largest economy in the world; in 2020, we were the fifth largest.[3] Our foreign reserves in 1991 were down to two weeks of imports; in 2020, they could pay for a year of imports. India's foreign trade had fallen to 0.5 per cent of global trade

---

2   Montek Singh Ahluwalia, *Backstage: The Story behind India's High-growth Years* (New Delhi: Rupa Publications India, 2020), 170.
3   India, Italy, France and the UK are all within 10 per cent of each other—so the fifth- to eighth- place ranking is affected by small changes in exchange rates and growth, and the impact of Covid. We went up to fifth place when we overtook the UK and France in 2019.

Table 4.1: India's Trade as per cent of GDP (1990–2019)

Year	Total exports of goods & services (US$ billion)	Total imports of goods & services (US$ billion)	Trade* (% of GDP)	Nominal GDP (US$ billion)
1990	23	30	15	321
1995	38	48	23	360
2000	60	73	27	468
2005	155	182	42	820
2010	348	439	49	1,676
2012	444	580	56	1,828
2015	429	492	42	2,104
2019	546	616	40	2,875

*Trade is the sum of exports and imports of goods and services measured as a share of gross domestic product.

Source: World Development Indicators (various years); available at https://databank.worldbank.org/source/world-development-indicators#

Figure 4.1: Trade in India, China and the USA

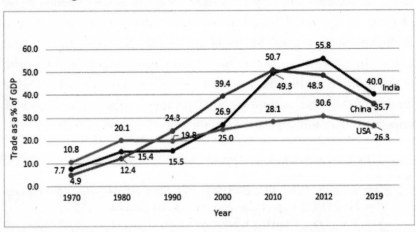

Note: Data reported as 1970 for China and USA is based on figures for 1971.

Source: World Development Indicators (various years); available at https://databank.worldbank.org/source/world-development-indicators#

in 1991, down from 2 per cent at Independence; we were at 1.7 per cent in 2020. Indian companies in 1991 were pygmies by international standards—the entire market cap of the top 100 firms on the Bombay Stock Exchange was $45 billion; in 2020 five companies—Reliance, Tata Consultancy Services, HDFC, Hindustan Unilever, and Infosys—*each* had a market cap over $45 billion.

By opening India up to the world, the finance minister was applying his academic specialisation. His doctoral thesis (submitted to Oxford University in 1962) had looked at India's export performance in the 1950s. He was later himself a professor of international trade at the Delhi School of Economics and Punjab University. Manmohan Singh's thesis contributed to the debate of whether India is best served by a trade policy that is outward-looking or inward-looking, a debate that is older than I am. From 1947 to 1991, our trade policy was characterised by what was called 'export pessimism'—we doubted our ability to export much, and thus had to conserve our limited foreign exchange and limit imports. From 1991 to 2017, India was increasingly open to the world, with tariff rates coming down, and fewer restrictions on foreign investment inflows and outflows. Exports were a substantial driver of our growth performance, contributing roughly a quarter of our record 8 per cent growth between 2000 and 2010. Since 2017, increasing protectionism has delivered a decisive reversal of our trade policy. It needs another reversal: India's long-term future requires an outward-looking policy. And, further, the long-term durability of an outward-looking policy requires a more confident and outward-looking Indian industry.

Free Trade and Its Critics

The case for free trade: Adam Smith argued that the wealth of nations depends on productivity, and that productivity depends on specialisation and the division of labour. 'The division of labour is limited by the extent of the market', written in 1776, is probably the most famous sentence in economics. Expanding the market *is* the case for trade. But do all countries benefit from trade? What if other countries are more efficient and productive than you are? David Ricardo's theory of comparative advantage argues that even if one country is more competitive in making everything than another, it still benefits by specialising in those things where it is relatively more efficient, exporting those items and importing the rest. Given that the theory of comparative advantage was first published in 1817, even Indian and American policymakers should have understood it by now.

Two hundred years after Ricardo, Professor Arvind Panagariya's *Free Trade and Prosperity* makes an unabashed argument for free trade.[4] Professor Panagariya is one of our most illustrious economists, a world-class academic, who served with distinction as the vice chairman of NITI Aayog for the first three years of the Modi government. As he says in his introduction, while arguments for free trade have often been made for the developed world, his book has the developing world as its focus. He deals systematically with all the arguments against free trade, and addresses the relationship between free trade and each of growth, poverty and inequality. A wealth of empirical data shows that higher rates of growth are strongly correlated with free trade, or at least freer trade. The systematic alleviation of poverty is not directly connected with free trade, but is directly connected with growth. And he shows that inequality is more connected with other factors—levels of primary education and health in particular—than with free trade.

Professor Panagariya then deals with the Asian Tigers (South Korea, Taiwan, Hong Kong and Singapore) before turning to India and China. In each case he shows how the opening of the economy is strongly correlated with more rapid economic growth. He concludes

---

4   Arvind Panagariya, *Free Trade and Prosperity: How Openness Helps Developing Countries Grow Richer and Combat Poverty* (New Delhi: Oxford University Press, 2019).

that there are no exceptions—*no* exceptions—to arguments in favour of free trade, and *no* arguments in favour of protection. The vehemence of the argument and the lack of qualification are unusual for an academic, but are refreshingly direct as a result. As a sometime teacher of economic development, and particularly of the role that technological capability-building plays in economic development, I found the book very interesting. For anyone who has ever taught economic development, with however market-oriented an outlook, one usually made an exception for the protection of an infant industry. In my own case, I usually accompanied an argument in its favour to foster essential learning, with a long quote from John Stuart Mill, the father of liberal economics:

> The only case in which, on mere principles of political economy, protecting duties can be defensible, is when they are imposed temporarily (especially in a young and rising nation) in hopes of naturalising a foreign industry, in itself perfectly suitable to the circumstances of a country. The superiority of one country over another in a branch of production often arises only from having begun it sooner. There may be no inherent advantage on one part, or disadvantage on another, but only a present superiority of acquired skill and experience ... But it cannot be expected that individuals should, at their own risk, or rather to their certain loss, introduce a new manufacture, and bear the burden of carrying it on until the producers have been educated up to the level of those with whom the processes are traditional. A protecting duty, continued for a reasonable time, might sometimes be the least inconvenient mode in which the nation can tax itself for the support of such an experiment. But it is essential that the protection be confined to cases in which there is good ground for assurance that the industry which it fosters will after a time be able to dispense with it; nor should domestic producers ever be allowed to expect that it will be continued to them

beyond the time necessary for a fair trial of what they are capable of accomplishing.[5]

Dr Panagariya refers to this quote somewhat testily in a footnote, and then has a full chapter detailing studies that argue against infant industry protection. Learning, he argues, can be fostered more effectively by other means than protection. While Dr Panagariya is as pure a free *trader* as you can find, allowing no qualifications or exceptions, his is not an argument for complete free *markets*. Market failures do occur, and when they occur need to be addressed through government intervention, but protection is not one of the ways to intervene.

The case for creating comparative advantage: Development economists have tended to less pure prescriptions. One of Professor Panagariya's particular targets, Dani Rodrik, in his book *Straight Talk on Trade*, published around the same time as *Free Trade and Prosperity*, argues for a more qualified approach to trade:

> Countries that managed to leverage globalisation, such as China and Vietnam, employed a mixed strategy of export promotion and a variety of policies that violate current trade rules. Subsidies, domestic-content requirements, investment regulations, and, yes, often import barriers were critical to the creation of new, higher-value industries. Countries that rely on free trade alone (Mexico comes immediately to mind) have languished.[6]

Abhijit Banerjee and Esther Duflo in their wonderful book *Good Economics for Hard Times* have a chapter titled 'The Pains from Trade'.

---

5   John Stuart Mill quoted by Sanjaya Lall in 'The East Asian Miracle: Does the Bell Toll for Industrial Strategy?' *World Development* 22, no. 2 (1994).
6   Dani Rodrik, *Straight Talk on Trade: Ideas for a Sane World Economy* (Princeton, NJ: Princeton University Press, 2018), 3.

Like all of the book, it is worth reading at least twice. There is insight on every page that combines equal mastery of theory and empiricism.

Instead of focusing on their differences, I'd like to point out the common ground between Panagariya and Banerjee/Rodrik.[7] Both perspectives share the same end objective: a future where firms compete without the need for protection, and export on the basis of their comparative advantage. Both also see trade as growth-enhancing and necessary. Growth-enhancing, as trade expands the market and provides opportunity for specialisation. Necessary, as a disciplining tool—as with Forbes Marshall, if you can be successful against competitors overseas, you can compete with them brilliantly at home.

Both perspectives also argue that countries and firms need to create future sources of comparative advantage in higher-value industries, but differ on how to do so. Dani Rodrik sees protection as a legitimate part of the toolkit[8] for creating future comparative advantage. Arvind Panagariya sees any compromise of free trade as dangerous, as a slippery slope to inefficiency, with the Indian experience clearly at the top of his mind. I appreciate Dani Rodrik's argument, and especially his plea for pragmatism instead of dogmatism. Both Dani Rodrik and Abhijit Banerjee argue strongly and persuasively that the biggest mistake in development policy is to think there is one right policy for all countries that applies at all points in time.

But I share Panagariya's fear, with the Indian experience also at the top of my mind. It is good to remind ourselves how far we progressed between 1991 and 2017, as the data at the start of this chapter showed. By opening up to the world, and by the removal of myriad other controls, Indian industry was transformed. And the transformation of Indian industry transformed India. The real

---

7   In so doing, I fear friends on both sides of the debate will hate me. Sorry Arvind, sorry Abhijit. A future in politics beckons!

8   But he does emphasise it's a *part* of the toolkit.

strength of Panagariya's book lies in its timeliness. I deliberately picked 2017 as the end date for this transformation, because things have since gone into reverse. We have had several rounds of tariff increases. This is a dangerous trend, one with the potential to derail our progress. We seem to be doing exactly what Arvind Panagariya says we should not, on the basis of both economic theory and empirical evidence. Dr Panagariya's best case is don't protect. We have started protecting. His second-best case is that if you do protect, then protect across products and the value-chain equally and modestly. We have been protecting completely variably, with tariff rates for some goods increasing three and four times in a few months, and huge variability between the lowest and highest rates. And his third-best case is that if you do protect variably, then protect the finished good, not the intermediate product. We are doing exactly the reverse—with high tariffs on steel and none on engineering products and higher tariffs on fabric than on garments. Surely, we deserve a better trade policy than fourth best.

Have Free-trade Agreements (FTAs) Helped India?

The world is full of various regional trade agreements (the WTO recognises well over 400 such agreements, and counting). India is no exception, we already have FTAs with Sri Lanka and Bangladesh, the Association of Southeast Asian Nations (ASEAN), Japan and South Korea, and were negotiating a trade agreement with Australia and New Zealand.[9] Such trade agreements cover similar ground. All address trade in goods, and often include some combination of trade in services, trade facilitation and classification, non-tariff barriers, intellectual property, competition policy, investment policy, and dispute resolution. Across industry and in government, a view has emerged

---

9   There were eleven trade agreements—including with Sri Lanka, Bangladesh, Singapore, Thailand, ASEAN, Less-Developed Countries, South Korea, Japan, Chile and Mercosur—signed by India between 2000 and 2012.

that these FTAs have not served India well, and even actively damaged Indian industry. Is this view correct? Tales of woe of specific sectors and individual firms abound. What does the aggregate data show?

The success of an FTA should be judged against its objective of enhancing trade. If the *proportion* (and not just absolute level) of *both* imports and exports between the countries concerned has grown, then an FTA is successful for both parties. That is its intended effect—to move trade in the direction of the FTA country relative to others. If only one of imports or exports have grown, then the benefits have been one-sided. If the proportion has stayed the same or fallen, then the FTA has had no effect.

India's trade patterns—to FTA or not to FTA? Table 4.2 shows India's trading volumes for 1999–2000 and 2018–19. Strong annual growth over nineteen years in both imports (14 per cent) and exports (12 per cent) has taken our trade volume from $85 billion in 2000 to $850 billion in 2018–19. Of this, $152 billion was with countries with which we have FTAs. Both exports and imports has grown. The India–Japan FTA would seem to have been completely ineffective for both countries, as our share of imports and exports have fallen substantially. The South Korean FTA seems to have worked to South Korea's advantage, with our share of exports staying the same, while our imports have risen. Our FTA with Bangladesh seems to have benefited India, with our share of exports growing.

Compare trade patterns with our major non-FTA trading partners: the US, EU and China. These three accounted for 32 per cent of our imports in both 2000 and 2019, and 50 per cent of our exports in 2000, falling to 38 per cent in 2019. The US has retained its importance for us in both imports and exports, while the EU has declined. The big winner is China. From 2.6 per cent of our imports and 1.5 per cent of our exports in 2000, China accounted for 13.7 per cent of our imports and 5.2 per cent of our exports in 2019, making it our largest trading partner after the US.

Table 4.2: India's Trade with FTA and Key Non-FTA Countries

Country	India's imports 1999–2000 (US$ million)	Share of total imports %	India's imports 2018–19 (US$ million)	Share of total imports %	India's exports 1999–2000 (US$ million)	Share of total exports %	Indian exports 2018–19 (US$ million)	Share of total exports %
ASEAN 10	4,600	9.2	59,000	11.6	2,200	5.9	37,000	11.2
Sri Lanka	44	0.1	1,500	0.3	500	1.4	4,700	1.4
Bangladesh	78	0.2	1,000	0.2	640	1.7	9,200	2.8
Japan	2,500	5.0	13,000	2.5	1,700	4.6	4,900	1.5
South Korea	1,100	2.2	17,000	3.3	480	1.3	4,700	1.4
Total FTA	**8,322**	**17.0**	**91,500**	**18.0**	**5,520**	**15.0**	**60,500**	**18.0**
China	1,300	2.6	70,000	13.7	540	1.5	17,000	5.2
EU countries	11,000	22.0	58,000	11.4	9,700	26.2	57,000	17.3
USA	3,600	7.2	36,000	7.1	8,400	22.7	52,000	15.8
Top non-FTA	**15,900**	**32.0**	**164,000**	**32.0**	**18,640**	**50.0**	**1,26,000**	**38.0**
India's non-oil import/export	50,000		510,000		37,000		330,000	

Sources: Department of Commerce, Government of India; Centre for Technology, Innovation and Economic Research.

What the trade data means: Overall, our FTAs have had little effect on our trade flows. They accounted for 16.3 per cent of our trade in 2000 and 17.9 per cent of it in 2019. They have not been a disaster for Indian industry, but we have certainly not seen the benefits from the FTAs that we expected. Three reasons why:

India is not the only country signing FTAs. ASEAN, South Korea and Japan have FTAs with many more countries than we do, including China. Some of these are much wider and deeper than ours—so-called zero-for-zero agreements, where zero items are excluded from the FTA and a zero tariff often applies in both directions. This enables close supply-chains to develop and prosper, for example in electronics, where components and subassemblies wander around Asia with tiny bits of value-addition at each step in each country. That's an altogether nice demonstration of Adam Smith's 'degree of specialisation being limited by the extent of the market'. By excluding many items from agreements, we limit the extent of the market and our ability to participate in these supply-chains.

Tariffs are not the only barriers to trade. My favourite non-tariff barrier from some years ago is when France required electronic consumer products to be imported only through the port of Lyon. This would have been fine, except that Lyon is not a port. Our pharmaceutical firms report great difficulty in getting approvals to sell in Indonesia, South Korea and Japan in spite of specific inclusion in the FTA. Sector-specific subcommittees are to be set up to address such issues, but have not been formed—still a clear opportunity.

Most importantly, trade patterns reflect underlying industrial competitiveness. It is no accident that we have seen the greatest growth in our imports from China (up fifty-four times), South Korea (up fifteen times) and Vietnam (up sixty-five times). We have no FTA with China, but we have grown our imports from China dramatically, so how can FTAs be blamed for our trade performance? China, South Korea and Vietnam are among the world's most competitive countries, and almost any country's trade balance has moved substantially in favour of these three. We might complain about non-tariff barriers and higher costs of doing business, but improving our competitiveness is the surest way of improving our trade balance. I will return to this point later in the chapter.

Who's afraid of RCEP? The Regional Comprehensive Economic Partnership (RCEP) brings together the ten countries of

ASEAN in South East Asia, Japan, South Korea, Australia, New Zealand, China and, until 2019, India. These sixteen countries account for almost half the world's population, a third of world GDP and trade, and are collectively growing at a rate that is double that of the rest of the world. The Indian economy is large, but the rest of RCEP is eight times the size. It is by far the most attractive market in the world today—and will be for the next twenty years. RCEP is not only ambitious in scale, but also in scope, going well beyond trade in goods. After protracted negotiations that began in 2012, the fifteen RCEP members (minus India) signed an agreement in November 2020. Our Prime Minister went to Bangkok in November 2019 for the final discussion on RCEP, with wide expectation that we would join. We didn't.

RCEP is good for India: Our negotiators had obtained a good deal for us in RCEP. Some say that we dropped out because of a need to protect the Indian farmer. This is surprising, as almost all agricultural items, including milk, were in the excluded list. Dairy *products* were included—so was it the Indian food-processing company, and not the Indian farmer, that we sought to protect? For industrial products, China was provided less access and a longer adjustment period than the other fourteen countries. For example, RCEP covered 90 per cent of all traded items (tariff lines, in trade negotiator jargon) for ASEAN, but only 74 per cent of all traded items for China. For ASEAN, most items had zero duty, but for China there was a long adjustment period of five, ten, fifteen, twenty and even twenty-five years. Finally, India asked for an automatic safeguard against a sudden surge in imports for any item from China, a unique provision. China had agreed for some sixty of our most sensitive items. We wanted more, but surely this could also have been negotiated to an acceptable conclusion.

In all trade deals, there are things to negotiate, interests to protect and advance, and domestic political concerns to satisfy. But if a decisive Prime Minister who likes to travel the world meeting other leaders, and heads a government with a strong majority, can't address these issues then who can? RCEP provided us with the stepping stones to integrate with the best in the world—a long adjustment period, graduated tariff reduction, hundreds of excluded items, and friends like Japan and Singapore that supported our negotiating position. The fear of being flooded with imports from China led many sections of Indian industry to argue strongly against RCEP. Our decision to drop out of RCEP reflects this desire to protect the short-run interests of Indian industry against the long-run interest of enabling it to compete with the world. So, what trade policy will further the long-run interests of Indian industry?

Old Wine in New Bottles? Atmanirbhar and Production-linked Incentives (AN–PLI)

As Covid and our stringent lockdowns wrecked the Indian economy in April and May 2020, the government announced a new economic programme, called Atmanirbhar (AN), or self-reliance. Launching the policy of self-reliance, the Prime Minister referred to two medical items (PPE kits and N95 masks) in his first speech on the subject. And in a second speech at the CII AGM in June 2020, he asked why we imported thirty per cent of the airconditioners sold in the country. All three examples have one thing in common: imports from China. We export $15 billion of goods to China each year, mainly raw materials such as iron ore. We import $75 billion of goods from China (the Covid-19 virus was supplied free), almost all manufactured goods, equal to around one-fifth of our national manufacturing output. China is a manufacturing superstar, with deep supply-chains across items.

The term self-reliance harks back to what was official Indian policy for over forty years. Jawaharlal Nehru made the memorable statement, 'I believe, as a practical proposition, that it is better to have a second-rate thing made in our own country than a first-rate thing we have to import.' That is exactly what the policy delivered for forty years, until Manmohan Singh's landmark budget of 1991,[10] except that some items produced could only be described as second rate if one was being extremely polite.[11]

The government says this rediscovered self-reliance is an outward-looking policy. But how can a policy that relies on tariff protection against imports be outward-looking? How can self-reliance help deliver a vibrant and competitive manufacturing sector?

The PLI scheme, launched in July 2020, aims to do this. Mobile phones have over the last three years been subject to an import duty of 20 per cent. The PLI scheme provides an incentive as a per cent of sales for firms that deepen supply-chains in a list of 'desirable' components or assemblies. Components for mobile phones will attract an incentive of 6 per cent of sales. A subsequent announcement incentivised the local production of fifty-three active pharmaceutical ingredients that go into the manufacture of drugs. Further schemes have been announced for medical devices and electronics manufacturing, and another half dozen sectors have been added. The PLI scheme aims to enhance competitiveness by deepening supply-chains. It will be partially financed by ending the Merchandise Export Incentive Scheme which this same government had introduced in 2015, which cost Rs 45,000 crore annually and did nothing to boost exports ($310 billion in 2014–15; $313 billion in 2019–20). Will PLI work?

---

10 Manmohan Singh's budget reversed decades of inward-looking, self-reliant policies. It was striking to me that he still felt compelled to refer to his budget as one for 'growth, equity, and self-reliance'.

11 Ashok Desai points out that protection was actually official Indian policy for over fifty years, if one counts the severe import controls introduced by the British on the outbreak of World War II in 1939.

This question has rekindled the old debate—are we better off with a regime of tariffs and import substitution, or a regime of trade liberalisation and export promotion? In AN-PLI, India is not alone. As *The Economist* points out, governments in many countries, China and India among them, have dusted off the old idea of import-substituting industrialisation.[12] It combines with that other old idea being 'dusted off': self-reliance (atmanirbharta). Perhaps the memory of being colonised by an MNC (the East India Company) and the freedom struggle powered by ideas of swadeshi are the reasons why self-reliance still has so much emotional and political resonance. Still, three-quarters of a century after the British left our shores, we should surely be more secure.

Making self-reliance work: The sociologist Ronald Dore was a great scholar of Japan. During a visit to Delhi in the early 1980s, he wrote a paper on self-reliance in India, subtitled 'Sturdy ideal or self-serving rhetoric'. It provides us with both the direction of what we must do to make self-reliance work (the sturdy ideal), and a clear warning of what to stay away from (the self-serving rhetoric). Dore's essential argument was that India needed to learn from the best in the world, that this learning required a systematic and considerable effort, and that in matters of self-reliance learning mattered more than creating.

Dore was writing at the time when self-reliance was key to Indian economic policy. It condemned us to substandard goods, sold at a high price. Some of us are old enough to remember that every new Premier Padmini or Ambassador we bought—with a five-year waiting list—was a twenty-year old-design, and that Indian Airlines published a timetable for the sole purpose of allowing passengers to calculate how late they were. My favourite cartoonist, R.K. Laxman captured things best with a brilliant cartoon from the 1970s:

---

12 *The Economist*, 'Why is the idea of import-substitution being revived?' 7 November 2020.

... and so the only small, economy, low-cost car with a high indigenous content capable of being mass-produced in the public sector, I can think of is ...

India in the 1970s was a miserable place for the vast majority of Indians. We must not go back there.

Will AN–PLI build world–competitive firms? There is much for us to learn from the experience of Japan, South Korea and Taiwan in the 1950s to 1970s.

The period of protection must be certain—and temporary: At the heart of self-reliance is tariff protection. Make no mistake, a tariff on imports is a tax on consumers who pay more than they would without the tariff. How do we justify such a tax on ourselves? Only if the tax is temporary (five years, say), and results in a world-competitive industry that needs no further protection—an industry the country would not otherwise have. Mill said this in 1848; let's follow it in 2022.

The government has imposed a tariff on both air conditioners and the components that go into them—compressors, controllers, evaporators, and such. A good phased manufacturing programme has a defined time frame for the protection to go to zero. But in India we have the tariff increasing over time—to 30 per cent from the current 20 per cent for the finished air conditioner and from 10 to 20 per cent for components. Should the Indian consumer really have to pay 30 per cent more than the world price five years from now?

The schedule of tariff reduction must also be fully credible. Robert Wade shows that Taiwan used tariff protection across many industrial sectors—textiles, steel, plastics, consumer electronics, semiconductors—in the 1960s, 1970s and 1980s.[13] All of those were successful in establishing globally competitive industries, as the tariff protection was dismantled. Their experience with cars was different, as protection was provided in the 1960s and early 1970s. The state then opened up the car market as scheduled, in spite of protests from local industry that it would be wiped out (it was, but subsequently every other industry believed more strongly that protection was temporary). So we need a phased tariff reduction for air conditioners to zero, and we need it announced transparently ahead of time and stuck to, so that firms know exactly what to expect and can invest in confidence of a clear and unchanging policy. Tariffs always have to be removed before firms are entirely ready to deal with the removal—competitiveness cannot be a choice left to firms.

Combine protection with exports: Japan, South Korea and Taiwan are models for the advocates of both import substitution and

13   Robert Wade, *Governing the Market: Economic Theory and the Role of Government in East Asian Industrialization* (Princeton, NJ: Princeton University Press, 1990).

export promotion. Any thoughtful study of Japanese industrialisation in the 1950s and 1960s, and South Korea and Taiwan's industrialisation in the 1960s and 1970s, shows how the governments actively intervened in protecting domestic firms.[14] But they did so in a very special way. Firms often received subsidies, like PLI, as they deepened supply-chains, and protection from imports as they entered new product lines. In return, they committed to specific export targets. In Taiwan, for example, firms had to export over half their output—if these targets were not met, the protection was removed. The great advantage of exporting is that it forces competitiveness, with all manner of beneficial feedback from demanding buyers. Firms also learn what product features are in particular demand, features which may take time to develop and which prepare the firm for future demand at home as well.

Protection is only worth doing if it results in useful learning: Competitiveness is a reflection of what firms do and how they respond to price signals and incentives. Making an AC compressor efficiently is a matter of learning. And learning, as Dore pointed out, takes conscious effort. When Hyundai Motors started making its first vehicles in 1968, their teams learnt how to manufacture efficiently by repeatedly disassembling and assembling the sample cars the company had imported. Samsung did the same when it started making microwaves as a supplier to GE—and eventually emerged as the world's largest manufacturer.

As we saw earlier, the purpose of protecting an infant industry is learning. All firms learn by doing; what matters is 'learning

---

14   Hirayuki Odagiri and Akira Goto, *Technology and Industrial Development in Japan: Building Capabilities by Learning, Innovation and Public Policy* (Oxford: Clarendon Press, 1996); Yung Wun Rhee, Larry Westphal and Gary Pursell, *Korean Industrial Competence: Where it Came From* (Washington, DC: World Bank, 1981); and, Wade, *Governing the Market.*

by doing in an appropriate environment'.[15] An export-oriented environment carries dual benefits. Export success also has a direct impact on technical capability. Exporting provides for a substantial flow of technology from demanding buyers. Studies of how South Korea and Taiwan built their technical capacity identified the most important sources of technology for firms. Technical flows from overseas buyers came in first—ahead of in-house R&D, technology licensing and domestic R&D institutes. This reflected the industries involved—textiles and garments, consumer goods, and as assemblers of electronic appliances for global brands. None of these required substantial investment in R&D. As the industrial structure changed towards automobiles, semiconductors, and IT hardware, greater investment in in-house R&D supplemented these flows of technology from buyers.

Anecdotal comments from the two industries in India that are strongly export-oriented (software services and pharmaceuticals) say that technical flows from demanding buyers have played a similarly important role. The absence of export orientation for much of Indian industry has deprived it of this flow of technology.

Self-reliance as a sturdy ideal goes much beyond protection: Self-reliance for essential medical supplies, like PPEs and N95 masks during a global health emergency, is a fine example of how idealism and challenge can deliver extraordinary results. In April 2020, when a team at CII started working on the supply-chain, India produced zero PPEs and N95 masks. Thanks to an extraordinary response from small and large Indian industry, India became the world's second-largest manufacturer of PPEs (500,000 per day) in eight weeks and started exporting them. The supply-chain of raw materials is also local. And the import tariff on masks and PPEs? Zero,

---

15   Jagdish Bhagwati's words, not mine, in *India in Transition: Freeing the Economy* (Oxford: Clarendon Press, 1993).

as it should be. This is India's future: to manufacture so efficiently that we do not need protection. Self-reliance must be our sturdy ideal, not self-serving rhetoric to justify protection.

As the government has increased import duties on over half of all tariff lines in the last four years, it can well argue that in doing so it is only listening to the pleas of Indian industry. That is true. But Indian industry has not changed what it is saying—we asked for protection in 1991, 2001, 2011 and now. What is new is that the government is listening to Indian industry, and protecting it.

Two Futures for Indian Industry

Indian firms have a choice to make. The firms we hear most on trade issues—such as those moaning about RCEP in our media—are inward-looking and focused on the Indian market. Food-processing firms worried about competing with the import of cheese from New Zealand and steel and chemical firms concerned about China were the most vocal in the run-up to dropping out of RCEP. They argued for, and obtained, either exclusion of their items from the RCEP free trade agreement, or highly extended adjustment periods. If we cannot be confident of competing effectively with China in ten, fifteen or even twenty-five years, do we deserve to be in business?

What it will take to compete: Let us start with costs. Material costs are largely similar around the world—unless one has to buy the item at a higher price from a protected domestic firm. If we protect our steel producers, we spread costs and inefficiency throughout our engineering sector. If we protect our fabric producers, we spread cost and inefficiency throughout our garment manufacturers. Low or no tariffs are the best way to ensure our firms get competitive inputs and our consumers get products at world-competitive prices. This ball is squarely in the government's court, and they have fumbled badly with their dozen rounds of tariff increases in four years.

Labour costs are a big variable between countries. As China has grown into a mid-income country, its wages have risen dramatically. Higher wages must be matched by higher productivity or one will be uncompetitive. We may look to the government for a better educated and skilled workforce, but the primary responsibility for training and productivity lies within each firm.

Trade policy must adopt a strong export-promotion stance, starting with a competitive exchange rate. A strong rupee may be good for our psyche, but it makes imports cheaper and exports more expensive. Around Rs 80 to the dollar would restore the rupee to the real effective exchange rate of 2014. Rs 100 to the dollar would remove all need for protection, and be an export incentive like no other.[16] Our export policy must also focus on markets where we have complementary strengths. We need FTAs with the US, EU and the emerging pan-African Free Trade Area. As we negotiate with the EU, we must ignore the growls from the auto industry and heed the opportunity of the auto-component and garment industries. And let us enable our exporters to scale up by raising the capital of the EXIM bank and the export credit guarantee cover to global levels.

The buck stops with industry: Ultimately, it is the choice we make in Indian industry which will determine our future. One alternative is to accept that after seven decades of Independence, thirty years since reforms began and another ten- to twenty-five-year adjustment period, we will still not be able to compete with the best in the world. We can then lobby against FTAs, demand protection from the government, and build a moat to keep the world out of India. This policy, which we followed for decades, protected incumbents and kept us poor. It was decisively reversed by Narasimha Rao and Manmohan Singh in 1991. The second alternative is to continue what

---

16   As of mid 2021, the exchange rate was Rs 73 to the dollar.

we began thirty years ago—to open up to the world, let the best in, and encourage our best to go out and build businesses that lead the world. Many Indian companies have been doing just this, but are still not typical. Competition from imports is the best way of ensuring that it is this type of firm that predominates.

A ten-year project: Let us set ourselves a project. In ten years, every Indian company must either be able to compete with the best in the world or does not deserve to exist. There are three types of Indian firms. There are those, mainly in commodity businesses with thin margins and little product differentiation, that are most affected by the cost of doing business in India. They need to turn from growling at FTAs to roaring at anything that adds to our costs—exchange rates, power tariffs, export paperwork, port congestion, fickle policies that change by the month, a new regulation from company affairs every other week. Then there are the Indian firms that are already today happily doing business around the world: our software companies, of course, but also companies manufacturing motorcycles, specialty chemicals and energy-saving equipment. They need to articulate their interests in FTAs, such as RCEP, so our government is encouraged to pursue them *today*. And lastly, there are firms that have built world-beating businesses that are domestically focused today, such as our private banks and NBFCs that are world-leaders. They need to state their interests in access to world markets. In ten years, even the Indian market will be too small for them and they will need the RCEP Asian market that is eight times larger than India's.

It is a question of confidence. Do we seek to hide from the world, secure and protected in our own fortress? Or do we have the confidence to let the world in and ourselves go out and compete with the world on its terms?

Indian industry must see its future in export. As the RCEP negotiation ran its course, in CII we held a series of discussions with different industry groups. We began each meeting by saying we had ample input on our defensive interests but needed input on our offensive interests. With no effect. There was overwhelming focus on protecting the Indian market and underwhelming interest in accessing Asian markets. This must change. We have dozens of great Indian firms that see the world as their market, but we need tens of thousands of Indian firms to export their way to greatness. We must use our technical talent to develop products and services that we seek to then sell around the world. An FTA enables access. It is for Indian industry to turn this access into opportunity. Instead of howling about imports, let us howl instead about anything—infrastructure, the cost of power, delays at ports, the strength of the rupee, non-tariff barriers, the ease of doing business—that comes in the way of our being great exporters.

Conclusions: Multinationals with Indian Roots

Today, Indian industry is responding to the AN–PLI initiative, submitting applications for subsidies, so that it can substitute imports and serve the Indian market. With every new industry that is included, requests arise for yet more to be included. A recent editorial in the *Business Standard* warned that 'India does not need a government subsidised, high-cost manufacturing industry that produces purely for the local market and does not export'.[17] We can all hope that this scheme will end with the development of deeper supply-chains that are world-competitive, and that Indian firms will then emerge as major exporters in these additional sectors. But I'm not holding my breath. An industrial policy where the state decides which sectors to subsidise, and which not to, worries me. Rather than picking winners, in most countries, at most times, the state has demonstrated much greater competence in picking losers. There are exceptions, such as the stories

---

17   *Business Standard,* December 2020.

from East Asia we discussed earlier. Intelligent use of state discretion seems to have enhanced learning and grown competitiveness over time. Indeed, Japan, South Korea and Taiwan seemed to constantly display so much foresight for so many industries in all studies, that one almost suspects the studies.

But is this right for India? As Montek Singh Ahluwalia says, 'retaining a system of discretionary control but operating it in a business-friendly manner is not the best way of building a strong private sector. In fact, it poses a serious risk of degenerating into cronyism.'[18]

We do not need a few dozen champion firms, supported by the government, that say 'Made in India' to the world. We need a thousand multinationals with Indian roots, in all sectors, operating and investing around the world. The future of Indian industry could look like Germany, with thousands of specialised firms, with deep proprietary technology, and an international presence. Motorcycle companies like Bajaj Auto exporting 40 per cent of their output, specialty chemical companies like Aarti Industries exporting over 50 per cent of theirs, and infrastructure companies like TVS Logistics acquiring companies around the world—this is the future of Indian industry, not firms seeking domestic dominance by getting into bed with the state. In CII International, we are focusing on helping firms enter markets overseas. We are working with around 130 Indian firms, in the $50 million to $2 billion range,[19] that aspire to be multinationals operating worldwide. We have established CII overseas offices in Cairo, Dubai and Jakarta, with Yangon and Hanoi in the near future. South America and West and East Africa have much scope too.

---

18 Montek Singh Ahluwalia's 'India's 1991 Reforms', in *India Transformed: 25 Years of Economic Reform*, edited by Rakesh Mohan (New Delhi: Penguin Random House, 2017).

19 $50–100 million would seem to be the minimum size for a firm to have the necessary bandwidth to establish an overseas presence. Beyond $2 billion, firms are large enough to enter markets on their own except for a few specialised places like Iran or Myanmar.

I began this chapter by talking about Tarun Das, CII and the 1991 reforms. Tarun's push for openness came not from ideology, but from his confidence in Indian industry. Tarun believes in Indian industry perhaps more than it believes in itself. I do too. The results that flowed post 1991 proved him right. We must believe in Indian industry's ability to compete with the best in the world—in the world.

5

Innovation: Transforming In-house R&D[1]

It is possible that he may have an idea. He nearly had one about three years ago.

—Uncle Fred in the Springtime, P.G. Wodehouse

Indian industry has changed beyond recognition in the last thirty years. From operating in a protected home market, often producing old designs of indifferent quality, in sector after sector there are today no product gaps between what is available in India and what is available in the rest of the world. We take this for granted now, but in 1991 as an affluent Indian I was fortunate enough to buy a new car which was only ten years out of date (replacing my old new car, which was

---

1   This is an updated, reader-friendly version of the more academic chapter that appeared in *India Transformed: 25 Years of Economic Reform,* edited by Rakesh Mohan (New Delhi: Penguin Random House, 2017).

twenty-five years out of date). I bought most of my clothes overseas. No decent cheese or processed food was available in the country, and we booked phone lines five years ahead of when we thought we might need them. Television meant Doordarshan, which consisted of state propaganda on everything from culture to animal husbandry. Contrast that with 2021, when what we enjoy in each large Indian city is on par with most large international cities. And if you take a flight today from New York or London to Mumbai or Delhi, you leave a third-class airport and arrive at a first-class one.

So India's product and service markets have been transformed in the last thirty years. Has India's innovation system been similarly transformed? If you are a macroeconomist, the answer is No. If you are a microeconomist, the answer is Maybe, somewhat. In brief, the macro innovation data shows at best a modest change in the proportion of GDP spent on R&D, in who spends on R&D, and in where it is done. There is some change in the sectors where R&D effort is concentrated. The import of technology shows rapid change. And some individual firms tell stories of transformation. In particular, a focus on learning has completely changed what products are made, and how often new products are introduced. And the basis of survival has dramatically changed the efficiency with which firms operate. We have already discussed Indian industry's opening to the world in the previous chapter, and how we must invest in a deeper international presence. This requires that Indian industry build the proprietary technology to deploy around the world. I will focus on learning and R&D, leaving discussion of design and the higher education system to chapters 6 and 7. In chapter 8, I deal with the public research system. In this chapter, I argue that India's unusual pattern of specialisation in skill-intensive and capital-intensive manufacturing demands much more investment by industry in innovation than currently happens.[2]

---

2   For a lower-middle-income, labour-surplus country.

A Personal Detour

When I started working on my doctorate at Stanford in 1983, my initial topic was to compare the ecosystem for technical entrepreneurship in Pune with what I saw around me in Silicon Valley. I soon realised that there were far too many variables in each geography, so I removed the comparison with Silicon Valley and focused on Pune. Since no work had been done on technical entrepreneurship in developing countries at that time, I necessarily had to read work done on developed countries. I also started to study and take courses in economic development and the economics of technology. I was asked to teach a course in 'Technology and Development', and found myself in a very exciting emerging area of work.

In the early 1980s, most published work on technology in developing countries was characterised by a decidedly Marxist perspective, with dependency theory dominating the field. Technology, it was thought, was the monopoly of a few large firms in rich countries. Developing countries needed to act to break this monopoly or they would remain permanently dependent on the rich world. But work was starting to appear that looked more empirically at what was happening in different countries. Some countries, in particular the Asian gang of four (South Korea, Taiwan, Singapore and Hong Kong), had grown rapidly precisely by developing their own technological capability. Particular industries and firms in Brazil, Argentina and India had done so too, while broader industrial capabilities remained uncompetitive.

Around that time I came across a new book, *Technological Capability in the Third World*,[3] which approached the subject from a robust empirical perspective. The book looked at how countries and firms had acquired technical capability; it remains one of the great books in the field thirty-five years later. There were three chapters on India,

---

3   Edited by Martin Fransman and Kenneth King (London: Palgrave Macmillan, 1984).

one each by Ashok Desai, Sanjaya Lall and Ronald Dore. I wrote to them and all wrote back, sending me more work they had done; all became long-term friends. Ashok Desai then introduced me to a study he was doing at the National Council of Applied Economic Research (NCAER) on imports of technology and technical capability in India. The book that came out of that study, *Technology Absorption in Indian Industry*, studied technology transfer from several countries to India and the technical capability that resulted.[4] Ashok's characteristically perceptive and brief introductory essay said: 'It is the policies that control competition—licensing, MRTP, preferences to state enterprises and small-scale industry—as well as those that control technology imports that are ultimately instrumental in making Indian industry technologically stagnant and dependent.'

Ashok is truly the pioneer of work done on technical capability in India. He did the first study on the import of technology in 1970 for NCAER. The study was published as *Foreign Technology and Investment: A Study of Their Role in India's Industrialisation*;[5] it was his follow-on study, done in the late 1980s, that he involved me in. I read Ashok's many papers on technical capability in India, including a very perceptive comparison of the machine tool industries in Taiwan and India. His work exemplified solid empirical research, where the data spoke and told its own story. Within a month of becoming finance minister in 1991, Manmohan Singh made Ashok Desai his Chief Economic Advisor. Over the years, Ashok had become a well-known newspaper columnist. The team of economists in the finance ministry, who had long seen Ashok as their fiercest critic, suddenly found he was their boss. One of the things Ashok did for Manmohan Singh was to set up an annual pre-budget consultative process with industrialists—

---

4   Ashok V. Desai, editor, *Technology Absorption in Indian Industry* (New Delhi: Wiley Eastern, 1988).

5   *Foreign Technology and Investment: A Study of Their Role in India's Industrialisation* (New Delhi: NCAER, 1971).

he included me in the first such meeting in 1992. I found myself placed between Ratan Tata and Mukesh Ambani, which meant I had to be included in the front-page photograph of every newspaper that wanted the two of them together. Later, when Farhad and I set up a supervisory board for our company, Ashok was in the founding group. At one of our board retreats, two board members put on a wonderful skit set in Ashok's schooldays, when Pupil Desai was being disciplined by the principal for his 'unhealthy regard for the truth'. That is a failing that has long bedevilled Ashok; long may it continue.

Returning to my romance with the study of technology in development, my path was to apply to developing countries what I learnt about the developed country experience in the economics of innovation. I found this a most rewarding direction. Between the time that I taught my first course in 1987 and turned the management part of it into a book (together with David Wield) in 2002, the field matured and the economics of technology in developing countries became a field in its own right.[6]

A Few Building Blocks to Understand Technical Capability, R&D and Innovation

The importance of technical capability to economic growth is well recognised. From the very first growth accounting exercises of the 1950s for the US economy,[7] through analyses of Japan, South Korea and Taiwan in their catch-up stories, to China today, technical change is estimated to account for over half of all economic growth.[8] Technical

---

6 The course was called Management and Technology in Newly-industrialising Countries. The book was *From Followers to Leaders: Managing Technology and Innovation in Newly Industrializing Countries* (London: Routledge, 2002). As the field matured, it became decidedly less interesting!

7 Carried out independently by Moses Abramovitz and Robert Solow.

8 Although the contribution of technical change to economic growth is well appreciated, it is still calculated as the residual in Total Factor Productivity calculations, left over from the contribution of capital and labour to total growth.

change shows up in the economy as innovation, as doing new things for commercial advantage. Innovation largely happens in firms, which makes this a story of Indian industry. The innovative capacity of firms is affected by both what they do themselves and the institutions around them. The trade regime can foster local production or an outward mindset. The education system provides skilled labour, engineers and researchers. Publicly funded research can enhance science; where it is done affects how it connects with industry. Public policy can provide incentives for investing in R&D, either directly or through patents. The culture of entrepreneurship affects investment in different kinds of capabilities. And broader cultural factors can influence how entrepreneurs define 'good'.

Although R&D is the most studied component of innovation, it is good to always keep in mind that industrial innovation—defined as something new for commercial advantage—is a much broader concept and applies to all firms in all sectors. Innovation matters just as much to a garment firm introducing a new design or a start-up launching a local transport app—activities which rarely involve R&D but are still highly innovative—as it does to a pharmaceutical firm developing a better cure for a disease involving years of research.

Learning is central to innovation: At the heart of innovation is learning, and learning largely happens within firms. How firms learn is affected by their environment—the policies that drive them to compete or protect them, the ease of hiring qualified people, the availability of finance for ventures and the ambition of entrepreneurs. But learning is also—indeed, even more—affected by the choices that firms make and the effort they put in themselves. When I taught my course, my organising principle was a diagram showing these relationships:

Figure 5.1: Indigenous Technological Capability

Technical capacity is a result of accessing knowledge from the outside (from another firm, particularly), the endowment (education, entrepreneurship and culture) one starts with, and the effort (learning) put in. Learning comes in two forms. First is learning by doing—a passive, automatic and costless by-product of production. Second is learning by investment, a result of deliberate choices that firms make. Learning by analysing requires a firm to carefully study what it is doing so that it can improve it. Reverse engineering—where one learns by taking apart a competitor's product—or documenting and standardising work practices is included. A firm can go further in deliberately trying to learn by sending people to other firms and countries for training or bringing in specialists to learn from. Last is R&D. Learning and building technical capacity applies to all firms. It is what makes them competitive in the long run. When does R&D matter?

For much of human history the world got new products and processes without anything that we would recognise as R&D. The great innovations of the late eighteenth and early nineteenth centuries, especially in the textile industry, gave Britain its incredible lead in global manufacturing (from chapter 1, remember, in 1870 Britain accounted for one-third of world manufacturing output). These innovations were a result of great ingenuity, but were not a result of R&D: organised efforts at innovation bringing together groups of people with specialised technical skills. The first in-house R&D departments appeared only in the 1870s in firms in Germany (in the chemical industry) and then in the US (in the chemical and electrical industries). It was no coincidence that organised R&D first appeared in these industries. The chemical and electrical industries required more specialised technical skills than those of a good generalist. As these first R&D departments showed their ability to produce innovative new products and processes, the need for R&D spread to other technology-intensive fields. This prompted the remark, in 1925, that 'the greatest invention of the 19th century was the invention of the method of invention'.[9] By World War II, R&D was a substantive enterprise and considered vital to innovation.

Today, R&D is the most directly connected with the study of innovation. It is particularly important for us in India because of our particular industrial structure. As Kochhar and her impressive roster of co-authors point out:

> ... it is striking that India's share in skill-intensive manufacturing, which was already high in 1980 despite its lower level of per capita income, has been increasing and is at levels reached by Malaysia or Korea at much higher levels of per capita income. There is also a striking contrast with China. China's share of output in skill-intensive industries is lower than India's and has been virtually flat whereas India's level has been higher and rising. The move towards skill-intensive goods is also reflected in India's exports: the share

---

9   By the British philosopher Alfred North Whitehead, in his *Science and the Modern World*, Lowell Institute Lectures (New York, NY: Macmillan, 1925).

of exports of skill-intensive goods has risen sharply from about 25 percent in 1970 to about 65 percent in 2004.[10]

It is entirely possible for an economy focused on labour-intensive manufacturing to grow rapidly for years. So long as wages remain low, that is the source of comparative advantage. The most successful development experiences that we discussed in chapter 2 (Japan, South Korea, Taiwan, Singapore, Hong Kong, China) enjoyed decades of rapid growth by exporting simple manufactured products—textiles and garments, footwear, toys, simple electronic items. Throughout the first twenty years of their rapid growth—1950–1970 for Japan, 1960–1980 for the Asian gang of four, and 1980–2000 for China—R&D was a very modest enterprise. Later, rising wages pushed a move to higher value-added sectors and with it forced investment in innovation. As Japan, South Korea, Taiwan, Singapore and China progressively entered more sophisticated industries, they expanded investment in R&D.

For various historical reasons, we have a more skill- and capital-intensive industrial structure than other countries at our level of development. Bangladesh has now passed India in per capita GDP. With the dominance of textiles and garments in its industrial structure (40 per cent of industrial value-added),[11] it is fine if its R&D investments are modest. But India, with the industrial structure of a much richer country, must invest much more in R&D if we wish to have a vibrant manufacturing sector.

---

10   Kalpana Kochhar, Utsav Kumar, Raghuram Rajan, Arvind Subramanian and Ioannis Tokatlidis, 'India's Pattern of Development: What Happened, What Follows?' Working Paper WP/06/22, (Washington, DC: International Monetary Fund, 2006), 22. This paper is worth reading both for its outstanding content and for the co-authors. Note also that the China comment reflects when the paper was written, in 2006. Today, fifteen years later, as wages have risen, Chinese industry has become more skill-intensive and we see the investment in R&D we discussed earlier. China has moved on, India much less so.

11   World Bank, *World Development Indicators*.

But what is R&D? We use R&D as a well-understood term, but it involves many different activities. For many decades in India, R&D meant indigenisation—if it was imported, make it locally. When Ashok Desai did his pioneering studies of R&D in India in 1969 and 1980, he found that research absorbed 2–3 per cent of corporate R&D, development around 30–40 per cent, and 'operational investigation' (problems of raw material supply, manufacturing, customer complaints) the rest. I can vouch for the accuracy of this definition of R&D. We have long had an R&D department in our own firm, Forbes Marshall. As I said in the previous chapter, after hearing Manmohan Singh's budget speech in July 1991, we resolved that R&D would from then on only take up products to develop which we could sell worldwide. Indigenisation was dead.

But if R&D is not indigenisation, then what is it? A three-level hierarchy: at the base level, R&D is learning from other firms. Some of this learning happens by buying technology. Some of it happens by reverse engineering products to see how they are made and do what they do. And some of it happens by feedback from demanding buyers that one exports to. At the next level, R&D is improving existing products. This is what firms call development, it is the great bulk of what firms call R&D, and it applies around the world. It involves prototyping, experimentation, design, which we will discuss in chapter 6.

Research, as an activity aimed at generating new knowledge, is deservedly in last place. It is what you do when everything else has failed. If an R&D engineer does not know how to do something, what does he do? He asks the more experienced engineer at the next desk. If she doesn't know either, they scout around the firm trying to find someone who does. If they can't, they look up some books and search the internet to learn what others have done. Along the way, they call a professor from their college, or someone knowledgeable at another firm. If no one seems to know, the firm might do some experimenting and research in-house to generate the knowledge themselves. When all else fails, they might then reach out to the best scientist they can access to mount an organised research effort. Research comes last.

This description of how innovation happens draws on both my own observation and several conversations with Stephen Kline, professor of mechanical engineering at Stanford. Steve came up with what he called the chain-linked model of innovation in the early 1980s. The field of innovation studies owes a great debt to Steve, a wonderful and generous human being once you got to know him.[12]

All of these activities, from learning to development to research, constitute R&D. Research may sound the most exciting, but it is best seen as a minor part of what firms do in their quest to innovate. Indeed, I've long argued (following Nathan Rosenberg) that R&D is more correctly D&R, or development and research, as development usually both precedes and is more important to the total project of innovation than research.

When firms report R&D data to their governments, and when people like me pull their numbers together in comparative tables, we include all of these different animals.

R&D Spending at the National Level

Table 5.1 shows that India was an early investor in R&D, with R&D as a percentage of GDP being higher than for countries that were considerably richer at that point in time. However, India's investment in R&D has stagnated over the last forty years, ranging between 0.6 and 0.8 per cent of GDP, while South Korea, Taiwan, Singapore, China and, to some extent, Brazil have seen a substantial increase. Mexico and Thailand (and Malaysia and Indonesia, as other leading newly industrialising countries) reflect much more subdued investment in R&D throughout.

---

12 Steve's last book—Kline, *Conceptual Foundations of Multidisciplinary Thinking* (Stanford, CA: Stanford University Press, 1995)—is a work of genius rendered in difficult and sometimes indecipherable prose. See chapter 8 for more.

Table 5.1: R&D as per cent of GDP over Time, in Leading Newly Industrialising Countries[13]

Country	R&D (% of GDP)				
	1980	1992	2004	2011	2018
South Korea	0.6	2.1	2.5	3.8	4.8
Taiwan	NA	NA	2.6	3.0	3.3
Singapore	0.3 (1981)	0.9 (1990)	2.1	2.2	1.9 (2017)
China	NA	0.6	1.2	1.8	2.2
Brazil	NA	0.8 (1994)	0.9	1.2	1.3 (2017)
India	0.6	0.7	0.7	0.8	0.7
Mexico	NA	0.2	0.4	0.4	0.3
Thailand	0.4	0.2 (1991)	0.3	0.4	1.0 (2017)

Source: *UNESCO Statistical Yearbook* (1999) for data from 1980–1996; UNESCO Institute of Statistics (various years), *UIS.stat*, available at: http://data.uis. unesco.org for data on China, India, Mexico, Singapore, South Korea, Taiwan and Thailand and Brazil (pre-2000); *Taiwan Statistical Data Book* (2019) for data on Taiwan.

R&D is highly concentrated: Research and development is hugely concentrated worldwide. Most R&D is done in a handful of countries—of a total of around $1.7 trillion spent on global R&D in 2019, the top five countries accounted for 73 per cent.[14] It is highly

---

13   The term 'Newly industrialising countries' almost always includes the eight countries in Table 5.1 plus Malaysia and Indonesia. Often, Turkey, South Africa and Hong Kong are also included, and on occasion Chile, Argentina, Colombia, Egypt and Vietnam.

14   Total global R&D in nominal terms for 2019 calculated using nominal GDP data from the *IMF World Economic Outlook Database April 2020* (available at: https://www.imf.org/external/pubs/ft/weo/2020/01/weodata/index. aspx), and GERD as a percentage of GDP from UNESCO Institute for

concentrated in a few industries. The top five—pharmaceuticals, automobiles, technology hardware, software and electronics—account for 72 per cent of all industrial R&D. And within those industries, it is highly concentrated in a few companies, with the top 20 companies accounting for 23 per cent of global industrial R&D (think about it, 20 firms spend over 20 per cent of what millions of firms do worldwide) and the top 300 companies for two-thirds.[15]

India as outlier in R&D spending: Table 5.2 shows that the bulk of R&D spending worldwide happens in firms (around 71 per cent of the total). The balance is publicly funded research, most of it done in universities (17 per cent), with a smaller share in autonomous R&D institutes (12 per cent).[16] India is an outlier on three counts. First, the share of industry in total national R&D is the lowest of any major economy at 37 per cent.[17] This share was 25 per cent in 1991,

---

Statistics, *UIS.stat,* (available at: http://data.uis.unesco.org/). The figure for total industrial R&D was obtained from the EU Industrial R&D Investment Scoreboard, 2020. Figures in euros were converted to dollars using the EUR-USD exchange rate of 1.12 as at 31 December 2019 as mentioned in the EU Industrial R&D Investment Scoreboard.

15 EU Industrial R&D Investment Scoreboard, 2020; Centre for Technology, Innovation and Economic Research, 2021.

16 There is a difference in many countries between who funds and who does research. In most major economies, the state funds the bulk of research undertaken in universities, whether public or private. In some economies like the US, Israel and the UK, the state also funds a substantial part of the defence research expenditures of private industry. In India, there is essentially no gap between who funds and who does—publicly funded research is done in government laboratories (overwhelmingly) or in government higher education institutes (to a minor extent). Private industry funds the great bulk of its own R&D.

17 There is a serious problem with Indian R&D statistics. No government agency can provide overall data. Centre for Technology Innovation and Economic Research (CTIER) estimates that if we include contract R&D done in India for foreign firms in the total, the R&D share as a per cent of GDP would rise to 1.2 per cent—with public and industry shares at 50:50 and the industry share in turn splitting roughly equally between R&D done for use within the country and as contract R&D that is exported.

Table 5.2: Who Does R&D? (2019)

Country	Total R&D expenditure (US$ billion)	GERD* as % of GDP	Corpora-tions (% of total)	Public research institutes (% of total)	Universi-ties** (% of total)
USA	584	2.8	73	10	17
China	292	2.2	77	15	7
Japan	162	3.3	79	8	13
Germany	122	3.1	69	13	18
South Korea	83	4.8	80	10	10
France	61	2.2	65	13	22
UK	49	1.7	69	6	25
Italy	29	1.4	62	13	25
Canada	27	1.6	51	7	42
Australia***	27	1.9	53	10	37
Brazil	24	1.3	—	—	—
Netherlands	20	2.2	67	6	27
Sweden	19	3.3	71	4	25
Israel	18	5.0	88	2	10
India	18	0.7	37	56	7
Spain	18	1.2	57	17	27
World	**1,725**	**2.0**	**71**	**12**	**17**

* GERD = Gross expenditure on R&D

** Also includes private non-profit

*** Data for 2017

Note: UNESCO uses the term business enterprise, government and higher education for corporations, public research institutes and universities respectively.

Source: UNESCO Institute for Statistics (various years), *UIS.stat,* available at: http://data.uis.unesco.org; Centre for Technology, Innovation and Economic Research (CTIER); Department of Science and Technology (DST), Research and Development Statistics at a Glance 2019-20, available at: https://dst.gov.in/sites/default/files/R%26D%20Statistics%20at%20a%20Glance%202019-20.pdf

so the rise (of a rapidly growing GDP) is significant but not dramatic, and keeps India an outlier.[18] Second, publicly funded R&D in India at 63 per cent is the highest among all major economies. It was also high in China, but in this same period the publicly funded share has fallen to 22 per cent (from 50 per cent in 1991).[19] Third, where publicly funded R&D is done is again dramatically different in India. The bulk of public R&D (85 per cent) is done by the government in its own autonomous R&D institutes. A small share of publicly funded R&D (15 per cent of the public share) is done within the university system, giving the Indian higher education sector the lowest share of national R&D (7 per cent) of any major economy.

---

18   Department of Science and Technology, India (various years).
      In 1991, the 25 per cent spilt was 15 per cent private and 10 per cent public sector. Today, the 37 per sent spilt is 30 per cent private and 7 per cent public sector.
19   OECD Statistics, 1991, *OECD.stat*, available at: http://stats.oecd.org/

Table 5.3: Industrial R&D by Sector for the Top 2,500 Global R&D Spenders (2019)

	Sector	R&D spending (US$ billion)	Share of sector in total R&D (%)	No of firms	India	China	South Korea	USA
1	Pharmaceuticals & Biotechnology	187	18.4	436	11	48	7	234
2	Software & Computer Services	160	15.8	288	4	62	3	153
3	Technology Hardware & Equipment	156	15.4	237	0	50	6	80
4	Automobiles & Parts	149	14.7	152	6	36	8	22
5	Electronic & Electrical Equipment	77	7.6	224	0	75	5	42
6	Industrial Engineering	36	3.6	187	1	42	2	34
7	Chemicals	26	2.5	130	1	25	5	27
8	Aerospace & Defence	23	2.3	45	0	5	2	14
9	General Industrials	23	2.3	75	0	17	5	16
10	Construction & Materials	21	2.1	65	0	30	2	4
Top 3 sectors		503	50	961	21	187	21	467
Top 10 sectors		858	85	1,839	23	390	45	626
Total (2,500)		1,013	100	2,500	29	536	59	775

Sources: EU Industrial R&D Investment Scoreboard 2020; figures in euros were converted to dollars using the EUR-USD exchange rate of 1.12 as on 31 December 2019, and as mentioned in the EU Industrial R&D Investment Scoreboard; CTIER.

Why Industrial R&D Lags in India

The top 2,500 firms worldwide account for over three-quarters of global industrial R&D spending. Table 5.3 shows data by industry for these firms. Note that of 29 Indian firms (to 536 Chinese firms and 59 South Korean firms), 21 are in just three sectors—pharmaceuticals, automobiles, and software. India has no firms in five of the top ten R&D-intensive sectors worldwide. So, India lags in not having any presence in half of the most R&D-intensive industries. Leading Indian firms also invest less in R&D as a percentage of sales than their global counterparts. But a much more dominant explanation is the absence of really large R&D spending firms. No Indian firm figures in the top twenty-five R&D spenders worldwide (Table 5.4). The world's top R&D investor, Alphabet invests more in R&D ($26 billion) than all of India—every public laboratory, university and firm put together. So does the top Chinese firm, Huawei ($19 billion). When I wrote a chapter on R&D for a book edited by Rakesh Mohan four years ago, I used this same table with data for 2014. The top firm worldwide then was Volkswagen, now at number six. Huawei was already the top Chinese firm investing in R&D, but then spent $7 billion on R&D, which more than doubled in five years. Also, while Alphabet makes almost all of its profit and most of its revenue from software (Google), its R&D spending is much more diverse— including autonomous vehicles, healthcare and mobile telephony. It is no accident that the firms that invest huge amounts in R&D are generally the most dynamic worldwide.

Table 5.4: Top Twenty-five Firms, Based on R&D Spend Worldwide (2019)

	Company	Country	Sector	R&D spending (US$ million)	R&D as % of sales
1	Alphabet	USA	Software & Computer Services	25,939	16.1
2	Microsoft	USA	Software	19,211	13.5
3	Huawei	China	Technology Hardware	18,718	15.3
4	Samsung	South Korea	Electronic Equipment	17,388	8.8
5	Apple	USA	Technology Hardware	16,168	6.2
6	Volkswagen	Germany	Automobiles	16,023	5.7
7	Facebook	USA	Software	13,559	19.2
8	Intel	USA	Technology Hardware	13,322	18.6
9	Roche	Switzerland	Pharmaceuticals	12,044	19.0
10	Johnson & Johnson	USA	Pharmaceuticals	11,321	13.8
11	Daimler	Germany	Automobiles	10,786	5.6
12	Toyota	Japan	Automobiles	10,145	3.7
13	Merck	USA	Pharmaceuticals	9,223	19.8
14	Novartis	Switzerland	Pharmaceuticals	8,639	17.2
15	Gilead	USA	Pharmaceuticals	8,281	37.0
16	Pfizer	USA	Pharmaceuticals	8,258	16.0
17	Honda	Japan	Automobiles	7,655	5.6
18	Ford	USA	Automobiles	7,378	4.7
19	BMW	Germany	Automobiles	7,189	6.2
20	Bosch	Germany	Automobiles	6,976	8.0
21	Siemens	Germany	Electronic Equipment	6,816	7.0
22	General Motors	USA	Automobiles	6,779	5.0
23	Sanofi	France	Pharmaceuticals	6,737	16.7
24	Cisco	USA	Technology Hardware	6,557	12.7
25	Bayer	Germany	Pharmaceuticals	6,303	12.2

Sources: EU Industrial R&D Investment Scoreboard 2020; figures in euros were converted to dollars using the EUR USD exchange rate of 1.12 as at

31 December 2019 and as mentioned in the EU Industrial R&D Investment Scoreboard; CTIER.

Why does Indian industry invest so little in R&D? A 2017 report from the World Bank, *The Innovation Paradox*, points out that the returns to R&D for developed countries are 40 to 60 per cent.[20] For developing countries, the returns are potentially in triple digits. Such massive returns should drive much more investment in technology. This is the 'innovation paradox' of the book's title: 'Developing country firms and governments appear to be leaving billions of dollars on the table, uncollected.' What is true for developing countries in general is true for us in India. Why?

Could it be that as manufacturing firms traditionally dominated R&D spending, it is our poor showing in manufacturing that reflects in our low industrial R&D? Partly so. China's manufacturing sector is today ten times that of India's ($3.9 trillion to India's $400 billion). But Chinese firms today invest over twenty-five times what Indian firms do ($225 billion in R&D to Indian firms' $7 billion). And the comparison extends beyond manufacturing.

Is it the scale and profitability of our firms? Are Indian firms just too small to invest in R&D? The general understanding is that there is a threshold level for R&D in firms. One needs to be above a certain minimum size to justify investment in R&D and benefit from it. But beyond that size, getting still bigger doesn't provide additional economies of scale to R&D. Indian firms in many sectors are today well beyond 'big enough'—our ten largest pharmaceutical, IT services, chemical, and engineering firms all have a turnover of over $500

---

20   Xavier Cirera and William F. Maloney, *The Innovation Paradox: Developing Country Capabilities and the Unrealized Promise of Technological Catch-Up* (Washington, DC: World Bank, 2017). https://openknowledge.worldbank.org/handle/10986/28341

million, which most would consider to be beyond this threshold level. Are Indian firms not profitable enough to invest in R&D? Even after eight years of slow industrial growth, corporate profitability in India (a typical return on sales of 10 per cent) compares well with China or South Korea.

Indian firms invest less in R&D as a per cent of sales than do their global counterparts. This is true in our two most R&D-intensive sectors of pharmaceuticals and auto, where our firms invest roughly half as much as a percentage of sales as the global leaders. And this is particularly true in software. Compare the software industry in China and India. The top ten companies in China invest over 8 per cent of turnover in R&D; in India the top ten companies invest 1 per cent in R&D. An obvious explanation is that India's software companies are software service firms, not product firms. But most Indian software companies are worried about how long the existing model of labour arbitrage combined with excellence in project execution can continue to drive growth. No one would consider TCS, Infosys or Wipro to be either small or unprofitable. They just invest little in R&D.

Writing in 1988, Ashok Desai said the results of his study of technology imports into India support the view that a major reason for the lack of technological dynamism in Indian firms is management.[21] Over thirty years later these controls have long gone. Some Indian firms have changed and are investing strongly in technology, but still too few for the change to show in the aggregate data.

---

21   In his 'Introduction' in *Technology Absorption in Indian Industry*, edited by Ashok V. Desai.

What Would Transformation Look Like?
A Comparison with South Korea and China

Table 5.5: R&D and Industrial R&D in India,
South Korea and China

Country		1970	1980	1990	2000	2010	2014	2018
India	R&D as % of GDP	0.4	0.6	0.6	0.7	0.8	0.7	0.7
	Share of industry in total R&D (%)	15	20	25	30	33	37	37
South Korea	R&D as % of GDP	0.4	0.8	1.9	2.7	3.7	4.2	4.8
	Share of industry in total R&D (%)	13	36	81	74	75	78	80
China	R&D as % of GDP	–	–	0.6 (1996)	0.9	1.7	2.1	2.2
	Share of industry in total R&D (%)	–	–	43 (1996)	60	73	77	77

Source: UNESCO Institute of Statistics (various years), *UIS.stat*, available at: http://data.uis.unesco.org/; World Development Indicators (various years), *Indicators*, available at http://data.worldbank.org/; Research and Development Statistics at a Glance, 2011–12, and 2019–20, Department of Science & Technology, India.

South Korea saw two transformations in the twenty years from 1970 to 1990. First, the proportion of R&D done by firms and the state essentially reversed. Second, the share of R&D in GDP rose strongly. The industrial share of total R&D increased from 13 per cent of national R&D spending to 81 per cent, at a time when R&D increased from less than 0.4 per cent of GDP to 1.9 per cent, when South Korea was growing at 8 per cent a year. Absolute investment by firms in R&D rose dramatically: a rising share, of a rising share, of a rapidly growing base means a triple multiple. My calculation says that South Korean industry was investing 1,000 times as much in real terms in R&D in 1990 as it was in 1970—the most rapid expansion worldwide of R&D investment ever. I've checked and rechecked that incredible multiple, but it seems to be right.

The comparison with China over the last twenty years points in a similar direction—the industrial share of total R&D almost doubles, at a time of a trebling of the share of GDP spent on R&D, while China was growing at over 10 per cent a year. My calculation says Chinese industry was investing 106 times as much in R&D in 2018 as it was in 1996. Indian industry has also expanded in-house R&D investment—but by a lower multiple of fifteen times in these same years. How has this transformation in industrial R&D happened? There is a double source. South Korea especially, but also China, has seen substantial structural change in lead industrial sectors. Textiles and apparel and food processing (low R&D intensity sectors worldwide) have seen their share in industrial output fall. Automobiles, semiconductors, electronics and IT hardware (high R&D intensity sectors worldwide) have seen their share rise. In India, automobiles is the only R&D-intensive sector to substantially increase its share of industrial output—a much more modest structural change.

In addition, *within* industrial sectors, both South Korea and China have invested more in R&D: semiconductors especially in South Korea. This reflects a deepening of technical capability within sectors and the emergence of some large firms. Note the growth of R&D spending at a few giant R&D spending firms, as Table 5.6 below shows. If we consider the top ten firms in R&D spending in each of South Korea, China and India, the emergence of firms like Samsung and Huawei (at $17 billion and $19 billion respectively, each over twice India's total industrial investment in R&D) illustrates the impact of a few large firms. And China is constantly widening the gap—from 301 firms in the top 2,500 R&D investors worldwide in 2014, to 536 firms by 2019. India, meanwhile, increased the number of its firms from 26 to 29.

It brings us back to our earlier point of R&D being highly concentrated: a few giant firms invest giant amounts in R&D. South Korea and China have seen their emergence as they have deepened their technical capability. India still needs to. Some of this gap is to India's entire advantage: the single big cost in R&D is people. Costs in India are still between one-fourth and one-half those of an equivalent engineer or scientist in South Korea or China, presenting an opportunity I will return to later.

Table 5.6: Top R&D Spenders in South Korea, China and India (2019)

Country	Company	Sector	R&D spending (US$ million)	R&D as % of Sales
India	Tata Motors	Automobiles	427	4.3
	Mahindra	Automobiles	380	4.9
	Reliance	Oil & Gas	342	0.6
	TCS	Software	229	1.3
	Lupin	Pharmaceuticals	228	13.9
	HAL	Defence	211	7.4
	Dr Reddy's	Pharmaceuticals	173	11.3
	Cipla	Pharmaceuticals	154	8.6
	Sun Pharma	Pharmaceuticals	138	9.3
	Bharat Electronics	Defence	128	7.3
China	Huawei	Technology Hardware	18,718	15.3
	Alibaba	Software	6,147	8.5
	Tencent	Software Services	4,336	8.1
	China State Construction	Construction	3,121	1.6
	BAIDU	Software	2,618	17.1
	China Railway Construction	Construction	2,358	2.0
	China Railway	Construction	2,356	1.9
	Petrochina	Oil & Gas	2,235	0.6
	Saic Motor	Automobiles	2,107	1.9
	ZTE	Technology Hardware	1,858	14.4
South Korea	Samsung	Electronic Equipment	17,388	8.8
	LG Electronics	Leisure Goods	3,106	5.8
	SK Hynix	Technology Hardware	2,707	11.6
	Hyundai Motor	Automobiles	2,602	2.9
	KIA Motors	Automobiles	1,359	2.7
	LG Chem	General Industrials	958	3.9
	Hyundai Mobis	Automobiles	831	2.5
	Korea Electric	Electricity	678	1.3
	Samsung SDI	Electronic Equipment	613	7.1
	DOOSAN	General Industrials	507	3.2

Sources: India's top R&D spenders data sourced from *CTIER Handbook: Technology and Innovation in India 2021*; other countries data is sourced from EU Industrial R&D Investment Scoreboard 2020; figures in euros were converted to dollars using the EUR–USD exchange rate of 1.12 as at 31 December 2019 and as mentioned in the EU Industrial R&D Investment Scoreboard; CTIER.

What's to be Done?

Indian industry needs to be competitive in the long run. As wages rise, as natural resources are consumed, as the easier catch-up options are exhausted, it is innovation that enables an economy to keep growing value-added over decades. This is particularly vital for India. We must massively increase investment in innovation over the next twenty years, just as South Korea did between 1970 and 1990 and China did between 1998 and 2018. It is instructive that near the *beginning* of this transformation, India already has a lower share of manufacturing coming from the labour-intensive sectors of textiles, apparel and food processing (19 per cent in 2018) than Korea (25 per cent in 1990) or China (22 per cent in 2018) near the *end* of theirs. Our manufacturing structure has long been out of synchronisation with our comparative advantage. Our skill-intensive and capital-intensive sectors require constant innovation, and constant and substantial investment in innovation, to be competitive over time. It is time our innovation system matched our industrial structure. What must we do?

Drive change in the structure of Indian industry: We need to see a much stronger presence in those sectors that are the most technologically dynamic worldwide. Table 5.3 listed the top ten R&D-intensive sectors—pharmaceuticals, auto, technology hardware & equipment, software & services, electronic & electrical equipment, industrial engineering, chemicals, aerospace & defence, general industrials and oil & gas. We have a small—or non-existent—manufacturing base in sectors like technology hardware, electronic equipment, and aerospace & defence. Our priority must be to establish a strong industrial presence in at least some of these sectors. The initiative to attract investment by firms such as Foxconn and Flextronics, the world's largest technology hardware manufacturers, or Apple and Oppo, is very welcome. As their presence grows, this should create demand for local supply of components. As the component manufacturers in turn grow, the competitiveness of other (and smaller, and higher value-adding) downstream assemblers can also be enhanced.[22] This must be our goal for the government's Production-linked incentive scheme. PLI could potentially deepen supply-chains, if disciplined by being linked to export targets with a progressive removal of protection.

Use the availability of skilled people to build a competitive position, based on R&D and innovation: India has long had a distinct advantage over every other country in the availability of skilled technical people at relatively low cost. This is the source of our software industry and the growth in IT-enabled services. The IT industry has drawn on India's massive production of over a million engineers annually—compared with annual US production of 230,000 engineering (including computer science) and 200,000 natural science undergraduate degrees.[23] At the height of the Indian software boom in 2000, when that single industry was recruiting over 100,000 engineers a year, it is striking that no Indian firm in any field had problems recruiting fresh engineers. They were still available in abundance, if not in quality.

Indian industry has long had the luxury of an abundance of low-cost qualified people. But while engineers have been cheap, they have also been treated cheaply—recruited to perform jobs with undemanding technical content. It is only as economic reform has created a demand for product innovation and as engineer remuneration has risen sharply (in 2020, a good graduate engineer with five to ten years of experience would earn about five times in real terms what he or she earned in 1991) that firms expect their average engineer to do more technically

---

22   The knock-on benefits from vertical integration is not a new idea. Albert Hirschman wrote about it in 1958 in *The Strategy of Economic Development* (New Haven, CT: Yale University Press).

23   National Science Foundation, *Science and Engineering Indicators*, https://www.nsf.gov/statistics/seind/

demanding work. Too few Indian firms, though, recognise the huge advantage they have of low-cost qualified people in reducing R&D cost, and so building competitive positions based on R&D. The pharmaceutical industry is a major exception—firms like DRL, Sun Pharma, and Cipla are betting on India's lower R&D costs as a basis for competing long-term in a research-intensive industry. So, too, are auto firms like Tata Motors and Mahindra and Mahindra. But they are still exceptions. Multinational investment in building strong R&D teams in India has been much more widespread. When I looked at this four years ago, 83 of the top 100 global R&D spenders were reported to have an R&D presence in India.[24] For example, AstraZeneca had one of their largest R&D labs outside Sweden in Bengaluru and all their work on tropical diseases is now done there. Cummins had a design centre in Pune that became its second largest (after the US) in three years. Emerson employed 4,000 engineers at their R&D centre, also in Pune. Bosch employed 13,500 R&D engineers in India, their second-largest facility worldwide, and announced a major expansion of their R&D presence in India. And GE's Jack Welch Research Centre in Bengaluru became its largest R&D facility worldwide, employing 5,300 people, including almost 2,000 PhDs (it had the largest concentration of chemistry and chemical engineering PhDs in the country).

So industry must recruit the best talent available and aim it at pushing forward product innovation in their field. This talent should aim to learn from the best firms and research worldwide. As firms invest more in research, the demand for graduate engineers and PhDs will also grow. This will tie in nicely with the focus on graduate programmes and research at the IITs and progressively at other leading educational institutes.

---

24 India has as many as 847 MNC R&D centres, representing 83 of the top 100 global R&D spenders and half of the top 500 global R&D spenders, http://www.rediff.com/business/report/column-fdi-can-spur-innovation-ideas-and-industries/20140808.htm; CTIER.

Our major software service firms have a long record of success with rapid growth and high profitability sustained over decades. As we saw earlier, this success has not been accompanied by substantial investment in R&D. As the opportunity of further growth built around labour arbitrage decreases,[25] the pressure to grow through innovation in both product and service will rise.

All this will amount to an increased investment in R&D by Indian firms. The obvious and powerful incentive that drives firms worldwide to invest in R&D is that they will otherwise be put out of business by competitors. When Tata Motors and DRL become more typical of their industries, as sectors such as software start investing a share of turnover in R&D that is internationally comparable, and as new R&D-intensive sectors such as technology and electronic equipment and defence grow, investment in R&D by firms will meet the 1 per cent of GDP set as a national target.

The role of policy: In chapter 8, we address the key policy role played by the state in R&D worldwide—to fund public research generously and broadly and to do so in the higher education system. We have discussed the value of focused effort to attract investment in those hardware manufacturing areas which are largely missing in India. There are two more roles that the state can valuably play to build technical capability. Many like to use the phrase 'technology policy'. Following Nathan Rosenberg, whose writing and teaching greatly enriched my understanding of technology and economics, I always hesitate to use it. The policies that affect the building of technical capability most fundamentally are beyond those specifically concerning technology. Trade policy and openness are usually more

---

25   Many in the software industry would argue with my use of the term 'labour arbitrage' today, pointing to the substantial capabilities built up in large-scale project management and execution excellence. I agree, but what share of our total software sector would exist if we paid salaries at the local level of the markets we sell to?

important than research policy. Education policy affects a firm's ability to build technical capability more directly than a tax subsidy for doing R&D.

The state can set the tone for discourse on technology. The great R.K. Laxman drew one of my favourite cartoons over forty years ago. It shows a doctor examining a patient's eye: 'You have some foreign matter in your eye. Would you like to keep it since it is foreign?' Three-quarters of a century after independence, we still have a nodding acquaintance with our colonial past. Some public-sector firms specify in tenders that some products must be made in Europe or the US, regardless of local availability of better products. Several new shopping malls reserve prime ground floor space for foreign brands, pushing Indian brands to upper floors. The state can help Indian brands and Indian technology, not by the socialist rhetoric of the past or by subsidies or by reserving procurement to local suppliers, but by setting a tone of wanting the best and encouraging local brands and technology to be that best. (It can also shame those errant public sector firms and private malls into change.) For many products, India is not a lead market—the product is developed for a different market and made available in India through import or local manufacture.[26] Can the government launch a series of projects on particularly Indian problems—building flyovers in four weeks, addressing waste and sewage across a hundred cities at a time, or providing clean drinking water to 600,000 villages? The government could fund R&D in both universities and private firms to develop solutions to these problems, thereby creating capabilities that could be used more broadly.

Just in case the reader thinks I'm heading in a self-defeating swadeshi direction, let me set the balance right with my next point.

We need a trade policy which embraces the world. For too many years, India's trade policy stance has been largely defensive, focused on limiting access of foreign firms to Indian markets. We need to adopt a

---

26 I owe this insight on lead markets to Gopichand Katragada, then the CTO of the Tata Group.

more positive and outward-looking trade policy. How can we improve access for Indian firms to emerging markets in South East Asia, Africa, Latin America and the Middle East? Can we propose FTAs with the emerging markets where market needs are similar to India's? And can we open our own market to foreign competition as the best way of forcing Indian firms to invest in technology? Thirty years after serious reforms began, we still impose high tariffs on automobiles, auto-components and a range of consumer products. As I said in chapter 4, since 2017, we have seen a decisive return to widespread protectionism. This is a big mistake. The threat of being pushed out of business is an impetus to invest in technology like no other.

And finally, to firm strategy and entrepreneurship: In the mid-2000s, a new confidence seemed to be spreading across Indian industry. This showed in international acquisitions, which ranged from disastrous (Tata Steel and Corus) to brilliant (Tata Motors and JLR). But it also showed in a few Indian firms choosing to become multinationals and combining this choice with strong investment in technology. No group illustrates this better than Tata, India's largest group, with over half of its over $100 billion in revenue coming from outside India and investing $3 billion in R&D worldwide. Tata is betting in sector after sector—energy, food and wellness, automobiles, digital consumer products—on building an international business resting on proprietary technology. Tata is not alone. Mahindra, Sun Pharma, DRL, Cipla, Kirloskar, Forbes Marshall, United Phosphorus, SRF, Triveni and a hundred other firms have all been expanding investment in both international markets and R&D. The slowdown since 2012 has dampened confidence but it has not retrenched ambition. As I said in the previous chapter, India needs a thousand multinationals, operating around the world, in every sector, building brands and reach. Our industrial structure, as we saw earlier, is already concentrated in skill- and capital-intensive sectors. Building leading international positions in engineering or machinery requires substantial investment in innovation. A hundred Indian firms must match GE, Bosch and Emerson in each employing thousands of engineers in R&D in India. Our design institutes must produce world-class graduates that define new product functionality. Research-intensive higher education institutes must provide a standard of graduate education second to none. And a combination of trade policy and firm strategy must push firms overseas, deploying their technical capability worldwide. As our firms grow into multinationals, a few could emerge as giant firms with the wherewithal to be true leaders in R&D. India can then emerge as a leader in innovation.

6

Design: The Scale India Needs

We Homo sapiens are creative. We have had to be, to come this far
with our puny teeth, lack of claws, and relative inability to move
quickly... We are not alone among animals in our ability to be creative.
I am always dazzled by the ability of rats to build a unique and
comfortable home in the back of my car engine using nothing but
sticks, insulation from the wires, and a bit of stuffing from the seats
... I am impressed, since the rat has a two-gram mind compared to
my 1,400-gram one. But humans' creativity equipment far outshines
that of other living beings. Rats can live in New York City, but they
could not have built it.

—Jim Adams

In 1935, Kasturbhai Lalbhai and two friends established the
Ahmedabad Education Society and set aside 1,000 acres in
the city for education. The Sarabhai and Lalbhai families have a
tradition of making extraordinary contributions to Ahmedabad,
and in particular to education in the city. The institutions that have

come up thanks to these two families are remarkable. Apart from the twenty-five institutions promoted directly by the Ahmedabad Education Society, they include the Indian Institute of Management, and the National Institute of Design, both founded in 1961. NID owes a great debt in particular to Gautam Sarabhai and his sister Gira. They brought the world-renowned designers Ray and Charles Eames to India in the 1950s. The document they prepared, *The India Report*, was taken to Prime Minister Nehru by Gautam Sarabhai and led to the foundation of NID. The Sarabhais and the Lalbhais gave the land for both IIM and NID, an act of private philanthropy for public institutions that stands in striking contrast to the present day when private institutions seek grants of public land.

In 1969, IIT Bombay started its Industrial Design Centre. For three decades, NID Ahmedabad and IIT Bombay were the only sources of trained designers in the country, and design was a small but high-quality affair. From the 2000s onwards, more and more design institutes began life, including three more NIDs and several design programmes at other IITs. A National Design Policy emerged in 2007, and led to the establishment of the India Design Council (IDC) as an apex body intended to spread design in the country.

For me, design has long been a passion, ever since my Stanford advisor and lifetime mentor Jim Adams first introduced me to it forty years ago. Good design has been integral to our own company's strategy for three decades. And it's long been something that I strongly believe must drive our future as a country. I was privileged to chair NID Ahmedabad (2016–19) and IDC (2017–20). NID is a wonderful institute with great faculty and world-class students. IDC has been playing a useful role in bringing in new design initiatives in the country. Through both I met some outstanding designers, people with huge talent committed to the cause of design in India. Many good things have been happening with design in the country, but I've also been humbled by how large our task is. In spite of recent growth, design is still a tiny enterprise in India. Design is key for environmental sustainability, looks, functionality and life cycle. However, too few companies prize it, too few of our products, services and public spaces reflect good design practices, and too few people in the country have better lives thanks to good design. Design is sometimes thought of as a luxury reserved for rich consumers. In fact, good design matters (and can make a difference) everywhere. But to make the average Indian's life better, design must scale by a factor of a hundred. I came away from my NID and IDC association both struck by the potential of design, and challenged by how much more there is to do. What we must do is the subject of this chapter.

I have known Jim Adams for over forty years. I took a course from him, on organisational behaviour, my first term at Stanford. He became my PhD advisor while still a dean in the School of Engineering and I was then based in the Science, Technology and Society Program, which he chaired, while I did my PhD. Jim is one of Stanford's legends. His courses on creativity, on technical literacy and on good products were consistently among Stanford's most popular. I have a hundred great Jim stories, but one of my favourites dates to when he was living in Palo Alto, a city known for its political correctness. Jim got tired of receiving constant callers, wanting to do good on behalf of this or that cause. So he installed a rifle rack on the back of his pickup. That was the end of all such callers. It did not matter that Jim has never owned a gun. Jim wears his brilliance lightly—he's read all the books, but will never be a typical academic and quote them. In the dozens of seminars I've attended with him over the years, you could count on him to ask the one question that really mattered. So too with design. He was one of the founders of the Stanford design programme, and has constantly helped it redefine its purpose. You will see much more of Jim in this chapter.

What is Design?

Design is the deliberate conceptualisation of a product or service to achieve certain desirable characteristics. Design enables companies to move up the value-chain and give the world great products. Great products are *'and'* products—products that are beautiful *and* functional. They are elegant *and* simple. They are high quality *and* accessible to a wide strata of the population. It is the task of great design to deliver on that *'and'*. So, not just elegance, but elegance with simplicity; not just beauty, but beauty with functionality; and not high quality alone, but high quality with accessibility for all.

In 2000, Jim Adams and I decided to turn our conviction of what good design could do into an experiment with Indian industry. Four companies—Godrej & Boyce, Godrej Sara Lee,[1] Tata Motors and Forbes Marshall—launched a shared year-long programme to develop great products. Repeated training sessions with five Stanford faculty, all donating their time for the pleasure of two twenty-five-hour flights, provided the necessary theory. An experienced Stanford design professional came and spent the year living with us in India, working full-time, rotating between the four companies. The projects ranged from a mosquito mat for rural India, to bedroom furniture, to a new dashboard for a car, to a boiler-efficiency meter. We figured that if an integrated design, manufacturing and marketability programme delivered results for such vastly different products, it had potential everywhere. Some very nice products emerged at the end of the year. But even more, the fifty or so Indian engineers in the programme came away with much learning and a deep appreciation of the power of design. All the companies involved subsequently set up their own in-house design departments, and some of the engineers involved went on to lead key businesses for their organisations. I will return later to some of the key design learnings we took away from the project.

So, given that design has much potential to contribute to the success of our firms, and to the lives of our people, what must we do to enable design to scale its impact? Four things: size, the quality of design, raising the priority for design in industry, and thinking about design for public purpose and fostering a sense of aesthetics across the country.

---

1   As it was then. It later folded into Godrej Industries.

Size: Making Design a Larger Enterprise

Hundreds of millions of people should see a difference in their lives as a result of what design brings, whether better products or a pleasanter built environment. To have scale and impact, design needs to be a much larger enterprise.

A few numbers: we produce around 20,000 designers annually in India from around 150 design institutes. We now have a handful of PhD programmes in design, including one at NID. Compare the 20,000 designers with three other numbers—one million engineers India produces every year (so a tiny drop in the broader pool of engineers); 25,000 designers South Korea produces each year (a country with a population 4 per cent of India's); and 300,000 designers that China produces each year (a country with the same population as ours). South Korea has fifty PhD programmes in design, 180 master's programmes in design and 250 bachelor's programmes in design.

Even more, consider the number of designers that work in industry. In South Korea about 25,000 designers work for design consultancies, but 240,000 designers work for user firms. We will come back to this number later when we discuss the priority of design in industry, as it is the essential thing we need to do. Designers need to be appreciated a lot more in industry, where design must find much greater prominence. We should have many more firms in the country that see design as their core strategy, and design should be a part of how citizens construct their daily lives.

South Korea and China are good countries for comparison, because they have both scaled fairly recently, South Korea in the last forty years and China in the last twenty years. Both explicitly grew design to achieve key objectives: to have more successful firms coming out with better products, to develop more proprietary products, to improve public spaces, and to use design widely such that people have healthier and better lives. China today accounts for roughly half of all design registrations worldwide, at 650,000 a year. India is in the twelfth position with 11,000 design registrations.[2]

Table 6.1: Design Applications for Selected Top Twenty Countries (2018)

Rank	Country	Design applications, 2018
1	China	708,799
2	EU	108,174
3	South Korea	68,054
4	USA	47,137
5	Germany	44,460
6	Turkey	42,320
7	Italy	36,024
8	Japan	31,468
9	UK	27,442
10	Spain	18,853
11	Iran	14,774
12	India	12,632
13	France	12,495
14	Switzerland	11,640
15	Russia	8,943
16	Ukraine	8,166
17	Australia	8,029
18	Canada	6,818
19	Brazil	6,111
20	Morocco	5,552

Source: World Intellectual Property Organization, IP Statistics, Industrial design – Application design counts for the top twenty offices, https://www3.wipo.int/ipstats/keysearch.htm?keyId=251

---

2   Table 6.1 has the number of design applications. Applications lead registrations by a year or two.

So to scale and have impact, design needs to be a much larger enterprise on all counts—the number of design firms and the number of designers they employ; the number of designers we produce each year; and the number of user firms with qualified designers on the payroll. This needs to show in multiplying the designs we register each year. In all of these areas, we need to think of ten times what we do now as our immediate challenge. How?

Design education: We must address both supply and demand. Demand is about the industry that employs designers, which I will come to later in this chapter. Supply is about education; we need to grow our annual output of qualified designers from 20,000 to at least 100,000 each year. We have around 150 design institutes in the country.[3] Outside of NID Ahmedabad and IIT Bombay, we have less than 148 qualified design faculty in the country. In other words, some of our design institutes do not have even one full-time faculty member qualified to teach design. This is where doctoral programmes in design come in. In 2014–20, we graduated fewer PhDs in design than we started new design programmes. One does not need to be brilliant to note the gap. Fortunately, the best designers usually do not have PhDs; they tend to be practitioners running successful consultancies. Can we find ways of enticing many of them to become full-time anchors and teachers, at least one each, for our design programmes and then grow the graduates by an order of magnitude? And can NID and IIT Bombay build strong faculty development programmes for the many faculty spread around the country teaching design? In a few years,

---

3   I apologise for the approximate numbers, but design programmes in India fall under many heads. The NIDs (and National Institutes of Fashion Technology) come under the industry department. Design programmes within engineering schools come under the All India Council of Technical Education, within the Ministry of Education. The design programmes at our IITs are not part of AICTE and independently report to the Ministry of Education. I have not been able to find one authentic, official figure. This reflects the great pluralism of our higher education system.

such an effort could provide the backbone for strong, good quality design education.

The Quality of Design: Jim's Rules

The second area is quality. What is good design? In 2012, Jim Adams published *Good Products, Bad Products*.[4] Based on a course Jim taught at Stanford for twenty years, and a lifetime of reflection of what makes products great, it is the best book on design or quality that I have personally read. Jim discusses various aspects of a product or service that make it good or bad. He articulates, with great insight, what every human being experiences daily. Consider the ergonomics of human fit: sounds like an esoteric subject? I am yet to check into a new hotel where I do not play the game of hunt-the-switch the first night. To put all the lights off, you have to find the switch for the one light that stays on. It is a design problem, and a simple one that we can directly address.

Jim identifies seven attributes of good and bad design:

1. Performance and cost: Fostering a feeling of getting more for less. Perceptions of performance in a car do not come only from the speedometer; the height, the noise, the responsiveness, the suspension and many other factors also contribute. The cost includes both the purchase price, as well as fuel, maintenance and insurance. Some luxury products appeal *because* they are expensive, not in spite of being expensive.

2. Human fit: Apart from the light-switch-in-hotel problem, we face ergonomic problems daily. Many have long complained that the height of kitchen counters is fixed by men for men but mainly used by women. The extreme of this is actually dangerous—apparently airbags in cars

---

4   James L. Adams, *Good Products, Bad Products: Essential Elements to Achieving Superior Quality* (New Delhi: Tata McGraw Hill, 2012).

were designed based on the height and weight of the average man, which means that they're actually significantly less safe for women. Remote-controls should not require a PhD in computer science to use. I personally have always taken the approach to any device I get of plugging it in, switching it on, and opening the manual only if all else fails.

3. Consonance with global constraints: Many companies now consciously package their products in a more environmentally friendly manner. I often buy whisky in cities that I travel to. As I've got older, I've paid increasingly absurd prices for bottles of some rare malt that I usually require to be at least one-third my age. These tend to come in such elaborate packaging—handcrafted wooden boxes, with hinges and latches—that is completely wasted. I throw away the box almost as soon as I get it, and it always leaves me feeling guilty at the waste. I find the Japanese whiskies have this sorted. The whisky is as wonderful, and the box does what it is intended to, which is to protect the bottle—without consuming a whole forest in the process. A fine social initiative, Satisfeito, enlists restaurants in a programme where you sign up to be served a smaller helping than normal. In return, the restaurant provides meals for the homeless each day.

4. Craftsmanship: The difference between two products may be just how they 'feel'. We expect good furniture to be well crafted. If you look at the most modern of cars, we find that they use an abundance of wood and leather. Why? These are materials that have been around for centuries and are normally associated with much more traditional technologies. We use them in cars, especially in expensive cars, because they convey craftsmanship, and a sense of quality. As Jim Adams says, 'Craftsmanship is the process of making things extraordinarily well. It involves fits and finishes, obsession with details, tender loving care, and pride."

5. Emotion: How does the product appeal to the emotions? Consider ads for various SUVs that convey how brilliantly suited

the vehicle is for driving at high speed through an animal park in Madhya Pradesh. That may have little to do with what it will actually be used for—which is to sit in a traffic jam on the road into Delhi from Gurugram—but it certainly makes us feel good. When Tata Motors launched its first car in 1998, the Indica, the company took out full-page ads in the papers saying 'Isn't it time for some Indian engineering?', an obvious and highly successful appeal to the emotions. (Never mind that much of the first Indica was actually designed by the Italian design house I.DE.A.) The same Tata Motors got its appeal to the emotions completely wrong fifteen years later when it launched the Nano. Cars are aspirational items in India, and no one (barring a few Parsis) wanted to buy 'the world's cheapest car'.

6. Elegance and sophistication: Is the product a clean and efficient solution? Does form match function? Is it visually elegant? Some Titan watches come in machined steel cases with leather sleeves—the case conveys the slimness of the watch. I have a fondness for cufflinks, completely idiotic devices that cost more, take more time to fasten, and keep tarnishing. I put up with all that because it appeals to my sense of elegance.

7. Symbolism: Can the product symbolise something beyond itself? I've often used Titan watches as gifts I take abroad for friends. I want to take them something beautiful that symbolises modern Indian industry and precision manufacturing, and not just our great craft traditions.

I recommend Jim Adams' book very strongly. Too often when we read books about quality, we get lost in things like 'six sigma' and the 'Toyota Production System'. We like to talk about products in clinical terms, in terms of technical specifications. However, what determines whether a product is bought or not, and especially how much we are willing to pay for it, is usually something much softer and more emotional. Toyota, we are told, makes the best-quality cars in the world—they certainly tick all the boxes of defects per million, generally never needing to be repaired, and such. But why are we willing to pay three times as much for an equivalent Mercedes or BMW? And why are we also willing to pay more for a Toyota Prius hybrid, or a Tesla electric car, than would ever be justified on any rational economic grounds, payback calculations, product finish or performance comparisons? Because good products delight us. Think of a product you really love, and ask why. The texture of a shirt, the softness of a sweater, the growl of a motorcycle, the smooth opening of an iPhone box—all these things delight. Our emotional response makes for product success. If designers wrestle with emotional issues, ergonomic issues, issues of symbolism and what products stand for, I think we will end up delivering better products. At the end of the day, good design is not just about artistic creativity, it is about doing something that really makes a difference to the user.

Putting these rules to work: Even before Jim Adams' book came out, we were applying it in Forbes Marshall's product development processes, with our engineers (most of whom had never met Jim) calling the attributes 'Jim's rules'. When *Good Products* was published, we decided to systematically use it across product development in Forbes Marshall. Over a three-month period, all our R&D engineers were grouped in project teams, and read and applied each chapter to their current development project. One group of young engineers (average age twenty-four) was at a very early stage of conceptualising a project, in the vague—and very technical—space of condensate recovery. This group was also the most systematic in applying each chapter step by step to their project, spending time on craftsmanship, aesthetics and emotional appeal. For each attribute they produced a new prototype showing how the attribute had been specifically applied. The final stage was a conference in Mahabaleshwar, near Pune, where each project team presented their final product concept. The young team won the first prize for a product that simply looked spectacular. It was tall, painted red, black and silver, and looked like a rocket. Forbes Marshall's Flash Jet Pump has gone on to be a great success, with sales around three times the numbers we expected and installations across twenty countries within two years. Soon after we launched the product and sold the first units, I was told a story of a plant in Surat whose owner saw the Flash Jet Pump installed on one of his dyeing machines. He asked that it be installed on all his other dyeing machines—without knowing what the product did. I provide this detail to make three essential points: first, that these soft principles of good design and appealing to the emotions apply to all products, including those industrial products we normally think are all about performance and efficiency. Second, that Jim's rules work. Applied with understanding and dedication, they can result in a product substantially different and better than anything else around. And third, that if you're trying to break boundaries, a younger team is more innovative as they can more than make up for a lack of experience with a willingness to try anything. They are not concerned about looking foolish, and therefore end up with something simply better.

Virtual design: Most designers these days use computer-aided design tools. These are great tools to enhance efficiency. But I have to give you my bias. I am yet to see one product that I liked and which did not go through several physical prototypes—not one product! And it is a constant struggle in our own organisation, where colleagues show me images of products on a screen, which don't do anything for me. One of my greatest regrets as I write this book is that our Covid-induced virtual existence keeps me from going to work and seeing and feeling real stuff. I *have* to see a physical prototype to be able to relate to it, to pick it up and feel it. We do industrial products, like boilers, steam traps, control valves and flow meters, and for these products too a physical prototype is essential. Indeed not one prototype, but many— multiple prototypes and alternative prototypes and doing them again and again and again. As any good designer knows, doing excellent design is hard work and, in my biased mind, the more time we spend on our computers, the less time we spend on design.

Need-finding or market research: Market research asks customers what they want. It does so using qualitative and quantitative techniques of data gathering, using sophisticated statistical tools to analyse the data and form a precise picture of customer preferences. The field of design has generally been somewhat contemptuous of market research. The general approach is that if you ask customers what they want, they will tell you they want what your competitors give them. As such, one would always be playing product design catch-up instead of product leadership. Instead, need-finding is a technique aimed at discovering customer needs rather than wants. If these needs are non-obvious and unmet by anything similar today, they will not emerge from however careful and thorough a depiction of wants in market research. Jim's rules help one explore needs that are difficult to articulate. By observing what customers do and what problems they struggle with, unmet needs can be captured. Having formed a rough idea of what one should develop, market research can then help one work out the detailed product specification.[5]

Raising the Priority of Design in Industry

There are fine examples of companies in India that emphasise design. The Tata Group company Titan entered the market for watches with outstanding design. They built up probably the strongest design department in the country, and some of their designers, such as the Foley brothers, established reputations for design in their own right. The Indian auto sector has firms like Bajaj Auto, Tata Motors, Royal

---

5   In our chapter on design in *From Followers to Leaders: Managing Technology and Innovation in Newly Industrializing Countries,* Dave Wield and I talk about how firms in developing countries can build design leadership.

Enfield and Mahindra & Mahindra that all have substantial design departments. Godrej and Boyce, and our own firm Forbes Marshall, see design as essential to our success in the engineering sector. We are all companies that have placed a high priority on design, and use it as a base for building proprietary technology. There are more Indian firms that are truly passionate about design, but I doubt if they number more than a hundred. That's too few. Given the size of India, the scale of industry, and the need to build internationally successful businesses, we need at least a thousand firms in the country that are design champions and compete head to head on the basis of design—as Bajaj Auto and Royal Enfield do in motorcycles or Tata Motors and Mahindra in SUVs. If the same kind of competition takes place in every industry, we will deliver great products for our people.

Remember South Korea again—25,000 designers working in design consultancies and 240,000 designers working in user firms. Those 240,000 designers working in firms take the ideas they get from design consultancies and put them to work in their firms to turn them into great products, and in turn act as a market for the design consultancies.

It starts with an aspiration within the company to develop great products—those *and* (no compromise) products we discussed earlier. I've found it powerful to ask design teams to conceptualise the world's best whatever—boiler, steam-trap, watch, engine, refrigerator. Relax all other constraints—such as cost. Once one comes up with what makes for the world's best product, one can start compromising with performance and cost factors to get something that appeals to customer emotion and also makes for good business.

In our book, *From Followers to Leaders*, Dave Wield and I argue that firms should build the capability of pushing out the design frontier within a particular technological paradigm. Our argument was that the design and technology frontiers were distinct, and that pushing out the design frontier was an attractive way of adding value in products without the risk involved in attempting to push out the technology frontier—let the world's rich firms make the expensive mistakes, in other words. But building design leadership takes serious investment in skills and building R&D competences that few Indian firms have today. That must be our mission.

Reputation: Design has a high reputational effect that works at the level of the individual designer, the firm and indeed the country. The design and production of an outstanding product positively affects other products. This leads to a virtuous circle which steadily increases expectations and performance. A designer in an environment where doing good design is the norm wants at least to meet the standards of that environment and, if possible, exceed them. This in turn leads to better designed products, which improves the environment, and so on. Finally, not just designers but everyone is motivated by working at a firm that is perceived as being good at design. They are proud to be part of an organisation known for producing outstanding and beautiful products.

To illustrate this argument, let's do an exercise. If a product were to be produced in one of the following countries—China, Germany, India, Italy, Japan, South Korea, Switzerland, the United States—for which country of origin would you be willing to pay more for the product?

Now answer the question—from which of those countries listed would you pay more for a car? A computer? A chair? A machine tool? A pair of shoes? And, a very real question this year, a vaccine?

This exercise produces several conclusions. First, some countries have a reputation that is cross-product. Countries like Germany and Switzerland have a reputation in general for high-quality products, a reputation that is worth billions. China has a reputation (held earlier by Japan and then South Korea) for cheaper products. Second, countries even more have a reputation for a particular product range, such as Germany for cars, the US for computers, or Italy for clothes (I was going to add China for viruses, but decided against it). If you get more specific, the effect of reputation is even more marked—luxury cars (Germany; Japanese carmakers have struggled for years to break in), raincoats (the UK, guess why), or precision lathes (Switzerland; think mechanical watches). Where does India start? We do not have a reputation for exceptional design either overall or in any particular product area. We must start by understanding that this national reputation is a reflection of the reputation of a collection of firms. We will need to build it one firm at a time, area by area. What will it take?

Building design capability is hard, involving many things. Good design requires that one conceptualise a new product that meets needs that no one else meets today. We then need in-house designers with high aesthetic standards who are willing to try out new things and turn the concept into something tangible. And then we need good manufacturing and business capabilities to make and sell the product effectively.

Jim Adams and I learnt four things from our design project for Indian firms. Dedicated product development resource was crucial, combined with a challenging project plan. One also needed excellent in-house aesthetic and design capability. The source could be external, but with enough internal resource to integrate the outside work. Then physical prototypes were key—early and repeated prototypes improved output and speeded up projects. And a product champion in top management made all the difference, not just supporting good effort but contributing time and ideas to drive the project forward. The Indica was developed at a time when Tata Motors had no full-time CEO. Ratan Tata, the chairman, would visit Pune once each month and spend a day reviewing matters; over half his time was spent in the design department reviewing product design in detail. Apart from the motivation the designers received, the rest of the company received a clear message that design was essential to the company's success.

The India Design Mark: A key initiative of the India Design Council was to launch the India Design Mark. The overall objective is to raise the profile of design in the country, by certifying products as 'Good Design'. In the eight annual rounds to date, we have seen a steady stream of products, some very interesting. But to have impact we need to receive thousands of entries a year. In 2020, we received fifty entries; around 500 good design marks have been awarded in total. Japan has awarded 35,000 products its good design mark, Taiwan 6,700 and Germany around 1,500 products each year. All this brings us back to the need for scale, and more scale.

Design for Public Purpose

Finally, some comments about design for public purpose. The one thing we can be assured of on our streets is vibrancy. Unfortunately, vibrant often also means messy. We suffer as a society from too few attractive public spaces. Whenever we provide an attractive public space, we see immediate take up. Take the River-Front Development Project in Ahmedabad. It did not exist ten years ago, but today is *the* place where people go to just spend time, for an organised event, or to walk in the parks created on either side of the river.[6] Each city needs public spaces which are attractive meeting places for people. If we don't create these spaces, people will make their own that will spill out onto the roads. Public space will infringe on road space and parking space and create the mess that exists in so many of our cities, instead of it being an area which is attractive to use.

Going with this is a sense of heritage. We have a tremendous architectural heritage in the country. Consider the diversity on offer. The temples of Madurai, Belur and Halebid, the Taj Mahal, Red Fort, Bahai Temple and Jama Masjid in Agra and Delhi, the Dutch Palace in Cochin, the Town Hall in Mumbai, are all magnificent architectural achievements. The abandoned cities of Hampi, Fatehpur Sikri,

---

6　I am making no judgement of the ecological impact of the dam that a full Sabarmati river depends on. I am solely arguing for the creation of pleasant public spaces in all our cities.

Champaner and Mandu, the 100 villages that make up Chettinad, are each the kind of tourist destination that cannot be matched anywhere. Look at our colonial heritage—Rashtrapati Bhavan or North and South Blocks or anything Lutyens and Baker did in Delhi. These are all a part of *our* architectural heritage. All must be preserved and treasured. By appreciating them as works of great artistic achievement, we can raise the general consciousness of design and aesthetics in the country. They can inspire us to do great design.

Combining our craft traditions with modern industry: Our greatest missed design opportunity is an inability to blend modern industry with our craft traditions. We have the richest of crafts, the most widespread and diverse of any country in the world. The work spreads across fabric, wood, metals, and metal alloys centuries old in their origin, each in unique combinations of finishes and design. These craft traditions are ingrained in communities, who learn generation to generation, master craftsperson to apprentice. And we largely ignore it all in modern industry. Product finish often appears as a problem in our products, as often as it sets apart the excellence of so many of our crafts.

I made this comment of the opportunity for design that rests in our crafts at a CII Design Summit. After the programme, an energetic and passionate young man came up and told me he was starting a new business to do just this. I've since met Rohit Naag several times as he has developed his business concept. His company, Stories of Intrigue, has begun with some fascinating offerings of home furniture—credenzas, lamps, tables. He draws on two great crafts, Bidri work from Bidar in Karnataka, and Etikoppaka from Andhra Pradesh.[7] Rohit has employed some of the world's most interesting modern designers, and is combining their designs with these traditional crafts. Rohit will make

---

7   Bidri work involves an etching process where silver comes through a black laminate on metal. Etikoppaka is a lacquer process on wood, traditionally for small children's toys.

dozens, not millions, of each piece as works of art. But we need many, many such examples to inspire others to bring our crafts together with modern product design.

I started this chapter talking about the Sarabhais and the Lalbhais and their contribution to Ahmedabad. Both families have established museums in Ahmedabad, which enrich the city. The Calico Museum is, put simply, amongst the world's great museums. Set up by the Sarabhais in the family house, it brings together textiles from all parts of India. The collections are breathtaking in variety, design and craftsmanship. Gira Sarabhai's passion shines in every detail of the exceptional collection, serene garden and brilliant guided tour. The Lalbhais recently converted Kasturbhai Lalbhai's house into a museum, getting the architect Rahul Mehrotra to renovate and add gallery space. The Tagore collection of Indian art is on permanent display in the house, and a new gallery provides rotating space for the display of modern Indian painters. Visiting museums is a way of developing one's own sense of aesthetics; it needs to be part of the design curriculum. Italy is known for great design. 'The light', and centuries of being surrounded by exquisite colours and architecture fosters a natural sense of aesthetics. We need to consciously cultivate a sense of beauty till it becomes equally widespread and natural. Our museums should attract a wider audience. By immersing ourselves in our heritage of arts, crafts and architecture, we can create a sensitivity to aesthetics, to what is good in our own surroundings, to deliver a truly well-designed future for India.

Ramblings on Institutions

7

Higher Education: Less State, More Quality

In the first place, God made idiots. That was for practice. Then he made school boards.

—Mark Twain

Together with a juvenile waistline, he still retained the bright enthusiasms and the fresh unspoiled outlook of a slightly inebriated undergraduate.

—*Uncle Fred in the Springtime,* P.G. Wodehouse

I loved college. I went to Stanford when I was eighteen and left with a bachelor's degree in Industrial Engineering and History, and a master's and PhD in Industrial Engineering. By the time I got my last degree, I had been in the Department of Industrial Engineering longer than half of the faculty and all of the furniture. If those who get doctorates are supposed to be highly focused, I was, briefly, a major in Civil Engineering, Mechanical Engineering, English, and—returning from a wonderful term at Stanford's campus in the UK—even British Studies.[1] And I did not leave the university when I graduated; I taught a course roughly once a year at Stanford for another seventeen years. The flexibility of the system to explore and discover interests; the range of outstanding professors so generous with their time, ideas, and hospitality; the informality where a nineteen-year-old undergraduate could address a Nobel prize winner by his first name; an honour code where students operated on trust and faculty were barred from proctoring or supervising students taking an exam; and a culture where bright students worked very hard but could never show it—all this is in my blood. Along the way, I had the great good fortune of getting to know both faculty and the academic leadership well; many became lifelong friends. My twenty-five-plus years at Stanford, as student and teacher, are even today my reference point for anything in higher education. There were many things wrong at Stanford, but many more things that were right, and anything different we come up with has to be better.

I had many wonderful teachers at Stanford, people who helped me define what great teaching is all about. Picking just one is a challenge, but I would pick the historian of France, Gordon Wright. I used Gordon's classic text on the history of modern France while spending a term at the Stanford programme in Tours. On returning to Stanford, I found he was teaching a course on crime and punishment in modern Europe. This was a subject I had absolutely no interest in, but I showed up for the first class just to see what it was about. There were just seven students in the class and there was no way I could insult this wonderful teacher by making it six. I stuck with the course; it ended up being one of the best courses I ever took, which fundamentally altered my views on everything from prison to capital punishment. As we were just seven students and met once a week for three hours, Gordon moved

---

1   To really demonstrate lack of focus, I continued taking courses while doing the research and writing for my doctorate. My subject was technical entrepreneurship in India; my courses were whatever I was interested in at the time.

meetings of the class to his home on the campus, where his wife Louise gave us lemonade and cake as we talked. In the ten weeks that the course met, all seven of us became increasingly liberal in our approach to crime, while Gordon constantly challenged our beliefs. We were never able to learn what his own views were; indeed, I had to read his book on the subject when it came out two years later to find out what he actually thought!

I subsequently took every course Gordon offered while I was at Stanford. This included a wonderful course on the history of Europe since 1945. In my final year as a PhD student, while writing my dissertation, I took Gordon's course on the history of nineteenth-century France. (As this had absolutely nothing to do with my thesis on technical entrepreneurship in India, I had to hide my taking the course from my advisor Jim Adams. Jim, having promised my parents that I would eventually finish my PhD, had this strange notion that I should graduate. I could not offer such glaring proof of straying by getting grades, especially good grades, in a course in French History.)[2] A lecture in this course was on the nineteenth-century French professor and politician Jean Jaures—a figure not only I but the entire class had never heard of. By the end of the lecture, when Jaures was assassinated, the entire class of hard-bitten Stanford undergraduates and graduates were in tears, crying for the loss of someone who died seventy years ago, whom we had never heard of before, in a country 8,000 kilometres away, that none of us were from. One of my abiding regrets in life is not having a recording of that lecture, but we at least have Gordon's essay in his collection *Insiders and Outliers*.[3] Gordon and Louise became close friends, and when I was at Stanford teaching, we would have dinner and go to a movie together at least once a week.

---

2   Gordon's course on nineteenth century France was not the only one. Another wonderful course I took 'unofficially' was on Jane Austen taught by Susan Morgan.

3   Gordon Wright, *Insiders and Outliers: A Procession of Frenchmen* (Stanford, CA: Stanford Almuni Association, 1980).

If Gordon defines great teaching me, my model of academic leadership is Gerhard Casper, president of Stanford from 1992 to 2000. The president is a long way away from a part-time faculty member at a great university, and one rarely interacts in any way. I was fortunate that Gerhard made the first visit by a Stanford president to India in forty years and I travelled with him for the ten days he was here. In his eight years as president, he not only addressed the serious financial problems he inherited, but redefined the university's commitment to undergraduate teaching, making it attractive for the most respected researchers to teach first-year students in small seminars. Along the way, he became Stanford's most architectural president, hiring world-renowned architects for all the new buildings on campus. He dug out and implemented a century-old plan for a science and engineering quadrangle that was part of the original concept of the university. And he created new vistas that open out the campus even as they pull it together. Gerhard's ability to substantially impact and improve an institution at the top of its game has always inspired me.

Gerhard is without doubt the most profound thinker I have met. I tell him that he is incapable of making a superficial comment about the weather. Some years on, he published a set of eight speeches he gave as president of Stanford, *The Winds of Freedom: Addressing Challenges to the University*.[4] The speeches range across the purpose of the university, the mission of Stanford, free speech on campus, research universities and affirmative action. Each is classic Gerhard, at once scholarly, deeply thoughtful and brilliant. Gerhard also added the subtext of each speech (what he did not say at the time the speech was given, and why), one or two postscripts (what happened later), and even the wider context (why he chose the topic) of the speech. (If you want to know the difference between subtext and context, read the book.) This book is, in my view, required reading for anyone who wishes to understand what a great university is all about. And, with

---

4   Gerhard Casper, *The Winds of Freedom: Addressing Challenges to the University* (New Haven, CT: Yale University Press, 2014).

wider application, it illustrates what deep thought on any subject is all about.

But back to the story. Soon after returning to India in 1986, I started to get involved in things related to higher education, especially through CII. I ended up on various academic boards—a private engineering college in Pune, IIT Bombay, the University of Poona Governing Council, an AICTE regional board, IIM Visakhapatnam, and chaired the board of NID Ahmedabad. In 2003, for a paper on India's higher education system for a Stanford conference, I looked at the subject in more depth. That paper led to subsequent shorter derivatives on more specific subjects. It culminated in a visit to India in 2011 by Gerhard Casper and some Stanford faculty who work on education—including Roger Noll, Ron Hanushek and Anjini Kochar—for a week of meetings and conferences on our higher education system. While most writings on our higher education system, now and twenty years ago, speak of it being in crisis and needing urgent repair, my conclusion was (and is) that we have a system with deep problems, but huge potential. Tapping that potential is the subject of this chapter. Let's begin with what got us into our current state.

Why Higher Education?

Investing in higher education has long been viewed as important to the development process, but school education is even more essential. Even the most free-market economists support public provision of primary and secondary education, among the clearest examples of market failure in economics. Many studies have shown that schooling plays a central role in national development. The returns to primary education can be enormous, well upwards of 20 per cent in poorer countries. Multiplied across a huge population such as ours, the gains can be dramatic. The returns to secondary education are also substantial—good schooling provided the essential foundation for the efficient manufacturing of the East Asian miracle. Higher education is more problematic, with results varying from the strongly positive to much more tenuous. I deal with higher education because it has more to do with industrial innovation and is essential to the success of individual organisations—and because I understand it better.

Over fifty years ago, the first edition of Gary Becker's *Human Capital* brought analysis of higher education into mainstream economic analysis.[5] The British economist Joan Robinson once said that whatever can be said about India, so can the opposite. Nowhere is this more true than in higher education. Excellence at a few institutes coexists with mediocrity (and worse) at many others. The social mobility of millions of Indians who get a college degree contrasts with the waste of millions who remain excluded from a system they cannot afford. And the dynamism of new institution creation combines with stagnant governance structures in our public universities.

As Devesh Kapur and Pratap Bhanu Mehta point out in the fine introductory essay to their book on higher education,[6] India at Independence had a small number of literates, but these literates were highly educated. Independent India invested further in higher education, with the explicit objective of economic development. Technical education was accorded pride of place, giving India the third largest pool of technically qualified people by 1980.[7] India's higher technical education system is correctly credited with its successful software industry and strength in IT enabled services.

Growth with concentration: Higher education has grown very rapidly in India over the last forty years, with the enrollment ratio of the relevant age group rising from 6 to 29 per cent. Only China has

---

5   Gary S. Becker, *Human Capital: A Theoretical and Empirical Analysis, with Special Reference to Education* (Cambridge, MA: National Bureau of Economic Research, 1964).

6   Devesh Kapur and Pratap Bhanu Mehta, editors, *Navigating the Labyrinth: Perspectives on India's Higher Education* (Hyderabad: Orient Blackswan, 2017).

7   After the USA and the erstwhile USSR, today India has the second largest pool of engineering graduates, after China.

shown an even more dramatic increase, from 4 to 50 per cent, in the same period. India's growth has been greatly concentrated. First, most of the growth has been in professional fields, particularly engineering and management. Second, the growth has been in teaching rather than in research. Public research in India is highly concentrated in autonomous, walled-off research institutes instead of the university system where professors and students can freely and creatively interact. Third, most of the growth has been in private institutes. And fourth, with the growth concentrated in professional education, the humanities and social sciences have been neglected.

Such rapid growth with such concentration has led to four challenges. These are quality, building graduate education and research universities, providing equity of access, and creating excellent universities in the humanities and social sciences. I discuss this skewed growth of the higher education system and the challenges it has led to. These challenges can be addressed; factors inherent to India and the Indian higher education system provide for great opportunity.

The Quality Problem

Engineering, pharmacy, business and computer applications have seen the bulk of growth. The number of engineering colleges and enrolment have both grown dramatically for decades. At the height of the boom, 1995 to 2010, India saw approximately one engineering college and one management institute open each day. Devesh Kapur points out that since 2000, India has opened 4.4 colleges a day, Sundays included.[8] India today has 6,100 engineering colleges and 3,000 management institutes. From 40,000 engineers graduating annually in 1983, India today graduates over one million.[9] The result is an abundance of

---

8   *Financial Times*, 'Covid piles pressure on India to embrace online degrees', 6 January 2021.
9   There are three numbers we must wrestle with—we have roughly 1.7 million engineering places approved, we enrol roughly 1.4 million, and graduate roughly 1 million annually.

engineers, but raising their standard of quality is a pressing concern. So, the first challenge is quality.

Various attempts have been made to address the quality problem, most focused on regulation, which specifies the physical infrastructure for institutes and the qualifications of faculty. For instance, a full-time appointment as an assistant professor now requires a PhD. More useful measures have taken the form of various schemes to attract Indians with PhDs working overseas (the Ramalingaswami Re-entry Fellowship Programme) and programmes to make a career in academics and research more attractive to recent graduates (the J.C. Bose National Fellowship Programme). These have some impact, but mainly at the top end of the institutional scale. The great bulk of institutes have well over half of faculty 'temporary', who do not have to meet the regulations, and to date have displayed little interest in graduate programmes or research. Trying to regulate quality into institutes has largely failed. Instead, a combination of market and institutional mechanisms has much greater potential.

For many years, with demand for professional course seats exceeding supply, there was little incentive to improve quality. Supply has now exceeded demand in India for over a decade in the southern states, and institutes are finally being forced to compete on faculty and facilities. Actual enrolment in engineering colleges in 2020 is just 55 per cent of the sanctioned intake, with enrolments down to 1.4 million from 1.7 million in 2013.[10] Relying on the market therefore will address much of the problem. The state can play a useful role, beginning by ignoring the cry from incumbent colleges to limit the number of new seats[11] and new institutes. A strong compulsory accreditation and assessment programme that publishes college quality indicators would go a long way in harnessing this market solution. One could emulate the US state university system of the second half of the twentieth

---

10   K.M. Pavithra, 'Enrollment in engineering colleges down by more than 20 percent in 7 years', Factly.in, 6 July 2019.

11   The term used in India to describe the number of student places is 'seats'.

century, where a few excellent (and cheap) state universities provided an excellent 'quality control' for more expensive private universities, which either had to be better or admit poorer quality students.

Table 7.1: Undergraduate Engineering Colleges by State

State/ Union territory	Annual student intake (2003)	% of total	Annual student intake (2013)	% of total	Annual student intake (2019)	% of total	Population census (2011)	% of total
Tamil Nadu	79,122	22	186,965	16	297,500	21	72,147,030	6
Andhra Pradesh*	64,300	18	207,134	18	274,859	20	84,580,777	7
Maharashtra	47,035	13	159,323	14	144,061	10	112,374,333	9
Karnataka	40,385	11	100,946	9	102,899	7	61,095,297	5
Uttar Pradesh	22,491	6	90,051	7	103,645	7	199,812,341	16
Kerala	17,858	5	41,503	4	55,845	4	33,406,061	3
Madhya Pradesh	12,970	4	60,164	5	78,913	6	72,626,809	6
West Bengal	10,709	3	22,624	2	36,713	3	91,276,115	8
Gujarat	9,559	3	65,243	6	61,556	4	60,439,692	5
Odisha	9,505	3	39,869	3	40,445	3	41,974,218	3
Haryana	9,385	3	45,329	4	41,873	3	25,351,462	2
Punjab	8,875	2	49,610	4	35,914	3	27,743,338	2
Rajasthan	7,807	2	40,722	3	45,793	3	68,548,437	6
Bihar	1,575	0	3,400	0	11,020	1	104,099,452	9
Others	19,720	5	53,584	5	73,604	5	155,379,615	13
Total	361,296	100	1,166,467	100	1,404,640	100	1,210,854,977	100

* Includes Telangana too.

Source: AICTE Statistics at https://facilities.aicte-india.org/dashboard/pages/dashboardaicte.php, State Census 2011 data at https://www.census2011.co.in/states.php

What evidence is there that relying on the market to improve matters in higher education will work?[12] We have already seen some improvement in the states where supply exceeds demand. And consider the geographical concentration of India's higher education system. When I wrote my first paper on higher education in 2003, the five southern states accounted for two-thirds of seats and less than one-third of the population. This was entirely a demand–supply issue. The five southern states had moved first in permitting private engineering colleges and student demand voted with its feet. Over ten years, five million students migrated from states like Bihar, Uttar Pradesh, West Bengal and Rajasthan to states like Karnataka, Maharashtra and Delhi in search of education.[13] That prompted other states to join in the private education boom to meet the demand of their own students. By 2013, many other states—such as Madhya Pradesh, Gujarat and Punjab—caught up and their share of engineering students was closer to their share in the population, reducing the regional concentration.

Is massification a problem? As higher education has expanded globally in the last sixty years, many have pointed to the problems of providing higher education to the masses. The English novelist (and college teacher) Kingsley Amis claimed in 1961 that 'more will mean worse' as he contemplated plans to expand university education.[14] Higher education has gone from being the preserve of a small elite to something much more widespread. The OECD countries today report gross enrolment ratios of 75 per cent; the US is at 90 per cent. As the norm becomes getting a college education, two concerns have arisen. First is the concern over quality, when millions are in college (China

---

12 In India, we always have to justify relying on the market, instead of arguing why we must not.

13 S. Chandrashekhar and Ajaya Sharma, 'Internal Migration for Education and Employment among Youth in India', WP-2014-004 (Mumbai: Indira Gandhi Institute of Development Research, 2014).

14 *The Economist*, 'University education: Making it pay', 18 September 2008.

has forty-five million students in higher education and India has thirty-seven million), standards are harder to maintain. Second, if everyone gets a college degree, is it worth it? As *The Economist* asked some years ago, 'Does education pay, or have the politicians merely been seduced by the professors?'[15]

Table 7.2: Proportion of College-age (18–24) Population in Higher Education

Country	GER in tertiary education (%)	
	1970	2019
China	0.1	54
India	5	29
Israel	20	62
South Korea	7	96
UK	15	61
USA	47	88

Note: Total enrolment in tertiary education regardless of age expressed as a percentage of the population in the five-year age-group immediately following upper secondary education. The population of the official age for tertiary education is estimated to be the five-year age-group immediately following upper secondary education. If the official entrance age to upper secondary is fifteen and the duration is three years, then the age group is eighteen to twenty-two years.

Source: UNESCO statistical yearbook

Few countries have seen a greater increase than India: five million college students became ten million in the 1990s and are now thirty-seven million. The New Education Policy of 2020 aspires to raise the proportion of the age group in higher education from the current 29 per cent to 50 per cent by 2035. This is indeed mass education, but is 'massification' such a problem? One of our most thoughtful observers and brilliant academic leaders, Pankaj Chandra, vice chancellor

---

15   *The Economist*, 'Coming top: A survey of education', 21 November 1992.

of Ahmedabad University, sees the purpose of higher education as improvement in livelihood, citizenship, and giving individuals meaning in life.[16] Even if the bulk of our system does not provide this in the right mix, we surely have to keep working at making our institutions better—improving the connect with the job market here, letting people discover for themselves what it means to be a true and freethinking citizen there, and even discovering their true passion and meaning in life somewhere along the way. Some will want a particular degree because it teaches them what they need to know, others because it signals they are worth hiring, and still others because they wish to develop as individuals. All are worthy objectives and, as we will see later in this chapter, our very diverse and entrepreneurial education system can evolve to meet the different needs of different individuals.

What kind of education are you getting? Did you really think that NRIs are those who responded to the Quit India call?

16 Pankaj Chandra, *Building Universities that Matter: Where are Indian Universities Going Wrong?* (New Delhi: Orient Blackswan, 2018).

The Need to Build Graduate Education and Research Universities

The concentration by field has combined with a focus on teaching programmes. Enrolment in undergraduate engineering programmes has grown over forty times in forty years. To even keep the quality of engineering education level with what it was in 1980 (hardly an ambitious goal), one would have needed to multiply the faculty base by a like factor. In this same period, graduate degrees in science and engineering have grown fourteen times (and, within that, PhDs five times), opening up a wide shortage of qualified faculty. The past decade has seen improvement, with the better private engineering colleges starting master's degree programmes and the IITs growing their PhD programmes in a big way. But we will need ten years of increased output to address the faculty shortages at the top technical institutes, and will not have begun to substantially address the faculty shortages that are rife across the mainstream technical education system. Even the best institutes—the IITs and IIMs—report chronic vacancy rates for faculty, and some newer and lesser institutes run with no permanent full-time faculty. A recent article indicates that the twenty-three IITs have 3,700 faculty vacancies, over one-third of the faculty strength.[17] So, the second challenge is raising the quantity and quality of graduate technical education, an issue linked to where public research is done. India was an early investor in public scientific research, but this investment went overwhelmingly into autonomous scientific research institutions. The end result of doing scientific research in autonomous institutions has been that research and knowledge generation has largely bypassed the university system.

---

17 *Indian Express*, 'High student intake, lack of quality teachers lead to staff shortage at IITs', 18 December 2019. The *Indian Express* stated that the 23 IITs had 9,718 sanctioned posts, of which 3,709 faculty positions lay vacant at the time of this report.

Table 7.3: Where is Public Research Done? (2019)

Country	Total R&D spending (US$ billion)	As % of GDP	Firms (% of total)	Public research institutes (% of total)	Universities (% of total)
USA	584	2.8	73	10	17
China	292	2.2	77	15	7
Japan	162	3.3	79	8	13
Germany	122	3.1	69	13	18
South Korea	83	4.8	80	10	10
France	61	2.2	65	13	22
UK	49	1.7	69	6	25
Italy	29	1.4	62	13	25
Canada	27	1.6	51	7	42
Australia*	27	1.9	53	10	37
Brazil	24	1.3	—	—	—
Netherlands	20	2.2	67	6	27
Sweden	19	3.3	71	4	25
Israel	18	5.0	88	2	10
India	18	0.7	37	56	7
Spain	18	1.2	57	17	27
World	**1,725**	**2.0**	**71**	**12**	**17**

GERD = Gross expenditure on R&D

* Data for 2017

Note: UNESCO uses the term business enterprise, government and higher education for corporations, public research institutes and universities respectively.

Source: UNESCO Institute for Statistics (various years), *UIS.stat,* available at:http://data.uis.unesco.org; CTIER; Department of Science and Technology (DST), Research and Development Statistics at a Glance 2019-20 available at: https://dst.gov.in/sites/default/files/R%26D%20Statistics%20at%20a%20 Glance%202019-20.pdf

A few leading institutes, especially the IITs, are focusing much more on research than in earlier years, but the bulk of publicly funded research is still done in autonomous institutes. Although research in the higher education sector has grown (from 1 per cent) over the last thirty years, the current level of 7 per cent compares poorly with an international norm of 15–25 per cent of national R&D spending. Instead, India continues to locate 85 per cent of its public research within autonomous institutes. Most other major economies concentrate public research within the university system.[18]

Good quality graduate education requires research, and combining research and teaching will benefit both. World-class graduate education requires that teachers do research. Indeed, great professors are attracted to universities by the opportunity to do research in addition to teaching. They benefit, too, from the availability of the highly skilled, cheap labour we call graduate students. In the best US universities it is not only graduate students but often undergraduates who get the chance to do original research, either by writing senior theses or working in a professor's laboratory. In even our best undergraduate institutes such as the IITs, all undergraduate study is based on classes and examinations.

One of the strongest arguments against locating research in the Indian university system is concern over how it would perform in the absence of a research culture. Building this research culture will be key, and not easy. Kenneth Arrow points to Stanford University, which went through this same process in the 1950s, with huge success but a great deal of pain. It is not easy to reward *only* those professors with promotions who do great research. India would need to start with a few of the better educational institutes. The IITs, with their high teaching quality, outstanding student pool, abundance of alumni-funding opportunities, and lesser intrusion from the political system

---

18 France is a partial exception, doing a significant share of government-funded research in its own autonomous laboratories.

are obvious starting places. But we would need to extend to the university system in general to build a few first-class institutes. Every college and university I have spoken to has said how much they want to do more research as a top, and in the IITs *the* top, priority. But are they really willing to change their own recognition and promotion systems to reflect that every faculty member must do research? Conversations with a few academics at our best colleges and universities suggest that they increasingly are, but the process of building a culture of research will need to be a highly focused effort of the wider higher education system spread over decades.

The benefits from combining research and teaching would not flow one-way to teaching. Research would benefit too. This is particularly important for India's innovation system. I will return to this point in the next chapter on public research as an institution. By combining research with teaching, the Indian economy will get the primary benefit of doing public research—availability of trained researchers.

This issue is simply not on the Indian reform agenda. At a minimum, we should grandfather the problem and allocate increases in public research spending to the higher education sector. Instead, the problem continues. In the eleventh five-year plan (2007–12), we started fourteen more autonomous public research institutes, and in the twelfth plan (2012–17), we started yet another seven public research institutes. One of four budget recommendations CII made in 2017 was to freeze the allocation to autonomous research institutes in nominal terms, and allocate the entire annual increase (some Rs 7,000 crore) to the higher education sector. This remains the most immediately solvable long-term problem with the Indian higher education system. I gave my first talk on this issue in 1986, soon after my return to India. I've talked about it ever since, including dozens of times when I was president of CII and had the opportunity to raise it with the President, Prime Minister, finance minister, science and technology minister, commerce and industry minister, HRD minister and all the secretaries of their respective departments. All listened politely—and nothing changed. I am depressed that we remain oblivious to something where contrary international evidence is so overwhelming, so well founded, and so well known.

Talent is the key output of a research university: As I have gone around banging on about this point for years, I get much agreement. But many think the key output we should be after is research; that research universities are great sources for new scientific understanding. They are. Stanford is correctly seen as an important contributor, some might even say the definitive contributor, to Silicon Valley and its technology giants. The university indeed deserves this reputation, but in my view it is not Stanford's research output that should get the credit. Let me be crass: if the world had never seen the benefit of any of Stanford's research output in the 125 years of its existence, it *might* be marginally worse off. But research is not the key output of this exemplar of research output. The key output is students. The number of great companies founded by Stanford students—Hewlett-Packard, Varian, Google, Yahoo, Uber, Twitter, Apple, and hundreds more—have contributed more to the economy than all Stanford's brilliant discoveries. And the contributions of hundreds of thousands of graduates over the years to the economy and to science, literature and every field, is a multiple of what these giant companies contribute. The same is true of every great university.

We have a few examples of combining world-class research with teaching. The Indian Institute of Science in Bengaluru particularly stands out. But the Institute of Chemical Technology in Mumbai, better known by its old name of UDCT (the University Department of Chemical Technology), is our most noteworthy example. Founded in 1933, UDCT has long prided itself on its research. But consider the contribution it has made through its alumni. Here's a quick list: Mukesh Ambani (Reliance), Anji Reddy (Dr Reddy's Laboratories), Madhukar Parekh (Pidilite Industries), K.K. Gharda (Gharda Chemicals), Ashwin Dani (Asian Paints), Nilesh Gupta (Lupin), Ramesh Mashelkar (director of NCL and DG of CSIR), N. Sekhsaria (Ambuja Cements) and M.M. Sharma (who himself later led UDCT and established its worldwide reputation).

Ever since Wilhelm von Humboldt defined the founding principles of the world's first research university, the University of Berlin, in the early 1800s, the purpose of a research university has been the search for knowledge. And to this we must add that that knowledge particularly benefits humanity when it walks out of the university's door in the heads of its students. That is why research must be done in the higher education sector. Doing it in autonomous laboratories deprives society of this prime benefit. As Gerhard Casper succinctly put it in his speech in Delhi, 'Outstandingly educated students are still the most meaningful contribution that university-led research can make to knowledge transfer.'[19]

Providing Equity of Access to All

The rapid growth in Indian higher education has been overwhelmingly private, leading to concern about equity and access. Engineering enrolment went from being 15 per cent private in 1980, to over 90 per cent private by 2013. Public growth in higher education for most of this period was small, with renewed investment only in the last fifteen years. The UPA government (2004–14) greatly expanded the number of central government institutions of higher education. The number of IITs went from seven to twenty-three, IIMs from six to twenty,[20] with five new Indian Institutes of Science Education and Research, ten new National Institutes of Technology, four new NIDs, twenty new Indian Institutes of Information Technology and seventeen full-

---

19 Gerhard Casper, 'Governance of Higher Education', Speech at the CII–Stanford Conference on Reform in Indian Higher Education (New Delhi, 11 October 2011).

20 Roughly half the new IITs and IIMs were set up by the UPA, and the remaining by its successor NDA government. The other institutions were all set up by the UPA government.

service universities (including the South Asia University in the centre of Delhi and Nalanda University).

Finding out just what proportion of spending on higher education is private in India is not easy. The official numbers say public spending on higher education is around 1 per cent of GDP. My rough estimate says private spending on higher education is an additional 2 per cent of GDP. A recent study of household expenditure shows spending on higher education is 2.6 per cent of rural consumption and 4.9 per cent of urban consumption. This is the average for all households, including those who have no member in higher education. Of households with at least one member in higher education, it is 15 per cent and 18 per cent of annual rural and urban household expenditure.[21] These large spending proportions demonstrate the great willingness of Indian families to invest in their children's education. They believe it provides for a better life.

Why does this spending not show in the official data? Many private engineering and medical colleges charge what are called capitation fees—collecting an amount as a cash donation to a related trust (with no receipt) before admission is provided. The amount charged varies considerably, based on course and institute desirability. A good private engineering institute in Maharashtra, for example, would charge Rs 1,00,000 ($1,500) per year as the official fee set by the state and Rs 10 lakh ($15,000) as an immediate one-time 'donation' to the trust before admission is granted. The fees for a medical college would be even more extreme.

All in all, higher education is increasingly private and increasingly expensive, in spite of state regulation on what can be charged and who can be admitted. The fact that private spending shows in surveys of consumer spending but not in official education data means that capitation fees, long made illegal, are alive and well. The conclusion

21   S. Chandrasekhar, 'Household expenditure on higher education: What do we know and what do the recent data have to say?' *Economic and Political Weekly* (18 May 2019).

is clear: in Kapur and Mehta's words, 'half baked socialism has given way to half baked capitalism'.[22] So, the third challenge is to provide equity of access for all Indians.

Only the very best performing poor (who get into some leading public institutes such as the IITs on merit) get access to good quality education. They cannot afford the bulk of private education on offer, and cannot access loans, as the fees must be paid unofficially in cash. As such, student loans cover under 10 per cent of students compared with over half in the US, the UK and Australia. For a few years, higher education loans grew rapidly. They were classified as priority sector lending for banks, and rules laid down which specified that banks could not ask for collateral for smaller loans (up to Rs 4,00,000). A growing default rate has since resulted in banks reducing the number of students getting loans while the amounts disbursed have grown. In the five years to March 2019, the number of student loans fell by a quarter to 250,000 while the amount disbursed rose by a third to Rs 22,500 crore. Loan defaults doubled in this period to over 12 per cent. Since banks are not allowed to ask for collateral for loans under Rs 4,00,000, they now seem to only be lending over that amount—the average loan in 2019 was Rs 9,00,000, up from Rs 2,60,000 in 2014.[23]

The reforms needed are clear—one should free all institutions to charge the fees they wish. The state could then guarantee all student loans, perhaps up to some generous upper limit, which could be made available through the banking system as now. Given the government guarantee, the loans should be made available at a lower interest rate—the RBI borrowing rate plus a modest processing premium, say of 1–2 per cent. These loans could be repaid in an equitable way.

---

22 Devesh Kapur and Pratap Bhanu Mehta, 'Indian Higher Education Reform: From Half-baked Socialism to Half-baked Capitalism', CID Working Paper Series 2004.108 (Cambridge, MA: Center for International Development, Harvard University, September 2004).

23 *Times of India*, 'Education loans in India shrink 25 percent in 4 years', 25 May 2019. A classic unintended consequence of well-meaning government intervention that achieves precisely the opposite of what it was supposed to.

The most interesting of these is the Australian Higher Education Contribution Scheme, where education loans at zero real interest rates are repaid through a cess on the individual's income tax. This has the merit of speeding up repayment for those earning more, and reducing or eliminating it for those in low-paying occupations. Finally, there is no case for the state to subsidise education for professional courses at the IITs or IIMs, where median earnings after graduation comfortably cover the cost of education. The money saved can be used to fund a loan or grant programme for poor students.[24]

Funding research in higher education: If there is wide debate on the government role in funding higher education, there is wide agreement on the need for the government to fund research. Kenneth Arrow made the case for the state subsidising research in 1961. And this is what even the most free-market governments worldwide have done. Consider the US system, with a broadly hands-off stance in regulating higher education. Research funding from the federal government is critical to the entire US university system, public and private. Take the case of Stanford University. In 2019, Stanford undertook 6,800 sponsored research projects, amounting to $1.6 billion. To place that sum in context, in the same year, research spending in India's entire higher education sector (over 700 universities) came to $1.3 billion. Sponsored research accounts for 24 per cent, the largest single share,[25] of Stanford's annual budget of $6.8 billion. Stanford has great connections with private industry, but industry funding of research is small; 80 per cent of the $1.6 billion of research funding comes from the federal government. Gerhard Casper was entirely serious when he said in his speech at our session in Delhi that even the

---

24 We can consider even more imaginative schemes. Can future employers fund students in colleges, with a student reimbursing the employer if she does not take the job?

25 Student fees are 15 per cent, and income from the endowment 17 per cent.

best private universities would 'have to close their doors' without this government support.

The New Education Policy 2020 proposes the creation of a National Research Foundation. This is a welcome move. It must be implemented as specified in the NEP, with grants provided on the basis of merit through peer review. The manner in which funds are provided is critical. Universities must compete for funds, but once they get them, they must have full autonomy in use. The government can audit whether the funds have been used honestly, but it should not determine how they are used.

Building World-class Full-service Research Universities

The concentration on professional fields had the corollary of neglect of the social sciences and humanities. 'India did not have one world-class full-service university.' I made that assertion in 2010 at a presentation on our higher education system at the erstwhile Planning Commission. After much heated discussion, a few held that we perhaps had one, in JNU (Jawaharlal Nehru University, in Delhi). For a country of our size to have arguably one world-class institution that included the liberal arts surely proved the point! We require many. The last ten years have begun to see private investment in liberal arts colleges and a few endowed universities. Much remains to be done, though, so the second challenge is to build full-service universities with excellence in the humanities and social sciences. Our abundance of political and intellectual freedom can help the liberal arts thrive.

Two paths to excellence: The most elusive feature of a world-class institute is excellence. Excellence is hard to define. Presidents of universities that have it say it is in the water. But excellence is sorely missing in Indian higher education. It is only at the IISc, the IITs, some IIMs, and some of our smaller specialised research institutes that one finds it in abundance. Creating a culture of excellence in an existing educational institution is, it seems to me, a much harder task than growing new fields in an institution that has it. As such, an immediate opportunity of creating a few world-class universities is to grow the IITs and IISc into full-service universities, where graduate and undergraduate education is combined, and where science, engineering, the social sciences and humanities are all of equal merit. This should be their project for the next twenty years. I proposed this to IIT Bombay some years ago when I was on their advisory board. The proposal was met with polite agreement from the faculty.[26] Fifteen years later, little has changed on this count and IIT Bombay is still a great engineering institution—and the liberal arts remain service departments for the engineering disciplines. They are respected, but the faculty who teach in them know they are second-class citizens in a first-class institution. The problem is not IIT Bombay, or the IIT system, or India. The problem is the inherent conservatism of faculty. John Hennessy, Stanford's tenth president (2000–16), when asked repeatedly on a visit to India to 'set up a campus here', always replied that he couldn't tell his faculty to do anything. Or rather, he could, but they'd ignore him. Getting professors to collectively move in a particular direction, John would say, is 'like herding cats. And there's only one way to herd cats—you have to move the food.' So if we want the IITs and IISc and IIMs to become full-service universities, the state must hold out large sums of money—say a thousand crores each—to enable them to add fields, hire great faculty in the humanities and social sciences, and become great universities.

The sociologist Alex Inkeles formulated Inkeles' Law from decades of visits to India. Inkeles' Law says that it is easier to start a new institution than to reform an existing one. Rather than reform the Indian university system, we started the IITs. Greenfield initiatives have the great merit of starting with no baggage. Several recent private philanthropic efforts may substantially change the map of

---

26   And the strong encouragement from the director at the time, Ashok Misra.

Indian higher education. Ahmedabad University, Ashoka, Krea and Plaksha are all great projects that must inspire emulation. Ashoka has done an outstanding job of recruiting great faculty. Krea is trying the tougher task of starting with an existing institution, and developing it into a full-service university. Plaksha, funded by IIT alumni, is coming up in Punjab and is focused on technical education, but with a cross-disciplinary perspective.

Ahmedabad University under Pankaj Chandra's leadership has begun a new foundation course for all first-year students that moves away from disciplines. Students learn to connect ideas across disciplines, build a doing-orientation, and frame the right questions. Six domains of knowledge (including communication, data sciences, behaviour, constitution and civilisation, and biology, life and materials) help build skills, perspectives and engagement with innovation. These domains are integrated into four themes that represent challenges facing the twenty-first century, delivered as experiential studios. The current studios are climate change and environment, democracy and justice, neighbourhoods, and water. This integrative learning brings liberal arts and the professions together to address complex issues facing society.[27]

India needs many exciting projects such as there. We need thousands of graduates with a broad education to provide us with our intellectual leadership.

The CII University Project: Writing this book is a labour of love, but it is a fling of passion, not a deeply committed relationship. For that, there's the Nayanta University project we began within CII. A series of conversations with friends who themselves, or whose children, had been undergraduates at some of the great American universities prompted the thought that we should start a university in India. I was president of CII around the same time and many conversations

---

27   Personal communication from Pankaj Chandra.

with Chandrajit Banerjee later, I found myself chairing the university project.[28] A meeting we had with the then chief minister of Andhra Pradesh, Chandrababu Naidu, prompted the thought that public policy must be an area of focus. Over the last two years, the project has taken shape. This book should appear before the university does, so here is what we plan.

Our goal is to create a world-class full-service university, beginning with the social sciences, humanities and physical sciences. The university would be entirely industry-funded by CII members. Rather than do our own individual smaller effort, we collectively can create something quite grand. We would begin with a small initial master's programme in public policy. The following year, we would start the four-year undergraduate programme. Other graduate programmes would follow. Once the university is well and truly established, we could add professional programmes in engineering and management. The essence of doing something world class is to place quality before quantity every time. To sustain standards of excellence, we will not expand until we can do so with excellence.

None of our core team has any interest in starting an institution for the rich. We will follow an admissions process that is need-blind, with a combination of loans and grants available to all students. We do not intend to follow any kind of reservations in student admissions, but instead run an active and large-scale programme of working with schoolchildren from socially disadvantaged backgrounds with the CII Affirmative Action Committee to grow a pipeline of talent eligible for admission on merit. Scholarships from industry are to be packaged with internship programmes in companies.

Learning from the Covid experience, we will blend physical and digital coursework. We hope to bridge the two cultures in combining

---

28 I'm privileged to be part of a wonderful team that includes Kris Gopalakrishnan, Bharat Puri, Raj Dugar, Nadir Godrej, Meher Pudumjee, Jalaj Dani, Farhad Forbes, Satish Reddy, Ashok Misra, Pankaj Chandra, Ramesh Mangaleswaran and Banmali Agrawala.

the liberal arts with technical literacy. International faculty and students are sought from the beginning.

The key differentiator with the fine comparisons of Ashoka, Krea and Ahmedabad Universities will be the industry connection. CII has, of course, deep connections across industry, but it also has memoranda of understanding with international institutions across continents, and works with most departments of the Union government and every state government. The idea is to build these connections into the actual coursework for students, so that theory and practice are a part of the curriculum from the first year on. Various career development connections will enable students to develop options for employment as they study. We hope this project succeeds in its goal of building talent across all fields for India, its place in the world, and eventually for the world.

Conclusions

A relatively small reform in the early 1980s of allowing private colleges in some states triggered a massive expansion of professional education, almost all privately provided. We should not underestimate just how impressive this expansion has been: the quality problem we face now is a direct consequence. The solution is not to limit expansion but to improve quality. In classic Indian style, our state manages to simultaneously overplay and underplay its role. The state over-regulates private institutes, limiting what can be started, how many students can be admitted, what fees can be charged, and the curriculum that is taught. It underplays in the public assessment of institute quality, continues to starve the university system of research funding by directing most of it to autonomous institutes, and grossly underinvests in the humanities and social sciences. Meanwhile the public agenda is dominated by debate and cases in the Supreme Court on reservations, fees, and equity—a dialogue that is 90 per cent political rhetoric and 10 per cent education.

The NEP 2020 has correctly identified the quality problem as the key issue to address. It suggests welcome reform for the 'what' of reform—move from the affiliated college system to larger multidisciplinary universities of a minimum size. Combine professional schools with the liberal arts to provide multidisciplinary education. Encourage the entry of foreign universities and attract foreign students to study in India. All this constitutes major progress and is welcome. But to have the result on quality we desire, it needs to be effectively implemented, which will demand more state capacity than we usually demonstrate. How can we get superb education quality without needing superb governance?

All higher education systems worldwide look to the US system with envy. A blended state and private system has led the world since World War II. Universities in the US attract the world's best students and faculty, produce the bulk of Nobel Prizes, and are generally acknowledged as the source of the best science. The most enlightened observers of the US university system, such as Gerhard Casper, attribute its success to two factors working in tandem—competition and autonomy. Autonomy extends across the university system: there is no central education authority or regulator and no national public university. The Federal Department of Education in Washington, DC determines neither curricula nor educational standards, and leaves even accreditation to 'an informal private process'.[29] Neither federal nor state government determines the fees a university can charge. The federal government's main role in higher education is funding—especially of research in private and public universities through the National Science Foundation and the National Institutes of Health.

As a newly minted PhD, when I taught my first course at Stanford there was no oversight of what I taught. No one looked at my course outline. It was left to me to decide how many units of credit students would get for my course, who to let in, what assignments to set, what assessment criteria were appropriate, and what grades to give. Students

---

29   From Wikipedia.

rated me on my teaching at the end of the term, and those evaluations were looked at by the department chair and dean. I was very conscious that I was fully responsible for the quality my students received.

But autonomy is not enough on its own. The US university system is also a hugely competitive system. Universities compete fiercely with each other. As in India, students compete fiercely to get into the right institution. But US universities themselves compete to attract the best students by offering funding and going out to sell themselves. They compete in fundraising, with offices of development staffed by hundreds of people. They compete to attract the best faculty, poaching from other universities with benefits, research funding, staff support— and weather. (Stanford's favourite tack is to recruit in January, when the contrast with Boston is at its most telling.) Faculty compete with each other in writing research proposals to get funded and to get tenure. All this competition can be brutal—many fine teachers do not get tenure and leave the university. And a department that does not rank consistently in the top few in the nation is merged with another or closed.

The NEP 2020 advocates 'light but tight regulation' (whatever that may mean!). Instead of trying to regulate our way to quality, we should rely on competition and autonomy to drive change. In professional education, when demand for seats exceeded supply, there was little incentive to improve quality. As we saw earlier, supply now exceeds demand in India in many states, and institutes are finally starting to compete on faculty and facilities. All colleges should be free to add fields and seats at will, ignoring complaints from incumbent colleges that there is too much capacity. A few fine state universities can provide an excellent quality control for more expensive private universities, which must either be better or make do with poorer quality students. The state should be generous in funding non-professional fields (such as the arts and social sciences) where markets do not adequately value skills. The IITs, IIMs, IISc and our other public 'institutions of national importance' should all be funded to become full-service universities, as it is easier to add fields than grow excellence. We must also free all institutions to charge what they wish, so long as it is transparent and student loans are freely available. Private universities should be freely permitted, whether they are driven by philanthropy or profit. Just make their objectives transparent to all. And, as the NEP again says, ensure a compulsory accreditation system, provided by competing public and private agencies. Make the full assessment public to enable parents and students to choose colleges that do a good job and avoid those that don't.

The NEP points in the right direction, but is weak on the 'how' of comprehensively addressing our quality problem. It assumes a new, reformed, regulator will be able to bring in quality—ignoring decades of experience to the contrary. Quality in an institution of excellence must indeed be forced—but by competition, not regulation. And competition must be accompanied with the complete freedom to do what it takes to compete.

We have in India a tremendous opportunity, an opportunity provided by a unique combination of huge availability of talent in student numbers; an educational system that with all its problems has demonstrated its ability to respond effectively to market demand; a strong social propensity to invest in education at great personal cost; and an abundance of political and intellectual freedom in which academic enquiry can thrive.[30] To produce over one million engineers a year with slight state support, is no mean achievement. We must move on four fronts: first, in building true research universities by moving public

---

30   In March 2021, two of our leading intellectuals, both quoted often in these pages, Pratap Bhanu Mehta and Arvind Subramanian, resigned as professors at Ashoka University. The founders apparently came under pressure from the government to push Pratap Bhanu Mehta out, and Arvind Subramanian resigned in protest. While this is obviously a major concern that must be addressed through stronger institute governance, the issue received wide coverage in our newspaper headlines for several days. Ashoka, shaken by the consequent student protests, has since promised to address the issue of governance and independence. We would not see this in China.

research funding from autonomous institutes to the university system. That will grow graduate programmes, which will simultaneously feed faculty to the education sector and trained researchers to industry. Second, by using the market more and more to improve quality in the largely private professional education system, with the state ensuring a compulsory assessment is made public so parents and students decide which institutes are of adequate quality to survive. Third, to ensure equity of access on merit by permitting institutes to set their own fees and recover them in a transparent manner, for which state-guaranteed loans are easily available. The state will need to step in to provide adequate support for non-professional fields, but there is no argument for subsidising education in an IIT or IIM or regulating what a private college can charge. Fourth, by focusing our higher-education investment on building a few world-class full-service universities that will produce our intellectuals of the future. We must not mess up this opportunity.

8

Public Research: Fund It, Let Higher Education and Industry Do It

The applications of science are inevitable and unavoidable ... But something more than its application is necessary. It is the scientific approach, the adventurous yet critical temper of science, the search for truth and new knowledge, the refusal to accept anything without testing and trial, the capacity to change previous conclusions in the face of new evidence, the reliance on observed fact and not preconceived theory ... this should be a way of life, a process of thinking, a method of acting and associating with our fellow man. It is the temper of a free man.

—*The Discovery of India,* Jawaharlal Nehru

It is science alone that can solve the problems of hunger and poverty, of insanitation and illiteracy, of superstition and deadening custom and tradition, of vast resources running to waste, of a rich country inhabited by starving people.

—Jawaharlal Nehru, addressing the Indian
Science Congress in 1937

Ask your average industrialist what India's key R&D priority should be, and he will tell you (she might tell you something much

191

more perceptive) that we must do more research. This stems from a popular belief that the relationship between scientific research and industrial innovation is simple—scientific research leads to discoveries, these discoveries permit the development of new technology, and this new technology feeds into production and the market. This mental model, referred to in the literature as the linear model of innovation, is attractively simple but dangerously simplistic.[1] Over the last sixty years, the work of Kenneth Arrow, Paul David, Stephen Kline, Richard Nelson, Keith Pavitt, Nathan Rosenberg, Chris Freeman, Walter Vincenti and Derek de Solla Price has greatly enriched our understanding of the true, and quite limited, role that scientific research plays in industrial innovation.

My PhD advisor, Jim Adams (who I spoke of in chapter 6 on Design), was the chair of the Science, Technology and Society Program at Stanford. STS was deeply engaged in these issues.[2] The relationship between technology, science and innovation was a constant theme in interaction at STS and in a weekly seminar on the economics of innovation. 'Technology is that form of human activity … whose root function is to expand the realm of practical human possibility. Science is that form of human activity … whose root function is to attain an enhanced understanding of nature.'[3] The distinction, then, is not so much in what a scientist or technologist *does* but *why*. Utility is at the heart of what a technologist, or engineer, does. Knowledge may result from a new development, but that's not

---

1   See, in particular, Steve Kline's many insightful attacks on the linear model in his reports: (i) 'Research, Invention, Innovation and Production: Models and Reality', Report INN-1C, Department of Mechanical Engineering (Stanford, CA: Stanford University, 1987); and 'Models of Innovation and Their Policy Consequences', Report INN-4, Department of Mechanical Engineering (Stanford, CA: Stanford University, 1989).

2   Walter and Steve were two of the four founders of Values, Technology, Science and Society, in 1971, which became STS later on. Our quip when the name changed was that we'd lost our Values.

3   Robert McGinn, *Science, Technology and Society,* Prentice-Hall Foundations of Modern Sociology Series (Englewood Cliffs, NJ: Prentice Hall, 1990).

technology's purpose. A scientist aims at generating new ideas or knowledge. Again, utility may result from a scientific discovery, but that's not science's purpose. Innovation is best defined as 'something new for commercial advantage'.[4] Whether that 'something new' is new to the world, the country, or the firm does not matter. As long as it provides a commercial advantage, it is innovation. In other words, the test of good innovation is commercial, not technical.

I have always found it very useful to use these definitions.[5] Being clear on what they mean can save firms much wasted work and public research much wasted effort.

The Case for Public Subsidy of Scientific Research

Sixty years ago, seminal papers by Kenneth Arrow and Richard Nelson made the economic argument for public subsidy of scientific research.[6] Society, they argued, would underinvest in research because the benefits would not be *apparent* enough, as research outcomes are inherently uncertain, or *appropriable* enough, as the benefits of a new discovery may flow as much to others as to the investor.

The mirage of relevance: Arrow and Nelson made their arguments at the midpoint of a consistent increase in research funded by the state from the 1940s to the late 1970s. The 1980s and 1990s

---

4   More correctly, *industrial* innovation is connected to commercial advantage. The impetus for military innovation or health innovation would be different.
5   The definitions of technology and science are by Robert McGinn, who succeeded Jim Adams and Walter Vincenti and chaired STS for two decades. The definition of innovation is from Nathan Rosenberg and Richard Nelson's 'Introduction' in *National Innovation Systems: A Comparative Analysis*, edited by Richard Nelson (Oxford: Oxford University Press, 1993).
6   Kenneth Arrow, 'Economic Welfare and the Allocation of Resources for Invention', in *The Rate and Direction of Inventive Activity: Economic and Social Factors,* edited by Richard Nelson (Princeton, NJ: Princeton University Press, 1962); and, Richard Nelson, 'The Simple Economics of Basic Scientific Research,' *Journal of Political Economy,* no. 67 (1959): 297–306.

saw much debate worldwide on the proper role of the state in research. Public funding of research in the US and the UK was under pressure, with attempts made everywhere to 'make research more relevant'. A British scientist even wrote a full book, *The Economic Laws of Scientific Research*, which argued that state funding had actively harmed British research, and that the proper role of the state in research was, essentially, nil.[7] A thirty-page review of this 'thoroughly bad book' ended by saying that the case for public subsidy of research was still to be answered.[8] 'Distinctions between "blue-sky" (i.e. probably useless) and "strategic" (i.e. potentially useful) research should be made with great caution and treated with great scepticism.'[9] Nathan Rosenberg argued that technical change was inherently uncertain. As such attempts to select or promote research on the basis of relevance are misplaced. Instead, 'Government policy ought to be to open many windows and to provide the private sector with financial incentives to explore the technological landscape that can only be faintly discerned from those windows', so it makes sense to 'manage a deliberately diversified research portfolio'.[10]

We can conclude that there is a strong argument for the state subsidising public scientific research. This investment should be as broadly targeted across alternatives as possible. Attempts to 'make science relevant' and choose between specific projects could have a negative impact on welfare. The fact that the results of research are both uncertain and imperfectly appropriable continues to justify state funding.

---

7   Terence Kealey, *The Economic Laws of Scientific Research* (London: Macmillan, 1996).

8   Paul David, 'From Market Magic to Calypso Science Policy: A Review of Terence Kealey's *The Economic Laws of Scientific Research,' Research Policy* 26, no. 2 (1997).

9   Keith Pavitt, 'The Social Shaping of the National Science Base', *Research Policy* 27, no. 8 (1998): 803.

10 Nathan Rosenberg, 'Uncertainty and Technological Change', *Conference Proceedings*, (1996), 108–9.

The Role of Research in Industrial Innovation

Steve Kline, Professor of Mechanical Engineering at Stanford, made fundamental contributions to the understanding of fluid mechanics. However, in the last twenty years of his life, he contributed equally fundamentally to our understanding of innovation. He advanced a chain-linked model of innovation to replace the simplistic linear model.

Figure 8.1: The Chain-linked Model of Innovation

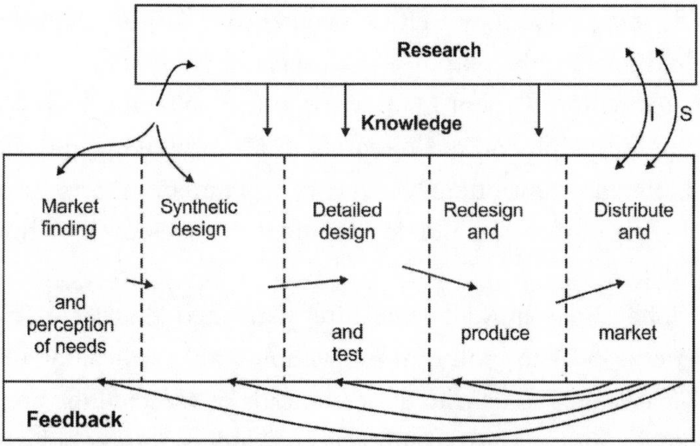

Source: Kline and Rosenberg, 1986.[11]

There are a few things to note about the chain-linked model. First, that innovation starts and ends with the market, with designing and testing as the core development activity. There are feedback loops all through the process, as one iterates between designing, testing, marketing, and redesigning. Second, that knowledge—both technological and scientific—plays a key role not as a trigger for innovation, but as a

---

11   Stephen Jay Kline and Nathan Rosenberg, 'An Overview of Innovation', in *The Positive Sum Strategy: Harnessing Technology for Economic Growth*, edited by Ralph Landau and Nathan Rosenberg (Washington, DC: National Academies Press, 1986).

repository one draws on during the innovation process to help solve problems. And third, that research, as an activity aimed at generating new knowledge, is what you do when the existing stock of technological and scientific knowledge is not enough to solve the problem. This ties in with the discussion in chapter 5 on how firms innovate. I said there, drawing on discussions with Steve Kline, that 'Research, as an activity aimed at generating new knowledge, is deservedly in last place. It is what you do when everything else has failed.' That statement is for research in firms, aimed at generating new *technological* knowledge. Scientific knowledge may well be needed too, but the chances are it will be old science, the output of past scientific research.

For this reason, I spent many years being pedantic: I would insist on saying 'development and research', and 'technology and science', instead of the conventional sequence.[12] Human history says that technology leads science, and development leads research, so that's the right order.

de Solla Price showed over fifty years ago that new scientific discoveries appear in industrial innovation with a typical lag of some twenty-five years. As such, an understanding of *old* scientific findings is adequate for most industrial innovation. Understanding old scientific research will usually be fully captured in course teaching, so science education matters much more to most industrial innovation than new scientific research.

Indeed, far from being the dominant source of industrial innovation, new scientific research matters to industrial innovation in just two exceptional cases. First, advancement in certain fields, like biotechnology and semiconductors, has a close connection with scientific research. Second, there is a broader role for scientific research as one of 'technology's wellsprings' to reinvigorate technical progress in a particular field.[13] This 'reinvigoration' typically takes the form

---

12 I've stopped. Age eats idealism for breakfast!
13 David Hounshell, 'The Evolution of Industrial Research in the United

of a new technological paradigm for industry, such as online music taking over from compact discs, or the jet engine from the propeller. As Nelson puts it:

> There is persuasive evidence that in many industries technological advance is what Winter and I have called cumulative, in the sense that today's new technology not only provides enhanced operational capabilities but serves as a starting point for tomorrow's efforts to further advance technology. Science may be involved as well, but in most industries science seems to be tapped as a body of general knowledge relevant to problem solving, with 'new' findings not playing a special role. Where new science is not particularly important, a steady flow of newly minted scientists and engineers suffices to keep the laboratory adequately up to date with the world of public science.[14]

So research is critical to technical advance in science-based industries and to the innovation of new technological paradigms. The results of research can be appropriated by other firms and indeed by other countries.

Scientific research should be seen, then, as the follower, not the leader, of industrial activity. Keith Pavitt made just this point:

> ... national technological activities are significant determinants of national economic performance as measured by productivity and economic growth. But what about the causal links between

States', in *Engines of Innovation: U.S. Industrial Research at the End of an Era,* edited by Richard Rosenbloom and William Spencer (Boston, MA: Harvard Business School Press, 1996).

14   Richard Nelson, 'The Role of Firms in Technical Advance', in *Technology and Enterprise in a Historical Perspective,* edited by Giovanni Dosi, R. Giannetti and P. Toninelli (Oxford: Clarendon Press, 1992), 175.

developments in national science and in national technology? Do they run from a national science base that creates the ideas and discoveries that the national technology system can exploit? Or do they run from the national technology system that creates both demands on—and resources for—the national science system? Our reading of the (imperfect) evidence … is that the causal links run from the national technology system to the national science system.[15]

In my book with David Wield, we identified a hierarchy of R&D in our firms. As we saw in chapter 5, R&D in firms begins with learning from other firms, progresses to improving existing products through development, and only then comes to research as an activity aimed at generating new knowledge. We did not imply that any of these roles for R&D are trivial: imitation or learning from other firms is not necessarily an easy process. Neither is 'mere' copying. Particularly if the product involved is complex and involves much tacit knowledge, imitation and learning to become competitive are hard. What matters for this chapter, though, are the demands in-house R&D makes on the public research system. Imitation, learning and incremental product improvement are all good roles for R&D but they have no connection with scientific research. In-house *research,* aimed at producing new knowledge, is a prerequisite for using the output of the public research system. So public scientific research could be justified in those areas where industry in the country is adequately advanced to be investing substantially in research in addition to development. Public scientific research can then serve as a wellspring for industrial innovation. Only when particular local industries approach the technological frontier is there a case for scientific research itself, and hence for publicly subsidising it.

---

15   Keith Pavitt, 'The Social Shaping of the National Science Base', *Research Policy* 27, no. 8 (1998): 802.

Public Scientific and Technological Research in India

India invested early in publicly funded research. In no other developing country was research accorded such high-level importance, or absorb so large a share of resources so early on. National laboratories were established in key areas before Independence, and the first non-Western Nobel prize in the sciences went to an Indian, C.V. Raman, in 1930.[16] By the late 1980s, India was spending just under 1 per cent of GDP on R&D, higher than the share spent by richer countries such as Singapore, Brazil, Mexico and Thailand. Among industrialising countries, only South Korea had reached a significantly higher share of R&D in GDP.

Indian policymakers saw the innovation process as the linear model of scientific discovery followed by technological innovation. Here is Prime Minister Nehru (also in the two lead quotes for this chapter), articulate on all matters and especially on scientific research:

> I am convinced that of all the big problems that face India today nothing is more important than the development of scientific research, both pure and applied, and scientific method. This is indeed the basis and foundation of all other work.... The extensive use of that method can only come through a properly directed education and a large number of research institutions which deal with pure science as well as the innumerable applications of it.[17]

In other words, technological progress first requires a scientific base. Nehru chose to do the research in newly founded autonomous public R&D institutes instead of the university system. There has been

---

16 The first non-Western Nobel Prize for anything also went to an Indian, Rabindranath Tagore, for literature, in 1913.

17 Jawaharlal Nehru, *Selected Works of Jawaharlal Nehru*, Volume 14 (New Delhi: Orient Longman, 1981), 558.

widespread dissatisfaction with the contribution that these autonomous research labs have made to industry, which I will deal with shortly.

The Union government is the major funder and doer of national R&D, with a 52 per cent share in 2017–18.[18] This spending takes place in autonomous R&D laboratories under different government agencies. The central government operates over 200 major R&D labs in Defence, Space, Atomic Energy, Industrial Research, Agriculture and Medicine (each agency, such as Defence Research and Development Organisation or Council of Scientific and Industrial Research (CSIR) consists of several independent laboratories focusing on different subjects).

In the US and most OECD countries, one needs to distinguish between funding and doing R&D. Publicly funded R&D in the US is paid for by the federal government but is done in private industry, public and private research universities, and public research institutes. Even including defence R&D in the picture does not change it, showing the relative importance of the state in funding, but not doing, R&D. In India, there is little difference between who funds and who does research, with sharp lines between public and private R&D. Publicly funded R&D is done in public R&D institutes. Privately funded R&D is done in private industry.

My argument so far, in this chapter and in chapter 5, has been that technological research should primarily happen in firms. In chapter 7, we saw that scientific research should primarily happen in universities. But that's not how we have seen it in India. The agencies for defence, space and atomic energy do technological research aimed at developing a new weapon system, satellite, or nuclear reactor. When the US, the UK, Germany or Japan do technological research of this kind, the government funds it, but it is generally done in private firms. We do it in autonomous government laboratories. When the world undertakes scientific research, the

---

18   CTIER 2021. 2017–18 is the most recent year for which this information is officially available (as of late 2020).

Table 8.1: Expenditure on R&D by Major Scientific Agencies under the Central Government

Agency	Spending in 2017–18 (Rs million)	% of total central government spending	% of national R&D spending
Defence Research & Development Organisation	152,000	26.7	13.4
Department of Space	91,000	16.0	8.0
Indian Council of Agricultural Research	54,000	9.4	4.7
Department of Atomic Energy	52,000	9.1	4.6
Council of Scientific and Industrial Research	46,000	8.1	4.0
Ministry of Environment, Forest and Climate Change	2,600	0.5	0.2
Department of Science and Technology	35,000	6.2	3.1
Department of Biotechnology	18,000	3.1	1.6
Ministry of Earth Sciences	11,000	2.0	1.0
Indian Council of Medical Research	15,000	2.6	1.3
Ministry of Electronics and Information Technology	3,900	0.7	0.3
Ministry of New and Renewable Energy	350	0.06	0.03
Total	**481,000**	**84.41**	**42.21**

Note:

1. The Ministry of Earth Sciences was formerly known as the Department of Ocean Development.

2. The Ministry of Electronics and Information Technology was formerly known as the Ministry of Communications and Information Technology.

Source: CTIER Handbook: Technology and Innovation in India.

government largely funds it, but it is mostly done in universities. There are exceptions—the Fraunhofer Institutes and Max Planck Society in Germany, the Industrial Technology Research Institute in Taiwan, or the Electric Power Research Institute) in the US—but they are just that, exceptions. India's scientific research is funded by the government and done in autonomous government laboratories.

Public investment in technological research—how effective? Defence, atomic energy and space account for over half of central government funding. India can point to major successes in space technology, with locally built satellites and a rocket-delivery system that costs a fraction of the US and EU equivalents.

In atomic energy, India has about 150 nuclear warheads, about the same as Pakistan. Apart from nuclear weapons, India has an ambitious atomic energy programme, with 7,000 MW of installed capacity and another 4,000 MW under construction.

In defence R&D, there has been some success at the low-profile end (ammunition, enhancement of older imported weapons technology) and some challenges. The two highest-profile defence projects have been the Light Combat Aircraft (Tejas) and the Main Battle Tank (Arjun). (I remember writing about these for a course on the economics of technology with Nate Rosenberg in the 1980s, so the projects date back quite a while.) The Tejas finally flew in 2001 and entered service in 2019. The Arjun entered service in 2004, but we have continued to order Russian tanks instead of the Arjun. Overall, India still relies on imported weaponry for anything halfway sophisticated; our country has long been the world's largest importer of arms. If you agree with my earlier argument of how innovation happens, our research effort in defence could be much more fruitful if it were funded by the government but principally carried out in industry. Some tentative moves towards sourcing defence supplies from Indian industry have been made in the last ten years, and we might finally see some change.

We must be self-reliant where arms and ammunition are concerned. This dependence on uncertain imports won't do!

In agricultural research, there have been major successes in many crops. India is today a major exporter of agricultural products, and the contrast with the food scarcities and fear of famines of the 1960s is a story of the green revolution written by agricultural research. The ICAR consists of seventy-nine research institutes that cover everything from agroforestry to sugarcane.

Public investment in scientific research—how effective?

CSIR: The government's industrial research infrastructure comes under various heads, including the Ministries of Science and Technology, Earth Sciences, and Electronics and Information Technology, and the Department of Biotechnology. These are the main funders, and doers, of scientific research. Chief among them is CSIR. CSIR consists of thirty-eight national laboratories with 4,000 scientists and 9,000 support staff. It advertises itself as 'the world's largest public funded industrial R&D agency'. It was set up by the colonial government in 1942 as an umbrella organisation for industrial research, modelled on the British Department of Scientific and Industrial Research, but its real expansion took place in the 1950s and 1960s.

There has long been serious concern about CSIR's connection with industry, the sole reason for its existence. Successive studies continued to show CSIR's poor impact. Here is a parliamentary committee report on CSIR's contribution:

> The constitution of our Committee was based on the obvious perception that the work of CSIR was out of step with the needs of the nation....
>
> In caricature form, the industrial sector believes that the CSIR laboratories are incapable of useful and timely research, while the CSIR system believes that manufacturing firms, which have no capacity for technology absorption and development, always prefer the soft option of importing proven technologies.[19]

Most knowledgeable observers would read those comments as a description of the situation today. They come, though, from the 1986 *Abid Hussain Committee Report*, which in itself was the fourth such parliamentary report.

A focused and serious attempt to improve CSIR in the 1990s was led by its director general, Ramesh Mashelkar. He spelt out goals of exemplary clarity with accountability unheard of in the Indian public sector, with targets for funding from private industry and international patents. Several laboratories—the National Chemical Laboratory (NCL), the Indian Institute of Chemical Technology, the National Institute of Oceanography—developed reputations for doing world-class work, and some of the world's leading firms sponsored research projects there. International patent filing rose rapidly.

---

19   Abid Hussain, Chair, *Abid Hussain Committee Report* (New Delhi: Government of India, 1986).

The better CSIR labs have many world-class scientists. Some of them, such as NCL in Pune, have close links with industry. In the mid-2000s, when I looked at NCL, it funded over half of its budget from contract research, with most coming from private industry. However, three-quarters of industry funding came from foreign industry. This is entirely consistent with our earlier analysis: research must follow industrial development, not lead it. If it leads it, then it will at best be useful to technology-leading industry, perhaps outside the country. As a report on the best research and technology institutes (RTIs) worldwide puts it:

> ....there is a constant risk of moving not *ahead* but *away from* market needs, which is one reason why strong industrial input is needed for the governance and management of RTIs ... Research tends to have a higher status than many more 'down to earth' RTI activities, so there is a constant tendency to do too much of it.[20]

CSIR continues to struggle. A recent article says that CSIR has not made its annual report public since 2014. The CSIR Society, the umbrella association, has not met in five years (its president is the Prime Minister and its vice-president is the minister for science and technology). Another article reports that in 2015, CSIR was 'ordered' to increase its non-government funding to 50 per cent by 2020.[21] From what I can gather, it was still struggling to cross 20 per cent in 2020.

My point is not to target CSIR, though I am tempted to ask what we would miss if it did not exist. It is instead that brilliant scientists

---

20 Howard Rush, Michael Hobday, John Bessant, Erik Arnold and Robin Murray, *Technology Institutes: Strategies for Best Practice* (London: International Thomson Business Press, 1996), 90.

21 T.V. Jayan, 'For 5 years now, CSIR has not made its annual reports public', *The Hindu BusinessLine*, 8 December 2019; and T.V. Padma, 'New head of Indian research to tackle funding issues and red tape', *Nature.com*, 25 October 2018.

and high-quality leadership are not the issue. An autonomous research laboratory simply has a negligible role in industrial innovation. With rare exceptions, scientific research should be done in one place and one place alone—the higher education system.

An Invigorated Higher Education System and an Invigorated Scientific Research System: Two Sides of the Same Coin

I return to my hobby horse from the previous chapter. Any attempt to reform the Indian research system must address the core issue of combining public scientific research with teaching in universities, instead of continuing to do it in autonomous research institutions.

Research universities matter because top-class graduate education requires cohabitation of research and teaching. Leading technical educational institutions, such as the IITs, provide as fine an undergraduate engineering education as Stanford or MIT or Caltech. The difference at the graduate level would seem to be driven by a difference in doing much less research.

Combining research and teaching will benefit both. The advantages of doing research in universities are manifold. The first is an apprentice–journeyman benefit as the graduates that industry hires come trained in doing research. Second, I am constantly invited to discussions on fostering industry–institute interaction. The well-meaning goal is to connect the work done in our research institutes with needs in industry. Every university has an automatic, costless and strong linkage with industry through students. Each time industry hires a fresh graduate, a new link forms. Students know their professors, and vice versa. And third, not only does teaching benefit from the research–teaching combination, research benefits too.

The unique benefits of the research and teaching combination are not a new idea; it was precisely the objective of Wilhelm von Humboldt for the University of Berlin in the early nineteenth century, the model for that great success story, the American research university.

American university presidents have been among the most articulate advocates of this combination. Donald Kennedy of Stanford spoke of the apprentice–journeyman benefit:

> Most of the basic science in America today is done by mixed groups of journeymen and apprentices; the result is that the nation's research trainees are being developed alongside the best scientists. That is the singular feature of our pattern of government support for basic science in the universities; to it, our most thoughtful European colleagues usually attribute our special success....[22]

Gerhard Casper, also of Stanford, was even more eloquent when he spoke, instructively, in Beijing:

> ... in countries in which research and teaching are fundamentally or even partially separated, much creative force lies fallow ... My point is not what goes without saying—university teaching should be based on university research—but that university research benefits from teaching, not just from teaching graduate students but also from teaching first-year students.[23]

Indeed, this research–teaching combination results in an automatic close linkage between research and industry:

> The most successful method of knowledge and technology transfer on the part of the universities lies in educating first-rate students who themselves have been engaged in the search to know—men and

---

22 Donald Kennedy, 'Basic Research in Universities: How Much Utility', in *The Positive Sum Strategy: Harnessing Technology for Economic Growth,* edited by Ralph Landau and Nathan Rosenberg (Washington, DC: National Academies Press, 1986).
23 Gerhard Casper, 'The Advantage of the Research-Intensive University', Speech, Peking University Centennial, (Beijing, 3 May 1998).

women who will then be in a position to take on leadership roles in industry and business. Students who receive their training in university-based research arguably have a greater influence on the economy than the patentable inventions of university scientists.

Outstandingly educated students are still the most meaningful contribution that university-level research has to make to technology-transfer ...

... technology transfer is a 'bodily contact sport.'

Note also that it is not sufficient that research be done at the university, with researchers and teachers being separate individuals. Researchers must teach: 'the link [between teaching and research] is also nullified when teaching at the university is primarily carried out by those who have no direct relationship to research'.

Pavitt calls trained researchers 'perhaps the most important' social benefit of basic research, and he further argues that it is this output of basic research that home countries can capture the easiest:

Such person-embodied knowledge is nowhere near as footloose as information: numerous empirical studies have shown that the links between basic research and application are inversely related to distance and directly related to common nationality. ... As a consequence, many of the benefits of nationally funded basic research stay at home.[24]

But, I must add, only if you do research in universities and your researchers stay at home too, attracted by jobs in research in industry and academia.

---

24   Keith Pavitt, 'Public Policies to Support Basic Research: What Can the Rest of the World learn from US Theory and Practice? (And What They Should Not Learn)', *Industrial and Corporate Change* 10, no. 3 (2001).

Finally, recall Richard Nelson's comment that 'a steady flow of newly minted scientists and engineers suffices to keep the [firm R&D] laboratory adequately up to date with the world of public science'.[25] It helps if this scientific knowledge reflects the current state of the art. If scientific research is done in universities, it will tend to be.

Our end objective is clear: we should have a few really world-class research-and-teaching centres. The current initiative of developing a few public and private universities into world-class institutions is most welcome. But where will we get our highly qualified research faculty from? I would suggest we bifurcate CSIR and make it part unexciting-but-useful institutions that provide industry with technical assistance (testing, certification, and so on), and part a large pool of professors. The 4,000 CSIR scientists would be a huge impetus to the national higher education system. As we saw in the previous chapter, even the IITs have faculty vacancies of over 30 per cent. Where are they all going to come from, except from such an initiative?

A National Research Foundation could disburse the state funding that is now going to CSIR and other government laboratories, with all disbursements on the basis of competitive grants and not budgetary support. The autonomous research labs must then sell their services and become totally self-funding, which would drive their work in the technology-assistance direction. Scientists could also compete for the national research funds with researchers from other institutes and from universities, and student participation could be an advantage in getting funded.

Some research laboratories could themselves become colleges. Several already run PhD programmes; all should be required to do so. But what is vital is that they extend their teaching role to master's programmes, and form permanent linkages with undergraduate

---

25   Richard Nelson, 'The Role of Firms in Technical Advance', in *Technology and Enterprise in a Historical Perspective,* edited by Giovanni Dosi, R. Giannetti, and P. Toninelli (Oxford: Clarendon Press, 1992),175.

institutes. That would ensure the research–teaching combination advocated in this chapter. The easiest reform would also be the most misleading: one could simply require every scientist to teach, full stop. That would probably lead to the scientist teaching in the university system, while continuing to do his or her research in an autonomous laboratory. As Roger Noll points out, while basic research in many countries outside the US has grown, conducting this research in autonomous laboratories means that 'it has not had a spillover benefit for higher education, *even though many of the researchers in national labs are also university professors*'.[26] This reform could mislead us into thinking we had managed to combine research and teaching. We would miss the prime benefit of doing research in the higher education system, training future researchers.

All of these reforms add up to very substantive change. We need a serious debate on what should be done to dramatically increase the share of research in higher education to international levels, eight times what it is now (0.05 per cent of GDP to 0.4 per cent). A rejuvenated scientific research system is the other side of the same coin of a university system that does dramatically more research.

Conclusion: Circling Back to Innovation

These previous four chapters have addressed innovation from different perspectives. Everyone wants to be more innovative, India as a whole and every firm in it. How? We can learn from the success of South Korea and Taiwan in building vibrant national innovation systems. The flow runs sequentially from industrial development to industrial in-house R&D to public scientific research.[27] An industrial sector

---

26 The emphasis is mine. The quote is from his introductory chapter, 'The American Research University: An Introduction', in *Challenges to Research Universities,* edited by Roger Noll (Washington DC: Brookings, 1998), 18.

27 See Keith Pavitt, 'The Social Shaping of the National Science Base', *Research Policy* 27, no. 8 (1998), mentioned earlier in this chapter.

competing with the best firms in the world in increasingly sophisticated industrial sectors is a requirement for sustaining investment in in-house R&D. Strong in-house R&D is a requirement for sustaining investment in public scientific research of value to industry. Since 1991, Indian industry has had to compete with the world's leading firms. This has driven investment in in-house R&D by specific Indian firms and industries such as pharmaceuticals and the auto sector. The more advanced technological sectors in Indian industry are only now capable of utilising, and therefore sustaining, public investment in scientific research. By combining research with teaching, the Indian economy will get the primary benefit of research—the availability of trained researchers.

It starts with the ambition and strategy of firms. Firms must want to build deep proprietary technology, investing in learning, R&D and design. And to then deploy that technology around the world. We have long had the goal of raising national investment in R&D from its current 0.7 per cent to 2 per cent, the world average. This requires that Indian industry increase its investment in R&D by a factor of five, from 0.3 to 1.5 per cent of GDP. And the state must increase investment in public research in the higher education sector by a factor of eight, from its current 0.05 to 0.4 per cent. As this chapter has argued, we have a great opportunity to progressively shift the 0.4 per cent of GDP that the state invests in R&D in its own autonomous laboratories to private industry (for defence and space research, for example) or higher education (what's done in CSIR and other agencies that do scientific research).

Our higher education system provides the potential for building a transformed innovation system. A visit to any manufacturing company or consultancy in the Middle East, South East Asia, or the US or UK, shows an abundant availability of engineers. I remember some years ago visiting the offices of Bechtel in London when they were working on the Reliance Jamnagar refinery. A few floors contained hundreds of Reliance engineers. A few more floors contained hundreds more of Bechtel engineers. They were almost all Indians. A transformed innovation system is within reach if we are willing to make the institutional changes necessary in private-sector participation and where we locate public research. Our supply of talent is the foundation on which an innovative India would rest.

9

Institutions: Strong, Independent, Inclusive

There was a time when development was believed to depend on the quantity of capital and labour. Today, we know that it depends as much on the quality of institutions and ideas.[1]

—Narendra Modi

The greatest dangers to liberty lurk in insidious encroachment by men of zeal, well-meaning but without understanding.

—Louis Brandeis

Margaret Thatcher could not see an institution without hitting it with her handbag.

—*The Economist*

Two articles appeared as I sat down to write this chapter on institutions. The first was an op-ed in the *Indian Express*, co-authored by three of our most respected economists, Shankar

---

1   Speaking at a NITI Aayog function on 26 August 2016.

Acharya, Vijay Kelkar and Arvind Subramanian. They argue strongly against the recommendation of an internal working group of the Reserve Bank of India (RBI) that industrial houses should be allowed to own and control banks. The second is from *The Economist*, 'India's diminishing democracy', with the strap, 'An increasingly dominant prime minister and the ongoing erosion of checks and balances'.[2] Both articles are about institutions. But what are institutions, and why do they matter so much? Why are they particularly important to us in India?

What are Institutions? Why do They Matter so Much to us in India?

When people use the term institutions, they mean a variety of things. Physical institutions include those of higher education and research, which we discussed in the last two chapters. The 2017 book, *Rethinking Public Institutions in India,* has chapters on more than a dozen institutions of state including the presidency, the Parliament, RBI, CBI, the Supreme Court, the Comptroller and Auditor General, the civil service and ECI.[3] It doesn't stop there. Institutions include formal law—for property rights, say—but also norms of behaviour that are enforced by social sanction rather than the force of government. In chapter 1, I used a definition by Douglass North, who won the Nobel Prize for Economics in 1993 for his work on institutions.[4] This broad definition of institutions,

---

2   Shankar Acharya, Vijay Kelkar and Arvind Subramanian, 'Why permitting large industrial houses to own banks is a bad idea', *Indian Express*, 27 November 2020; *The Economist,* 'India's diminishing democracy: Narendra Modi threatens to turn India into a one-party state', 28 November 2020.

3   Devesh Kapur, Pratap Bhanu Mehta and Milan Vaishnav, editors, *Rethinking Public Institutions in India* (New Delhi: Oxford University Press, 2017).

4   Douglass North, 'Economic Performance through Time', Nobel Lecture, (Oslo, 9 December 1993): Institutions are the humanly devised constraints that structure human interaction. They are made up of formal constraints (rules, laws, constitutions), informal constraints (norms of behaviour,

covering physical institutions (such as universities and schools, courts, industry associations, the civil service, constitutional bodies), rules (such as laws, law enforcement, property rights) and social norms (such as trust, social capital) forms the fabric of development. The simplest statement about institutions is that they make up the 'rules of the game', shaping the incentives of each person and entity, and how one interacts with the other.

A large and diverse country like India particularly needs strong, independent institutions. In a rowdy democracy like ours, progress happens by checks and balances from autonomous institutions such as universities, the ECI, the courts, a free media, an effective opposition and (in India as well as in other federal countries such as the US, Canada and Germany) a structure where power is shared with the states. Instead of a strong leader determining what's right, independent institutions frame the rules. We need independent institutions that balance incentives with protection, and economic freedom with social responsibility. Our aim must be to liberate the enterprise of millions of animal spirits and not rely only on one state animal. The process may be messier and less efficient than in an authoritarian state, but it is likely to be much more powerful as well as more enduring. How do we get there?

Where's 'There'? Vijay Kelkar and Ajay Shah, at the end of their fine book on economic policy that we met in chapter 2, tell us that 'the path to becoming an advanced country lies in many generations of sustained improvement in institutions'.[5] In this chapter, I will argue that our limited state capacity requires that it focus its effort on only a few areas. Those areas must be selected

---

conventions, and self-imposed codes of conduct), and their enforcement characteristics. Together they define the incentive structure of societies and specifically economies. Institutions and the technology employed determine the transaction and transformation costs that add up to the costs of production.

5   Vijay Kelkar and Ajay Shah, *In Service of the Republic: The Art and Science of Economic Policy* (New Delhi: Penguin Random House, 2019), 381.

solely on the basis of being things which only the state can do. If a private institution or an NGO could handle matters, it should be left to them. If the state can set up a public institution, give it full autonomy, and then let it operate fully independently, that removes any further draw on limited state resource. Institutions must thus be designed for independence, and the government must operate with the norms and culture that enhances the authority of the institution. The state can then focus its capacity on those limited operations only it must do, and therefore must do well—primary education, public health, the criminal justice system, the judiciary, and the tax system. Finally, institutions can be politically and economically inclusive or they can be extractive. We must systematically design for inclusion, and I give some examples of how.

State Capacity

I have often asserted in this book that India has low state capacity. This assessment derives from both personal experience and reading:

- When I did the research for my doctoral thesis, I went around interviewing entrepreneurs in Pune. I carried with me a large, heavy, 200-page compendium called, I think, *Policies and Procedures for Small-scale Industry*. This contained the various incentive schemes that were available to small-scale industry. Except that small industry was unaware of them—the typical take-up of each scheme was under 10 per cent.
- In the previous chapter, I quoted from the *Abid Hussain Committee Report* on the functioning of CSIR. This was the last of four parliamentary committee reports on CSIR between 1953 and 1986. They broadly cover the same ground. Thirty-five years have passed since the last report—it is still largely unimplemented.
- Higher education reform has been the subject of several committees. A National Knowledge Commission was set up in 2005 under Sam Pitroda. Rather than implement its recommendations,

another committee was set up under Professor Yash Pal in 2008. And rather than implement those recommendations, yet another committee was set up under Professor Kasturirangan in 2017. All three reports covered similar ground, and have much in common in what they recommend. A National Education Policy was finally announced in 2020. Let's hope it gets implemented without yet another committee.

- GST: We saw repeated postponement of linking supplier and buyer invoices online. Deadlines came along only to be replaced by new deadlines. The linking finally came into force with a two-year delay, and introduced several exemptions that opened up substantial loopholes in the chain of tax. We will return to how we can fix GST later in this chapter.

- In 2009, Lant Pritchett of the Harvard Kennedy School wrote a paper provocatively titled 'Is India a Flailing State?' He defined a flailing state as one:

> ... In which the head, that is the elite institutions at the national (and in some states) level remain sound and functional but that this head is no longer reliably connected via nerves and sinews to its own limbs.... The brains of the Indian state can formulate excellent policies and programs in nearly every domain ... yet ... the capability of the Indian state to implement programs and policies is weak ... In police, tax collection, education, health, power, water supply,—in nearly every *routine* service—there is rampant absenteeism, indifference, incompetence, and corruption.[6]

I emphasise his use of the word 'routine'. Kapur, Mehta and Vaishnav's introductory essay to their book on public institutions refers to Pritchett's paper. The Indian state can organise highly

---

6   Lant Pritchett, 'Is India a Flailing State? Detours on the Four Lane Highway to Modernization', Faculty Working Papers RWP09-013 (Cambridge, MA: Harvard Kennedy School, May 2009).

complex tasks like running an election with a 900-million electorate, they say, but 'our record in providing basic public services, from health to education and water to sanitation, ranges from modest to dismal'.[7]

• Or take the official view of this current government. The 2017 *Economic Survey* identifies weak state capacity as one of the three key challenges that India must address: 'A second distinctive feature of the Indian economic model is the weakness of state capacity, especially in delivering essential services such as health and education ... Of course, nearly all emerging markets started off with weak state capacity at independence. But as their economies developed and prospered, state capacity improved, often at an even faster rate than the overall economy. In India, by contrast, this process has not occurred. Fukuyama ... argues that the Indian State has low capacity, with high levels of corruption, "clientelism", rules and red tape.' The 2018 *Economic Survey* repeats this without the need to reference others: 'Limitations on state capacity (Centre and states) affect the delivery of essential services such as health and education.'[8]

'Low state capacity changes policy design': In a chapter with this title, Kelkar and Shah say we should have 'the largest possible state that is feasible while achieving competence, and this is likely to be a very small state'.[9] They argue that reform requires giving

---

7   Devesh Kapur, Pratap Bhanu Mehta and Milan Vaishnav, editors, *Rethinking Public Institutions in India* (New Delhi: Oxford University Press, 2017), 7.

8   Ministry of Finance, *Economic Survey* 2016–17, 44–5, and 2017–18, 8. The references quoted are from: Angus Deaton, *The Great Escape: Health, Wealth, and the Origins of Inequality* (Princeton, NJ: Princeton University Press, 2013); Francis Fukuyama, 'What is Governance?' *Governance* 26, no.3 (2013); and, Akshay Mangla, 'Bureaucratic Norms and State Capacity in India', *Asian Survey* 55, no. 5 (2015). The other two challenges are ambivalence about the private sector and property rights, and inefficient redistribution.

9   Vijay Kelkar and Ajay Shah, *In Service of the Republic: The Art and Science of Economic Policy* (New Delhi: Penguin Random House, 2019), 270.

people fair warning, going step by step, slowly and transparently, with abundant advance notice, gathering feedback along the way. Sudden moves are dangerous and can cause entirely unnecessary damage. A weak and cogitating government that eventually (having exhausted all alternatives) does the right thing, is far better than a strong and decisive one that blunders. Think of demonetisation in November 2016 that removed 86 per cent of the currency in circulation from a cash-dependent society. Think of the world's most stringent Covid lockdown in March 2020, in a country with no safety nets and a hundred million informal workers in our cities. Both with no deliberation, no seeking out of expertise, and four–hours' notice. And think, too, of the farmer protests against the agricultural reforms of September 2020, which I will return to later.

So what should one do?

Start by doing no harm. The burden of proof is on the state for showing that intervening in any area will provide multiple benefits. Kelkar and Shah suggest we limit the role of the state to just those things that only it can and must do; reduce the number of transactions that must be completed; pick the simpler alternative, which demands less discretion and judgement by bureaucrats; reduce the stakes, so that deterrence is highly limited as one learns; use incentives more and punishment less, all the while building institutional capacity; and work in the open.

State Capacity and Institutions

I used to go around saying that India should not seek better government, we should seek less government. As I've got older, and benefited from reading, among others, Kelkar and Shah, and Kapur and Mehta, I believe more nuance is called for. Our low capacity means the Indian state should seek to do far fewer things, but by focus do them far better.

What must the state do? Reform must enable the right private action. Post 1991, the state 'simply stopped trying to do what it was flailing to do anyway'.[10] So private airlines got going alongside Indian Airlines and Air India, private mobile operators began alongside the public-sector phone company and private oil refiners competed with public-sector oil companies. By retreating from various activities, the state created space for the private sector to step in and do the job, usually a lot better.

Yes, the departure is at 7 a.m. but the scheduled delay is about two hours and the actual take-off will be about 12 noon if everything goes well.

Private actors should be encouraged to play the role a strong and capable state would normally do. Running the national skill-development effort through NSDC should be handed to a private industry association like CII, all education statistics should be officially produced by an NGO

---

10 'Is India a Flailing State? Detours on the Four Lane Highway to Modernization', Faculty Working Papers RWP09-013 (Cambridge, MA: Harvard Kennedy School, May 2009), 32.

like Pratham, employment data should officially come from CMIE and we should rely for our national R&D data on a think tank like CTIER.

But that still leaves things that only the state can do, such as public health and primary education, which are essential tools for social inclusion. Dealing with a once-in-century (one hopes!) pandemic like Covid and organising a nationwide vaccination programme demands a role for the state. It must, however, get its role right. The state underplayed its role in not placing orders for enough vaccines in time: as of January 2021, we had ordered 16 million vaccines for 1.4 billion people, when the US had ordered 600 million for a population of 300 million. This, when India had by far the world's largest vaccine manufacturing capacity of any country. It then overplayed its role in trying to control which hospital could vaccinate whom and in which age group, instead of leaving it to the states. And then completely misplayed its role by signalling that Covid protocols were unnecessary. In a frenzy of hubris, speeches by the political leadership claimed victory over Covid. A massive religious festival was brought forward by a year (apparently for political reasons) with millions of people allowed to gather for the Kumbh Mela. And then, as cases surged, the political leadership spent April campaigning for state elections, appearing in sixty rallies in West Bengal alone, with barely a mask in sight. By underplaying, overplaying and misplaying its role all at once, the Union government directly contributed to the disastrous consequences of India's second wave.

But focusing on fewer things like public health means, first, being clear of what the state should not do.

What the state should not do: Even if the state cannot do good, it should, at the minimum, do no harm. The most dangerous question in Indian public policy is 'What is the government doing?' We constantly look to the government for solutions to all our problems. The monsoon fails. What is the government doing? Consumers are buying fewer biscuits, banians and cars. What's the government doing?

And while my worry is that we look too much to the government for solutions, my great fear is that they might actually respond and Do Something. Unless one has solid theoretical and empirical evidence that an action by the government will actually help, the right action is inaction. Governments should and can enforce the rule of law, ensure it is fairly applied to every citizen, protect our borders, and invest in widespread health and education for a better future. A government cannot make markets, and when it tries to control how they move, it almost always makes things worse.

Consider that vital question of national public policy, the price of onions. In October 2019, the price of onions shot up in a few months. The right action by the government was to do nothing. Instead, the government invoked the Essential Commodities Act, made the stocking of onions beyond a low limit a criminal offence and banned their export. All this was done during a visit to Delhi by the Prime Minister of Bangladesh, placing onions on the agenda for discussion between the two Prime Ministers.

What happened to the price? It went up further and then, as every year, in came a harvest and the price came crashing down. In September 2020, one of the agricultural reforms put through by the government was to limit the application of the Essential Commodities Act. This was a mistake. It should have been scrapped. The government retained the power to invoke its provisions if prices double in less than a few weeks. Onion prices range from Rs 3 to Rs 30 per kg each year. So, in October 2020, after the passage of the agricultural reforms, the price of onions rose again as it had the previous year. Once again, the government swung into action, invoked the Act, limited stocking, and banned export. Once again, onions were the subject of discussion at high levels of government between India and Bangladesh.

Indeed, an abundant supply keeps prices low; limiting stock has the opposite effect. Exporting grows the market, both supply and demand, reducing the impact of domestic changes. In other words, the knee-jerk actions of limiting stock and banning exports make for precisely the wrong action in the medium term.

Take another example—the reopening of liquor shops post the March 2020 Covid lockdown. For some reason, perhaps the high morals of the Union government official concerned, liquor shops were closed for forty days. When the Punjab state government permitted them to open, the Union government issued them a notice forcing them to close. Less than a week later, they were permitted to reopen everywhere in the country outside containment areas. But only 20 per cent of shops were permitted to reopen at a time, for limited hours, and with the threat they might be made to close again. The long queues and chaos that resulted would have come as a surprise only to the bureaucrat who formulated the policy.

The national interest is often better served by doing nothing. Should our government really use its limited implementation capacity to make seventeen changes in the export policy on onions in just one year? A wise government, conscious of its limited capacity, would sharply limit its interventions in both time and space. If it wished to go further, it could seek to strengthen institutions, both public and private. It can then leave it to them to independently make the rules of the game work better for all, without placing a burden on its own implementation capacity.

What Makes for a Successful Institution?

Institutions collectively define the incentives for each person and entity to act in a particular way. However, Kapur, Mehta and Vaishnav point out that how well institutions themselves function depends on their 'internal norms, cultures, financial wherewithal, patterns of hiring and firing, and leadership selection'.[11] I will add independence to that list. Let's consider these criteria.

---

11   Devesh Kapur, Pratap Bhanu Mehta and Milan Vaishnav, editors, *Rethinking Public Institutions in India* (New Delhi: Oxford University Press, 2017), 2.

Norms: Laws constrain or permit behaviour in a formal sense. 'Norms of behaviour, conventions, and self-imposed codes of conduct' are as important in constraining or encouraging behaviour. When we consider the question of why Pakistan, born from the same source one day apart from us, has lived under martial law for over half its time as an independent country, we should credit not only our Constitution, laws, or formal institutions. We should equally credit the norms of behaviour that our founding leaders established as conventions to be followed, in particular, our first Prime Minister. Jawaharlal Nehru may have got much wrong in economic policy and science policy, but he established institutions in every sense of the term. He had almost unchallenged authority, with Congress controlling 75 per cent of the seats in Parliament after the first election in 1952. But he was never less than respectful of parliamentary procedure, appearing for question time and answering questions raised by the Opposition, including a young Atal Bihari Vajpayee. Nehru's respect for the institutions of the new republic—whether this was providing the ECI with the necessary authority to do its job, or the Indian Army having no role in politics—was the making of them. The historian Ramachandra Guha writes of clear messages from Nehru (within a day of Independence) and Vallabhbhai Patel (a year later) to the British generals commanding the Indian Army immediately after independence that the army was subservient to the government of India. Guha also has a wonderful story of India's first army chief, General Cariappa, who in his last year started offering comments on various national matters, such as economic policy. Nehru saw this as straying from the army's remit to be independent of politics. Guha writes that within three months of retirement, Cariappa was appointed high commissioner to Australia. By the time he returned he 'was a forgotten man. Nehru's foresight was confirmed, however, by the statements the general made from time to time.'[12]

---

12   Ramachandra Guha, *India After Gandhi: The History of the World's Largest*

Consider the saga of the transfer of power from the 45th to the 46th president of the United States. Donald Trump's refusal to concede the election violated norms set by every president before him, both Democrat and Republican. His action was probably not illegal, but it undermined the fabric of the institution of elections being accepted by the full electorate. Whatever bitterness exists between Narendra Modi and Rahul Gandhi, in 2019 Rahul Gandhi conceded defeat and congratulated his rival. When Atal Bihari Vajpayee lost the election in 2004, he similarly congratulated Sonia Gandhi. That is how democracy works. It gains legitimacy by such norms of behaviour. Donald Trump went much further by inciting a mob of his supporters to storm congress in a direct attack on the institutions of democracy. The court system stood up to Trump. All sixty legal challenges raised by him were dismissed, including by the Supreme Court that Trump had appointed three justices to. It's called 'doing your job'.

Culture: As president of CII, one is a frequent visitor to the finance ministry, housed in North Block. North and South Blocks are architectural masterpieces, sitting on top of Raisina Hill. Every time I have been to North Block, I have winced at the upkeep of the place. The passages and public areas are a shambles,[13] with wires strewn across magnificent architecture, and crooked switches, failed bulbs and cracked panes. Across the road is South Block, built at the same time, and presumably kept up by the same maintenance contractor. It isn't perfect, but it seems cleaner, brighter and less abused. I've always wondered why. I cannot think of any explanation except that South Block houses the defence ministry and the PMO and standards might

---

Democracy (New Delhi: Pan Macmillan India, revised edition, 2017), 759–60. One of my five favourite books of all time, whether fiction or non-fiction. You will meet two more in the next chapter.

13   The offices of the minister and senior bureaucrats are just fine. I am talking of the public areas.

be higher there.[14] The same applies to a comparison of the ministry of commerce and the ministry of external affairs. Maintenance standards just seem far better in MEA, which I speculate has nothing to do with formal rules and regulations and everything to do with the culture of the place. As a manufacturer, I am a firm believer in the principle that you cannot make a good-quality product in a dirty factory. Could the culture of maintenance of government offices reflect a deeper attitude of caring about performance in general?

Financial wherewithal: As the chair of the governing board of NID Ahmedabad, I was struck by the finances of the institution. The government is represented on the board through a joint secretary from DPIIT, which NID comes under. The interest DPIIT takes in NID appeared to depend greatly on the individual. Those who were interested and participated, were helpful and contributed. Some did not attend a single meeting during their tenure, even if the meeting was held in Delhi. NID now meets over 60 per cent of its budget through its own resources—fees, consulting income, and the like. I was very keen that we work towards becoming fully independent of the government by raising fees and attracting donations for endowed professorships. So was a very supportive joint secretary, for most of my tenure, from DPIIT. But NID itself was less keen, as government funding has built most of the infrastructure. Institutions must seek independence, with all that goes with it. Being financially independent is the foundation, and enables charting one's own course.

Patterns of hiring and firing: Over the years, I've been part of many government institutions—NID, India Design Council, IIM Visakhapatnam, a review committee of IIT Hyderabad, and so on.

---

14   The Prime Minister does not work from the PMO so that has nothing to do with it. He or she works from the residence at Race Course Road, or from an office in Parliament. Narendra Modi is now building a grand residence for the Prime Minister on Rajpath.

I've always been struck by two things. The government tells you that the institute is autonomous, but it retains the power of selecting the director and the entire board. So where is the autonomy? The term of all board members ends at the same time. The government often selects an entirely new board with no overlap of members, thus needlessly losing institutional memory. This second aspect is easily fixed—let one-fifth be appointed each year for a five-year term. Whenever I have raised it as a suggestion with the concerned minister, it has always been enthusiastically received, and promptly ordered. The order, however, has never once been executed.

Here's how these confused practices can play out. When IDC was set up, a subcommittee worked on our Articles of Association. We did not succeed in getting a clause through that gave the institution control over the selection of its own board and secretariat. The net effect has been twofold—ten years after its formation, IDC still has no permanent secretariat. A proposal to have the secretariat handled by an independent industry association at no cost, CII to begin with, never happened. And after the term of the third council ended, no new council has been notified or serious work undertaken in over a year.

Take another example or two: appointments of directors of even our IITs and NIDs tend to be grossly delayed. Consider the case of a highly successful director of an IIT who should have been a shoo-in for a second term. He checked a couple of times, was always promised it would happen by a certain date, which passed. He then took a position in the private sector, which of course prompted the government to push his term through, but it was too late. This left the institute scrambling to find a successor—all completely unnecessary. In another instance, the director of a leading institute was reaching retirement age at the end of his second term. A search committee for his successor, constituted as usual somewhat late, had identified potential successors. But the department could not make the appointment without the PMO approving its choice. The PMO obviously had better things to do (dealing with China's aggression, say), so the approval came through three months after the director's term ended. The governing board, of this supposedly autonomous institute of national importance, had no power to approve the extension while we were waiting for the new director to be appointed. Neither did the concerned department secretary, who could approve a Rs 50 crore grant but not a three-month extension. The extension again needed the PMO's approval, which did not happen in time. On the day of the director's retirement the most senior faculty member of the institute was made acting director—to his own, the retiring director's, and the governing board's surprise. For three months. This, clearly, is not how our leading higher education institutions should be run.

Control does not come free. If the department retains control, it is fully accountable for failing to exercise it or if it exercises it badly. But why not pass on the control to the institution and its governance structure? Build true autonomy with control, responsibility and authority all with the institution. Retain the right to appoint an ombudsman who can investigate financial matters and adherence to purpose whenever called for. But leave governance to the institution itself, and to the board that is purely focused on the institution, instead of this being one more item in a list of hundreds the department must handle, let alone thousands the PMO handles. Control is a two-edged sword. By hanging on to it and centralising it in Delhi, and then concentrating it in the PMO, we do grievous damage to our institutions.

Leadership selection: Is the leader picked purely on the grounds of being the best for the job? Strong populist leaders often appear to value loyalty over competence. That has been the criticism of appointments made (or not made) by both Donald Trump and Narendra Modi. But is that just sour grapes, from those whose friends weren't selected? Or is there something to it? My metric is speaking with an independent voice. If leaders from many institutions have a view that is independent of (this does not necessarily mean opposed to) the government of the day, it says to me that individuals are selected more for competence than loyalty. If most leaders of institutions feel bound to jump to the defence of every government folly, or criticise only the Opposition, it says the opposite.

Does the leader matter? Kelkar and Shah argue against relying solely on a good leader of the institution: 'The capability of an institution lies not in personnel choices but in the arrangement of information, incentives and power.' My reaction is 'yes, but'. Yes, in that one should not solely rely on a good leader as the solution for institutional ills. But it does seem to me that personnel choices matter. When T.N. Seshan was made head of the Election Commission of India in 1990, he reinvented the role. As Sridharan and Vaishnav point out, he took advantage of a strong opposition, and mobilised public and media, to drive change.[15] The ECI's Model Code of Conduct had long specified limits on what could and could not be said on the campaign trail (causing communal disharmony is explicitly forbidden, for example) and proscribed anything that might entice voters through giveaways or threats of what might happen if they vote for the other candidate. Post Nehru, the ECI had become excessively subservient to the ruling party, looking the other way at violations of the Model Code. Seshan changed that, and those of us who lived through his censuring of practices and threatening to ban candidates who violated the code, witnessed a renewed faith in a constitutional institution. Sridharan and Vaishnav cite a poll in 2008 that had 80 per cent express a high degree of trust in ECI, second only to the army. Seshan set a precedent of independence from the ruling party that his successors, such as James Lyngdoh, were happy to follow. But in recent years that independence seems to have waned. The recent article in *The Economist* on democracy in India says:

---

15 E. Sridharan and Milan Vaishnav, 'Election Commission of India', in *Rethinking Public Institutions,* edited by Devesh Kapur, Pratap Bhanu Mehta and Milan Vaishnav.

During the 2019 general election, which Mr Modi won by a landslide, his opponents sharply protested when the prime minister and other top BJP leaders repeatedly escaped serious censure for issuing what amounted to communal dog whistles, whereas the ECI promptly sanctioned rival candidates for lesser infractions of its strict rules of conduct. One of the body's three top commissioners did object, but was overruled. His family subsequently found itself being investigated for alleged tax evasion. The official quit the ECI before the end of his term.[16]

And things have since gotten worse. In the April 2021 assembly elections for five states, voting in West Bengal was spread out by the ECI over eight phases and five weeks—ostensibly to allow the Prime Minister to campaign more widely. The ECI further closed its eyes to rampant flouting of safety norms and Covid protocols by all political parties, prompting the Madras High Court to ask if it should be charged with murder for fostering the spread of Covid. So perhaps an individual can push an institution forward in establishing norms of independence, but one needs the right 'arrangement of information, incentives and power' to sustain it in the long run. A more independent ECI might have implemented its own Covid safety protocols in the April 2021 state assembly elections, even if that irritated the powerful. But wouldn't those same powerful have preferred that irritation to the domestic and international abuse heaped on them as a consequence of our second wave? One of the purposes of independent institutions is to protect us from ourselves.

Institutions and the 'Primal Function' of the State

Kelkar and Shah tell us 'the four primal requirements of a state are the criminal justice system, the judiciary, the tax system and financial

---

16   *The Economist*, 'India's diminishing democracy: Narendra Modi threatens to turn India into a one-party state', 28 November 2020.

regulation. Our prime objective should be to learn how to be a capable state in these four areas.'[17] Building institutional capacity is at the heart of each. They advocate 'simple interventions that are easy to implement'. Let me illustrate each with an example.

The criminal justice system: *The Economist* starts its article on democracy in India with a recent case:

> In early November justices at India's Supreme Court turned their attention to an urgent plea. Arnab Goswami, a prominent journalist, had been dragged from his home and hurled into jail. Government ministers decried the arrest as an assault on free speech, demanding that Mr Goswami be granted bail. The hearing was brief.[18]

He was released that evening. Arnab Goswami had been arrested on grounds that were specious. He had been charged with abetment to suicide, as one of three people named in a note written by an interior decorator. The case had been dropped under the previous state government led by a BJP chief minister, and reopened by the successor government led by his—now—opponent. (The politics is murky, even byzantine.) The institutional concern is with the police (a state subject in India), who too often follow the demands of their political masters. Equality before the law is a fundamental principle of any justice system. It dates back over two thousand years to the ancient Greeks and is enshrined in Article 14 of the Indian Constitution. It is core to any effective criminal justice system.

---

17   Vijay Kelkar and Ajay Shah, *In Service of the Republic: The Art and Science of Economic Policy* (New Delhi: Penguin Random House, 2019), 388, 276.

18   *The Economist*, 'India's diminishing democracy: Narendra Modi threatens to turn India into a one-party state', 28 November 2020.

The judiciary: If equality before the law is core to any effective criminal justice system, it is even more so to the judiciary. Back to the Arnab Goswami case. The article in *The Economist* continues:

> ... the court's ruling was not surprising. What shocked was the speed of its intervention. Mr Goswami spent just a week in detention, and his case had hardly touched the lowest rungs of courts, yet the country's topmost judges ignored the court's backlog of some 60,000 cases to schedule a bail hearing within a day of the anchor's appeal ... When Mr Modi clamped direct rule on the erstwhile state of Jammu and Kashmir in August last year, thousands of its residents were detained. Out of more than 550 writs of habeas corpus such as Mr Goswami's that Kashmiris filed, courts have disdained to look at all but a handful ... Even more striking is the court's foot-dragging over constitutional questions. In 2017, Mr Modi slipped through parliament a controversial law that created 'electoral bonds', asserting that as a budgetary matter it need not be scrutinised by the upper house, which was not then in BJP control. The Supreme Court still has not examined the constitutionality of this innovation ... Other big questions its judges have yet to take up include the imposition last year of direct rule in Kashmir and some 140 legal petitions against the Citizenship Amendment Act 2019, which by inserting religion as a criterion for citizenship undermines the secular nature of the Indian state.

By giving one politically connected person so speedy a hearing, and delaying the hearing of many constitutional questions that affect hundreds or thousands, we violate the principle of equality before the law.

The tax system: Kelkar and Shah point out that 'tax officials obtained draconian powers under the excuse that these were essential for increasing the tax/GDP ratio'. But, they conclude, 'The importance of tax officials have gone up, but the tax/GDP ratio has not.'[19] Simplicity has much to say for itself. In the 1970s, Indira Gandhi's government raised the maximum marginal rate of tax to 97.5 per cent. No guesses that collections were abysmally low. In the 1990s and 2000s, income tax rates for companies and individuals were brought down step by step. Tax collections increased with each reduction. I remember a discussion CII had with the finance ministry three years ago. Total collections from corporate taxes were around 18 per cent of profits, against a marginal rate (including surcharges) of 35 per cent. The difference, of course, is that firms take advantage of various exemptions and incentives. CII recommended reducing the corporate tax rate to 18 per cent and then removing *all* exemptions, with no grandfathering. An official from the finance ministry at that meeting said that if that was the basis, she could 'have the law done by Monday and it will be just three pages long'. In September 2019, the government went part way—the rate was reduced to 25 per cent for existing companies, and 18 per cent for new manufacturing companies. Exemptions were substantially reduced, but not completely eliminated. Our analysis says that it is large firms that take advantage of exemptions; smaller firms pay the maximum marginal tax rate. By going for a simple, exemption-free, low-tax system we will simultaneously bring in simplicity for all and a level playing field for small firms. This is a policy of inclusion. A policy of higher taxes with exemptions that only larger companies have the capacity to claim is a policy of exclusion.

The same applies to the GST. GST finally became law in 2016 with cross-party support in both houses of Parliament, and all state legislatures passing it. GST replaced excise duty, sales tax, luxury tax, octroi and myriad other taxes and duties, which varied across states in quantum and implementation, with one tax. This was fundamental progress. To provide a complete set-off for all input taxes was an

---

19   Vijay Kelkar and Ajay Shah, *In Service of the Republic: The Art and Science of Economic Policy* (New Delhi: Penguin Random House, 2019), 288–89.

essential contribution to competitiveness. These two changes made GST a landmark policy reform that took the country forward.

Having said that, several major problems must be addressed.

In a chapter titled 'Building the perfect GST in a low-capacity state', Kelkar and Shah propose a single flat rate of 10 per cent GST with a comprehensive base. They figure that with a coverage of 70 per cent of the economy, with no exemptions beyond agriculture, it would give us 7 per cent of GDP as tax revenue. That is a lot more than this year's *budgeted* GST revenue of 4 per cent of GDP (the actual is even lower).

The government went about it quite differently, and took the path of 'fitting' the multiple old taxes into a set of rates. This convinced everyone to go along, from both the finance ministry and states, but has led to too many rates. We have seven in all—0, 3, 5, 12, 18 and 28 per cent, and then the cess items. By fitting, instead of unifying, we have repeated the earlier complexity. Take just two examples: a restaurant can carry a different GST rate if it is in a hotel with a room tariff over Rs 7500 or an independent restaurant.[20] And footwear that sells for less than Rs 1000 carries a GST of 5 per cent, with other footwear at 18 per cent. Further, as the passage of GST required their support, states insisted that GST returns also be filed separately in each state where one wanted to claim set-offs.

Multiple rates combined with multiple registrations and filing of returns have hugely complicated GST. This has had two consequences: smaller firms have struggled to cope with the system, and the GST system has struggled to automate the matching of input invoices with output invoices. The GST Council has responded by postponing when returns must be filed for smaller firms, reduced smaller firm filing to once in three months instead of each month, and raised the exemption limit repeatedly so that a turnover up to Rs 1.5 crore can now be exempt by paying a 1 per cent tax. Electronic invoice matching is still

---

20 We earlier even charged a different tax for independent restaurants by whether or not they were air-conditioned.

not done over a thousand days into implementation. And the onus of the correctness of the supplier's invoice and actual tax payment has been transferred to the receiving firm (how a firm can be held responsible for the accuracy of some other firm's invoice and accounts will probably end up in court).

This complex system creates a large incentive to stay out of the tax net (there are stories of firms whose business is fake invoices). The net effect is that GST collections have consistently underperformed, missing their budgeted target by Rs 1,50,000 crore in each of the last three years, almost 1 per cent of GDP annually. So GST must be reformed. How?

Simplify, bring down and make comprehensive: We should have at most three rates—0 per cent for essential food items, 12 per cent for everything else, and a high tax for 'sin goods' such as aerated drinks, tobacco and alcohol. Registration and filing of all returns should be with one authority—with the Union government and states having equal access to the data. Then make it comprehensive and bring the remaining items into GST—fuel, construction, alcohol. Have everyone file every month, but in one place alone instead of in twenty-nine, and drastically lower exemption limits from Rs 1.5 crore to, say, Rs 10 lakh. Use the economic census of business enterprises to ensure *all* firms are registered for GST, and prompt an inspection only if a firm is not paying GST broadly in line with its declared number of employees. We should close the door to exemptions that facilitate evasion, instead of bringing in draconian penalties to deter walking through an open door. Bring everyone into the net and make the filing (and, therefore, e-linking of invoices) simple. GST was a major reform, helping firm efficiency and tax buoyancy. It still has the potential to be transformative, provided we simplify, lower, remove exemptions and make the administration benign.

Financial regulation: I began this chapter with a recent recommendation of an internal working group of RBI that industrial houses should be allowed to own and control banks. Economists have been almost uniformly against the proposal. The concern is over the allocation of capital. The growth of the economy will be constrained by how efficiently one puts capital to work. In *The Third Pillar*, a book about the balance we need between the state, the market and local communities, Raghuram Rajan, a former RBI Governor writes:

> When parts of the economy become uncompetitive, modern economies rely on the financial sector to identify troubled firms, shut them down, and reallocate resources from them to healthier ones. Thus markets, rather than the state, allocate resources, and they do so based on who can use the resources better in the future rather than on the basis of who has the best connections.[21]

It is no accident, as Urjit Patel, another former RBI Governor reports, that public-sector banks have much higher NPAs (13.9 per cent) than private-sector banks (3.8 per cent).[22]

The Economist reminds us of a joke about central bankers. 'A student visits his former professor, who has become one. The phone rings. "No...no...no...no...yes...no...no," says the central banker. Hanging up, he explains that the caller was the finance minister. "What did you answer 'yes' to?" wonders the student. "He asked if I could hear him."'[23] The message, of course, is of central bank independence.

Kelkar and Shah argue, also, for speedy closure and reallocation of capital, but they also point to a much wider danger for enterprise in general:

---

21 Raghuram Rajan, *The Third Pillar: How Markets and the State Leave the Community Behind* (New Delhi: HarperCollins India, 2019), 262.

22 Urjit Patel, 'Data on Gross Non-Performing Assets for December 2018', Presentation (Stanford: Stanford University, June 2019).

23 *The Economist*, 'Why an excess of democracy can lead to poor decisions', 13 February 2020.

The willingness of entrepreneurs to start a business requires an economic environment of limited liability, where the entrepreneur will be able to give up, put the firm into the bankruptcy process, and walk out of it with nothing more than a bruised ego, reputational damage, and valuable experience. *A society that pillories entrepreneurs, and turns business failures into protracted disputes or entanglement in agencies, is one which will have less entrepreneurship.*[24]

That is why the Insolvency and Bankruptcy Code of 2016 was so important. It was specifically introduced to speed up the process of insolvency. It has helped, but not at the pace that was intended. The code runs up against two challenges. Earlier in this chapter I cited our 2017 *Economic Survey* which identified state capacity as one of the three 'meta-challenges' of the Indian economy. Another meta-challenge is 'stigmatised capitalism', a term Chief Economic Advisor (2014–18) Arvind Subramanian made his own. He argued that 'India is affected by stigmatised capitalism, where there is not enough trust in the private sector or in the ability of the state to regulate the private sector.'[25]

This combines with another challenge: most enterprises are limited liability companies. Limited liability was one of economic history's great institutional inventions, as it limits the liability of a shareholder to his or her investment in the enterprise. But too often in India, banks ask promoters of companies to provide personal guarantees for the loans the enterprise takes out. This makes a mockery of limited liability. Combined with stigmatised capitalism, it directly affects speedy resolution of stressed assets. How? Why? Consider that highly visible and, in my view, thoroughly bad business, the airline industry.

---

24   Vijay Kelkar and Ajay Shah, *In Service of the Republic: The Art and Science of Economic Policy,* (New Delhi: Penguin Random House, 2019), 78. My emphasis.

25   Interview in *Mint*, 9 July 2018.

We have had two excellent airlines fail in the last few years. Kingfisher Airlines, promoted by Vijay Mallya, failed in 2012. The joke at the time was to ask how Vijay Mallya became a millionaire. Answer: he was a billionaire, and started an airline. Vijay Mallya famously left India and has been living in the UK ever since, with the Indian government pursuing his extradition. Jet Airways, promoted by Naresh Goyal, stopped flying in 2019. Both airlines have seen their aircraft parked around Indian and foreign airports for years. We've given up on Kingfisher, but every three months there is talk that Jet Airways is about to be revived.

Now how should such a matter be resolved? In both cases the promoter and all shareholders should lose their investment in the enterprise. Another firm should come in and run the enterprise, or its assets should be disposed of to the highest bidder, with the company's creditors getting a share of the liquidation. But because of personal guarantees, the promoter hangs on to the company, keeping it from being put into formal receivership—which would prompt the guarantees to be invoked. Speedy closure and restructuring can preserve jobs and assets. Even if Jet Airways does fly again, I would be very reluctant to fly in a plane left unused for years. A combination of the state wanting to solve every problem (if a private airline goes bankrupt, why does it concern the state?) and stigmatised capital leads to great waste. We are afraid of the public outcry that would follow the cancellation of a personal guarantee and moving on. We seem to prefer rampant waste—visibly symbolised by dozens of motorcycles literally rusting into the ground outside most police stations, and abandoned planes scattered around Mumbai airport. My own view is that industrialists should collectively refuse to provide personal guarantees—and be prepared to walk away from a loan and a project if a banker insists on it. Bankers should rely on judgement, not guarantees.

The Insolvency and Bankruptcy Code of 2016 was a major reform. It needs to operate more independently and much more quickly to have the desired impact. The RBI is the banking regulator. It can force banks to recognise bad assets in a timely manner and insist that the IBC work to its required time frame of a resolution within six or nine months as specified by the Act. Appeals should not be permitted, and exceptions should not be made.

Institutions of Extraction, Institutions of Inclusion and Inclusive Politics

Before we pull things together on institutions, we need to cover one additional concept. A 2012 book by Daron Acemoglu and James Robinson, *Why Nations Fail,* draws a distinction between extractive and inclusive institutions. Extractive institutions are defined in the negative: they exclude the majority of society from the process of political decision-making and income distribution. But institutions can also include most of society in economic and political life. 'Rich nations are rich largely because they managed to develop inclusive institutions at some point in the last three hundred years.' Inclusive economic institutions are open: people with good ideas can start businesses where their property rights will be protected, workers can undertake activities where they can be more productive and earn more, and more efficient firms will replace less efficient ones: 'Inclusive economic institutions also pave the way for two other engines of prosperity: technology and education … The ability of economic institutions to harness the potential of inclusive markets, encourage technological innovation, invest in people, and mobilise the talents and skills of a large number of individuals is critical for economic growth.'[26]

Countries can grow for extended periods with extractive political institutions. Acemoglu and Robinson cite the examples of Argentina in the 50 years to 1914, the USSR in the 30 years to 1960 and China in the 40 years since 1980. All were among the world's fastest-growing countries in that period. Economic and political institutions tend to

---

26   Daron Acemoglu and James Robinson, *Why Nations Fail: The Origins of Power, Prosperity and Poverty* (New York, NY: Crown Books, 2012), 79, 372, 442.

reinforce each other. Extractive economic institutions (a fairly small group of people controls and benefits from most economic activity) rely on extractive political institutions where power isn't shared. Inclusive economic institutions are first inspired by, and then reinforced by, inclusive political institutions.

In the last forty years, China has combined extractive political institutions with inclusive economic institutions, where economic benefits were more widely shared: 'The growth process based on catch up, import of foreign technology, and export of low-end manufactured products is likely to continue for a while ... history and our theory suggest that growth with creative destruction and true innovation will not arrive, and the spectacular growth rates in China will slowly evaporate.'

Inclusive economic institutions come from inclusive political institutions, and more plural systems of governance deliver a more inclusive political system. The great economist Gary Becker, who won the Nobel Prize in 1992, wrote a blurb for *Why Nations Fail*: 'The authors convincingly show that countries escape poverty only when they have appropriate economic institutions, especially private property and competition. More originally, they argue countries are more likely to develop the right institutions when they have an open pluralistic political system with competition for political office, a widespread electorate, and openness to new political leaders.'

'Nations fail today because their extractive political institutions do not create the incentives needed for people to save, invest, and innovate.'

If pluralism is at the root of inclusive political institutions: Ramachandra Guha describes India as the world's most plural country. We have no national religion, no national language, and no one approach to institutions. Public-sector banks compete alongside private-sector banks. Poor-quality state schools compete with poor-quality private (but English-instruction) schools, both existing alongside excellent state schools competing with excellent private ones. Our higher education system is amongst the most complex in the world, with private, public and 'state-aided' institutions, an affiliated college system, some completely philanthropic private institutions and some that are completely venal. As Guha points out, our ability to compromise is a great strength. And yet, much of his description of India as a greatly plural country is in a chapter titled 'A 50:50 Democracy'. We are indeed a democracy, but a flawed one. Addressing our institutional shortcomings can go a long way towards fixing those flaws.

Conclusions: The Power of Institutions

Intellectual property: All definitions of institutions agree on the central importance of property rights. Property rights were invented for intellectual assets as an artificial construct to foster innovation. Patents are the key intellectual property right.

The modern patent system developed in Venice in the fifteenth century and then, step by step, in England in the seventeenth and eighteenth centuries. Patents are seen as essential to innovation, by providing a temporary monopoly for a period of ten (Venice) to twenty (current law) years. A patent needs to meet the three tests of being novel, non-obvious and useful. Debate, especially between developed and developing countries, focuses on the strength and period of protection. This property right provides the incentive for investment in innovation. But too little attention is given to the reciprocal requirement of disclosure. The purpose behind a patent system is that humanity benefits not by the creation of a novel invention, but by its diffusion and use. Society provides a temporary monopoly to the inventor in return for permanent benefits from the invention after the patent runs out. Diffusion and use can only happen through widespread disclosure. The inventor has to be incentivised to disclose the invention, hence the property right of a patent.

Let us return to the discussion in the previous section on extractive and inclusive institutions and apply it to the patent system. In eighteenth-century England and nineteenth-century USA, patents were taken out by individuals, most of them from humble origins and practically trained with no formal education. The invention and patent was a ladder of progress, their means to upward mobility and wealth. Today, with the 'invention of the method of invention' we discussed in chapter 5, patents are overwhelmingly taken out by companies, especially large companies. A prolific individual inventor, such as Thomas Edison, held over 1,000 patents in his individual name. The Chinese company Huawei applied for 4,500 international patents in 2019 alone. A few dozen companies worldwide each apply for a thousand or more patents a year. Companies—especially in the pharmaceutical industry—argue vigorously for longer and stricter patent laws to reward their investments in R&D. They neglect disclosure.

On any CII visit to the US one can count on the issue of intellectual property coming up, in particular, patents. As this book has made amply clear, I believe we have many, many things to fix in India. But our patent laws are not among them. One of the most contentious issues between India and the US is the evergreening of patents that seeks to extend their life through small improvements in efficacy. The US permits evergreening; Indian patent law does not (we are fully TRIPS compliant).[27] But many in the US, including legal scholars and economists, argue that evergreening and frivolous patents aim at keeping competition away. These actually harm innovation. I used to take great pleasure in pointing out to our US friends arguing for evergreening on behalf of their pharmaceutical industry that India's position was shared by several leading Americans, including one Barack Obama, then inhabiting the White House. So in designing the institution of patent rights, we should make it as inclusive as possible.

---

27   TRIPS, Trade Related Aspects of Intellectual Property Rights, is a 1995 international legal agreement under the WTO for IPR compliance by countries.

That means balancing disclosure with protection, and encouraging diffusion as much as we encourage innovation. Intellectual property rights can be an institution of extraction or inclusion, depending on how you design it.

Competition policy: The same applies to competition policy. Antitrust legislation in the US broke up, famously, the Standard Oil Company in 1911 under Theodore Roosevelt. AT&T was similarly broken up in 1984. In the 1990s, a failed attempt was made to break up Microsoft. There is discussion under way at present whether Google, Apple, Facebook and Amazon should be similarly broken up. Across sectors, concentration metrics have increased significantly in the US in the last twenty years, along with a substantial increase in corporate profitability and a declining share of wages in value added. *The Economist* insightfully connected increasing corporate concentration in the US with rising corporate profitability and declining productivity. It did this study in 2016, following it up with a study of the UK in 2018, where it found the same thing.[28] Firms invested in buying each other, reducing competition and increasing prices, instead of investing more in technology, training and productivity enhancement.

In India, the Monopolies and Restrictive Trade Practices Commission was a textbook case of how not to do competition policy. MRTP targeted bigness, not concentration or market power. The finance ministry under Manmohan Singh scrapped it in 1991. The Competition Act of 2002 under the Vajpayee government set up the Competition Commission of India (CCI), which became fully functional in 2009. It seems, though, to be very quiet, playing no role in examining, for example, market dominance in sectors such as telecommunications

---

28   See three articles in *The Economist:* (i) 'Too much of a good thing: Profits are too high. America needs a giant dose of competition', 26 March 2016; (ii) 'A lapse in concentration: A dearth of competition among firms helps explain wage inequality and a host of other ills', 29 September 2016; and (iii) 'Like America, Britain suffers from a lack of competition', 28 July 2018.

and airports. An independent and active commission could help make our industry more competitive, and thereby more inclusive. Applying the criteria we discussed (on what makes an institution successful) may help—the norms that the CCI follows of what is good performance, the culture of probity and independence, and where its leaders come from and go to.

Agricultural reform: As I wrote this chapter, a massive farmer's protest was under way in and around Delhi. Many thousands of farmers from Punjab, Haryana and Rajasthan gathered to protest the agricultural reforms of September 2020. Freeing farmers to sell to anyone anywhere in the country, instead of just their closest mandi, was a useful reform and in the interest of farmers.[29] It was not as if these reforms came from nowhere. Drafts of model Acts and letters were sent to the states over many years. Several states reformed their own agricultural markets, with useful changes in laws in Madhya Pradesh, in Maharashtra (private mandis) and in Bihar (abolishment of mandis). But when the government passed these reforms, they came as a surprise. The laws were passed on a Sunday without debate permitted in parliament and on a voice vote. Agriculture is a state subject in India, and implementation depends entirely on what states do with the changed laws. If we had followed Kelkar and Shah's approach, of working step by step, creating alternative mandis in Punjab, putting drafts up for discussion and debate, allowing the Opposition to have its say in Parliament, perhaps things would have been different. There should at least have been an attempt to discuss matters with the Modi government's own coalition partner from Punjab, the Shiromani Akali Dal, which resigned from the NDA coalition saying publicly that its letter to the Prime Minister had not even been acknowledged. The Opposition helped GST get implemented smoothly and quietly.

---

29 A mandi is a rural market, usually dedicated to a particular commodity. Various regulations limited farmers to selling only via their local mandi. The mandi usually fixes the price at which each item is sold on that particular day.

The Bill was passed unanimously. The contrast with the agricultural reforms is stark. The government had the necessary majority in Parliament to pass the bills without Opposition support, so why bother with discussion?

The 1991 reforms were aimed largely at industry. They directly affected entrenched industry interests, and caused much debate. The Bombay Club, an informal group of leading industrialists, argued strongly that the reforms were selling out the interests of Indian industry and would be disastrous. CII's role (as mentioned earlier in chapter 4) helped make them stick. Constant communication between CII and the finance ministry at the time encouraged the reforms to move ahead. This communication with a leading representative of the affected parties built constituencies of support for reform, and the right reform drove inclusion.

As I wrote this, I did not know how the farm laws would turn out. Would they stick, or would the government give in to the farmers?[30] Some compromise may have resulted. But a more institution-minded approach, especially one that respects India's Union–state sharing of power, could have seen these essential reforms implemented in the manner intended, instead of scenes of the police hosing down farmers in the Delhi winter. By violating the federal structure of our Constitution, negating norms of debate and damaging a culture of discussion, we put at risk a useful reform. Institutions matter. So does culture, the subject of our next chapter.

---

30 As this book goes to press, the government has given in to the farmers and repealed these useful reforms.

JUST RAMBLING

10

Culture: Building Unity in Diversity

India is a pluralist society that creates magic with democracy, rule of law and individual freedom, community relations and [cultural] diversity. What a place to be an intellectual! ... I wouldn't mind being born ten times to rediscover India.

—Robert Blackwill[1]

Understanding the atom is child's play compared with understanding child's play.

—Paul Streeten

For an organisation, culture is 'the way we do things around here'. For a society, culture reflects beliefs, preferences and values. The role of culture in economic development has long been studied. In 1998, the economic historian David Landes wrote *The Wealth and Poverty of*

---

1   Robert Blackwill, as he was departing India as US ambassador. Quoted by Ramachandra Guha as the lead quote in *India After Gandhi: The History of the World's Largest Democracy* (New Delhi: Pan Macmillan India, revised edition, 2017).

Nations, an obvious hark back to Adam Smith's book from two centuries earlier. The book is typical of anything Landes wrote, combining historical mastery with economic insight and flowing narrative. Equally typically, Landes does not hide or qualify his opinions, which are served up with enough wit to make a five-hundred page read most enjoyable. It is also one of my five favourite books. Here is Landes talking about industrial development in Europe, why some countries (Portugal, the Netherlands, Britain, Germany, and in Scandinavia) moved ahead, while others (Russia, Spain, the Balkans) lagged behind:

> … political economists and economic historians … think in terms of core and periphery: the rich center vs the surrounding dependencies. But that is not the relevant metaphor or image. Europe's development gradient ran from west to east and north to south, from educated to illiterate populations, from equality to hierarchy, and so on. It was not resources or money that made the difference; nor mistreatment by outsiders. It was what lay inside—culture, values, initiative. These people came to have freedom enough. They just did not know what to do with it.[2]

I have long believed that we are ill-served by blaming our ills on the past. I make no excuse for colonialism, or those who ran previous governments. Bad is bad, and if we learn from the past to correct mistakes in the present, that is fine. But if we use the past to justify poor performance today, we are condemning ourselves to continued mediocrity.

Like Landes, I believe it is what lies inside—culture, values, initiative—that matters. But culture needs to be talked of with care. Culture is itself about values, and my own values influence my analysis.

---

2   David Landes, *The Wealth and Poverty of Nations: Why Some Are So Rich and Some So Poor* (New York, NY: Norton, 1998), 243.

I believe culture is an important, even vital, influence, but have never thought it determines economic success.

So why study culture? I have also long struggled with explanations of what worked and did not work in development. As I studied the stories of success and failure in South Korea, Taiwan, Brazil, Mexico, Malaysia, Thailand, Indonesia and China, with the Indian experience constantly in my head, it appeared that the same development policies had very different results in different countries. Why did infant-industry protection develop deep technical capabilities in South Korea and Taiwan, but result in aged infants in India and Brazil? Why did collaboration between government and industry lead to world-beating export powerhouses in Japan, South Korea and China, but inward-looking inefficient firms in India and Mexico? Why did firms that began with export assembly in China and Mexico, making the same product, for the same market, end up with such different trajectories—in China, growing design capabilities and their own brands, while in Mexico the *maquiladoras*[3] continue with low-wage assembly forty years on? Why did the protection of IT hardware in the 1980s lead to a world-beating industry in Taiwan, and negative value-added in India?

I believe that it is the interplay of policy with many other things—institutions, culture, luck—that delivers success or failure. I certainly don't believe that culture determines success, but I do believe that culture can shape which policies will work and which do not. I also believe that India's culture can provide the foundation on which leadership would rest. But this means we must be clear about how

---

3   The *maquiladoras* are export assembly plants in Latin America, largely for duty-free access to the US. The typical *maquiladora* is just across the border in Mexico from the US, assembling low-value-added items such as consumer electronics and garments. They account for almost a fifth of employment and half of Mexico's exports, but suffer from limited deepening of local supply-chains in spite of having operated for decades.

our culture can be a strength and help us achieve world-leadership. At the minimum, we must not formulate policy that depends for its success on Indian firms and Indians behaving like Japanese, Chinese or Koreans. Culture does evolve—I'll provide some amusing examples from Landes later—but fiddling with it can be dangerous. It can be harnessed for development, but, again, this has to be done with care.

Apart from David Landes, my other major source in this chapter is the sociologist Ronald Dore, a specialist in Japan. The first paper by Ronald Dore that I read, 'Technological Self-reliance: Sturdy Ideal or Self-serving Rhetoric', was his single one on India.[4] That paper was the only one that remained in the reader for my course for the twenty years I taught it. Ron's paper described what I, as an industrialist, knew first-hand to be happening in India, instead of some armchair academic's theorising. I subsequently read whatever Ron wrote; his observations on Japan, India, Latin America, the UK and more have been hugely influential in my own thinking.

Ron was the quintessential humanist, placing an understanding of people at the heart of whatever he was studying. He believed in solid empirical research, wanting his theories to fit the facts, the essence of a good academic.[5] This was important, because as a sociologist, Ron studied culture. *Shinohata: Portrait of a Japanese Village,* is a gem of a book, describing the changes in a village over twenty years, as fast trains reduced the 100-kilometre distance to Tokyo, and as industry moved in and replaced agriculture as the main employer. It should be required reading for anyone who wishes to understand Japanese development, but also anyone who wishes to understand development itself. *British Factory, Japanese Factory* compared industrial relations in the 1970s between two factories of similar sizes making the same product, to tease out the relationship between industrial performance and the wider culture of the country and quality of company

---

4   In Martin Fransman and Kenneth King, editors, *Technological Capability in the Third World* (London: Palgrave Macmillan, 1984).

5   The corollary, of bending facts to fit the theory, is the hallmark of populist politicians.

management. *The Diploma Disease* was a most entertaining diatribe on higher education. For this chapter, I have found most valuable his observations on development in East Asia and Latin America, seen through a Japanese lens.

What Matters in Culture?

How homogenous is the country? I made the comment earlier on that India was the most diverse country in the world. Ramachandra Guha prefers the word pluralism to describe us. We have a plurality of religions. In a country which is 80 per cent Hindu, 'between 2004 and 2007, the president of India was a Muslim, the prime minister a Sikh, and the leader of the ruling party a Catholic born in Italy'.[6] Guha talks next of our pluralism of language 'graphically expressed in the country's currency notes.... The note's denomination ... is printed in words in Hindi and English (the two official languages), but also, in smaller type, in all the other languages of the Union. In this manner, as many as seventeen different scripts are represented.' Guha goes on to a fascinating discussion of how different the Sri Lankan and Pakistani experiences have been from India's. An emphasis on the ruling party's language—Sinhala, Urdu—prompted a civil war. He ends with the observation that 'Had Hindi been imposed on the whole of India the lesson might well have been: "One language, twenty-two nations".'

Ronald Dore argues that in a homogenous country like Japan, decisions by the leader will be accepted as more legitimate and in the national interest, and not a conspiracy to benefit some interest group. My ranking of a few countries on a homogeneity-to-heterogeneity scale would run: South Korea – Japan – Taiwan – China – USA – Mexico – Brazil – India. I would not argue much if you want to exchange a country with one away from it, but I would if you flipped the sequence around.

---

6   Ramachandra Guha, *India After Gandhi: The History of the World's Largest Democracy* (New Delhi: Pan Macmillan India, revised edition, 2017), 754, 756. One of my five favourite books.

Consider how this plays out in policy for the two countries at the ends of the scale. Around 1970, India and South Korea passed remarkably similar laws regulating the import of technology—but with very different results. Reading descriptions of firms that imported technology in each country, the gap was striking. In South Korea, firms and government departments discussed how the regulation could be used to get more access to technology from the foreign firm. In India, the Indian and foreign firms agreed what needed to be put into the agreement to get the Indian government to approve it.[7]

So does this then say that heterogeneity is bad and homogeneity is good? Not at all. The difference is one of culture, not morals. It implies that the very scope for detailed government intervention is more limited in a heterogenous society. Heterogenous countries have other strengths—but close government–industry ties seen as legitimate are not among them. I would also not make too much of South Korea's close government–business relationship. While I am a great admirer of South Korea's achievements in almost every aspect of development, their habit of charging previous presidents with corruption—usually involving their largest and most successful firms (Samsung is only the most recent example)—reflects what happens when a close government–business relationship goes too far.

Sources of motivation: Dore points out that entrepreneurs in Japan were not motivated purely by money. People who started small businesses like the Great Japan Match Company, the National Progress Soap Company or the National Laundry Works certainly did so to make money, but also from a sense of patriotism. They were not alone, of course. The story of Jamshetji Tata founding the Taj Hotel in Bombay, after a friend of his was refused entrance to the Grand Hotel as an Indian, or Jamnalal Bajaj's and Ghanshyam Das Birla's support for Mahatma Gandhi and the Indian independence movement came

---

7   Dave Wield and I dealt with this in some detail in *From Followers to Leaders: Managing Technology and Innovation in Newly Industrializing Countries* (London: Routledge, 2002).

from a deep sense of patriotism. Perhaps the robber barons in the US were inspired more by money, but having made great fortunes, they then turned around and used their wealth to create such nation-building institutions as the Rockefeller Foundation and Carnegie-Mellon University.

Our learning should not be that we need a culture of patriotism—which is actually more widely shared and in wider supply in more places than we think. Honour, everywhere, stems from more than just money, and our policies need to be in synchronisation with the key sources of honour in the country. A heterogenous society like India will have many such sources, so we should respect them all. I worry when I hear disparaging remarks about a 'trading mentality' of Indian entrepreneurs. Traders are valuable economic agents; it is they who compete, make goods and services cheaper, and make manufacturers reduce costs. We should respect all legitimate avenues of entrepreneurship, whatever our personal preferences might be.

Did you see how depressed and miserable that businessman looked? That shows our industrial policy is working.

Expectations and the will to develop: Lee Kuan Yew was asked in an interview some years ago if economic reform in much of the world would permit other countries to enjoy the same kind of growth as East Asia:

> Getting the fundamentals right would help, but these societies will not succeed in the same way as East Asia did because certain driving forces will be absent. If you have a culture that doesn't place much value in learning and scholarship and hard work and thrift and deferment of present enjoyment for future gain, the going will be much slower.[8]

In India, we placed most ills at the door of colonial rule. This meant that independence in itself raised expectations of democracy and progress. That made it very difficult to defer gratification. Dore contrasts Japan, where the population:

> ... did not expect the state to provide a minimum level of welfare for every citizen, in the way that this is normally expected even in the least developed countries today. So it was possible for the Japanese government to hold back consumption and concentrate on long-term investment, making the Japanese people forego jam today in order that their grandchildren could have more jam in the distant future, in a way that is rarely possible for the developing countries of today.[9]

One of my intellectual heroes, the historian of France, Gordon Wright, who I talked about in the chapter on higher education, made

---

8   Interview of Lee Kuan Yew with Fareed Zakaria, 'Culture is Destiny', *Foreign Affairs* (April 1994): 116.

9   Ronald Dore, *Japanese Industrialisation and the Developing Countries: Model, Warning or Source of Healthy Doubts?* (Singapore: Institute of Southeast Asian Studies, 1971).

a very insightful point in his assessment of why Britain did so much more poorly than France in the decades after World War II. Britain came through the war on the winning side, with its institutions intact. Then why change? France came out of the war an occupied country, with its morale shattered. The impetus for catch–up was much greater, while Britain settled into genteel decline. It took Margaret Thatcher to wake the country up after thirty-five years of falling behind first Germany, the Netherlands and Scandinavia, then France, and finally Italy, before the trajectory changed.

Japan, South Korea and Taiwan too had this will to develop—which Dore describes superbly in a paper called 'Reflections on Culture and Social Change'.[10] The will to develop came out of a sense of backwardness, a sense that one had to catch up. I have for years tried to do my bit in this regard, including in this book. We must not forget that in 1991 India was in the bottom fifth of countries in per capita GDP; today, after thirty years of the highest growth in our history, we are in the bottom third (at least until the Covid collapse). That is a fine improvement, but to be in the bottom third is surely not good enough. Repeatedly pointing out that China is now five times richer than we are from a similar start forty years ago is meant to foster just this sense of shame about economic backwardness. Perhaps, with Bangladesh having overtaken India in 2020, the message will finally hit home. I keep repeating all this not to depress us, but to foster a will to develop and catch up.

Dore points out that not only is a sense of backwardness important, but that this must be shared—across society. Both India and Latin America have long had elite enclaves at world-class levels. Nobel Prizes in science (C.V. Raman and Venky Ramakrishnan), literature (Tagore), peace (Mother Teresa) and economics (Amartya Sen and

---

10 Ronald Dore, 'Reflections on Culture and Social Change', in *Manufacturing Miracles: Paths of Industrialization in Latin America and East Asia*, edited by Gary Gereffi and Donald Wyman (Princeton, NJ: Princeton University Press, 1990), 361.

Abhijit Banerjee) justifiably fill Indians with pride. If we combine the pride with some soul-searching of why the most recent awardees— Sen, Ramakrishnan, Banerjee—did their work in institutes of higher education overseas instead of in India, then the urge would be wholly positive. But if pride in our great intellectuals lessens the urge to pull the farmer in the field up with us, we dilute a common will to develop. I've always trusted politicians who treat citizens as adults with a sober and hard-nosed assessment of where we stand in the world instead of selling them snake-oil. Setting reasonable expectations, emphasising our shared sense of backwardness and common interest in rapid growth can foster the will to develop that we need. Focusing on how wonderful we are ('India is the world's fastest-growing large economy') or were ('India invented the zero and plastic surgery') dilutes the message.

Dore's description of Latin America's elite enclaves resonated with me as an Indian. I recall a discussion from the early 2000s, when the treasury secretary of Mexico was visiting Stanford. I asked him about Mexico's performance and why there seemed to be no public objective of convergence with the US. He said that for his last budget he presented the financial numbers in a document, and talked instead of where Mexico was now and in 1970 vis-à-vis all the East Asian countries. His aim, like mine, was not to depress but to share a sense of backwardness and galvanise action. He said his speech was greeted with deafening silence. Manmohan Singh, as our finance minister in the early 1990s, drew similar comparisons of India with South Korea, pointing out that we did not matter to the rest of the world. He was the first minister to draw public attention to our poor growth and development record—every other minister till then always talked about how well we had done since Independence. Farmers and informal labourers live the experience of poverty and backwardness. As political leaders and industrialists, we need to share in this sense of backwardness even if we do not experience it ourselves. From it can spring a shared urge to catch up, a will to develop.

Learning and humility: As with too many of my fellow citizens, I like a good acronym. Here are two more. We need to avoid NIH and FIB. NIH is the not-invented-here syndrome—if we didn't do it, it couldn't be any good. This keeps one from learning from others. As we saw in the chapters on technology and research, imitation is a subset, indeed the first step, of innovation. We first learn what others do, how they do it, and why they are successful doing it. And not only must we learn from others, but we must then be as efficient as those who came before. NIH is an illness of leaders: if we think we are the best, why bother to learn from anyone else? (It is, equally in my experience, an illness of people who think they are smart.) During the heyday of the industrial revolution in Britain, when it was growing faster than anyone ever had before, it was a net importer of technology from the rest of Europe. It was only after relative industrial decline set in relative to Germany, the Netherlands and the US in the mid-1850s, that Britain became a net exporter of technology. As Joel Mokyr tells us, 'Technological creativity, defined as the application of new ideas to production, began to slow down in Britain. The ideas themselves were still forthcoming, but the economic environment slowly became less receptive to them.'[11]

In India we sometimes have added to NIH another acronym—FIB. FIB is Foreign is Better. NIH + FIB is a lethal combination—we do not need to learn from others, unless the others are foreign, because foreign is better. Here's Laxman, again:

---

11 Joel Mokyr, *The Lever of Riches: Technological Creativity and Economic Progress* (Oxford: Oxford University Press, 1992), 263–64.

There is some foreign matter in your eye. Would you like to keep it since it's foreign?

How do we avoid this? We need a combination of openness to outside ideas combined with pride in our own culture. We need openness to learn from the best. But we then need enough confidence to improve on what we've learned. 'Learn from the best, improve the rest' is a good axiom.

Openness to outside ideas and keenness to apply them:

David Landes details Europe's historical keenness to learn from the rest of the world. The three inventions of fundamental importance to the modern world—the compass, gunpowder and paper—were all Chinese. But it was Europe that took advantage of them. The Chinese used their gunpowder to make brilliant fireworks to entertain the emperor. The Europeans learnt to corn it (to compress it into a ball) and use it as a weapon. Landes lists the instructions given for the Portuguese exploration of Madagascar in 1508[12]:

1. The fleet was to follow the circumference of the island, with special attention to the west coast (the side facing Africa); enter and study every port, reconnoitre means of entry and exit, explore the possibilities of anchorage with reference to winds, currents, and nature of bottom; and *write all of this down* (my italics).

2. First contact with the natives: show them a range of articles and metals (spices, wax, copper) to see if these things are known on the island; and if there, ask how to get to them and trade for them. Find out what they would want in exchange.

3. Find out if any other ships come into these ports. Where do they come from? What do they carry? Do they trade these in other islands or carry different things to different places? Where do the merchants and crews of these ships come from? Are they Muslim or pagan ('*gentiles*')? White or black? How are they dressed? Do they come armed?

4. Are these other ships big or small? What kind? What are the seasons of their coming and going? The rhythm (annual, more often)? Their way of navigating?

5. Does the island have its own vessels, and if so, where do they go, what do they carry, what do they seek?

6. What does the island produce, what will the natives take for it? Are these things dear or cheap?

7. Political structure: what kinds of kings or lords, whether Muslim or pagan? How do they live? How do they administer justice? What do they possess? Do they hold treasure? What kind of state and dignity, and how they maintain it? What military force and arms: elephants

---

12   David Landes, *The Wealth and Poverty of Nations: Why Some Are So Rich and Some So Poor* (New York, NY: Norton, 1998), 92–98.

or horses, weapons, firearms, artillery of any kind? Are the soldiers timid or warlike?

8. Are there Muslim rulers apart, independent; and do they recognise the pagan rulers?

9. Is the population Muslim or pagan? If the latter, how do the Muslims live with them? Are there Christians as in India?* Do they know St. Thomas?

10. What are the customs? Are they, in part at least, like those of the Malabars?

11. Are there cities, towns, or villages of special importance? Are they fortified? How is the land inhabited?

12. Money? Is there some standard tender, or are there simply 'moneys', like those of Manicongo [in Africa]? In this regard do they make copper as a commodity, and in that case, what things are made of it? In particular, is it used for casting guns and if so, what kind? Also in that case, how do they make gunpowder?

This is curiosity about the world writ large. Contrast this with Landes' wonderful description of the fifteenth-century Chinese naval expeditions:

> From 1405 to 1431, the Chinese undertook at least seven major naval expeditions to explore the waters of Indonesia and the Indian Ocean. These voyages aimed to show the Chinese flag, bestow awareness and knowledge of the Celestial Kingdom on the barbarians, receive homage and tribute, and collect for the Emperor those few rarities not available within his borders ...
>
> The first of these fleets, that of the eunuch admiral Cheng Ho in 1405 consisted of 317 vessels and carried 28,000 men. From 1404 to 1407, China undertook an orgy of shipbuilding and refitting ... Over a period of three years, the Chinese built or refitted 1681 ships. Medieval Europe could not have conceived of such an armada. Yet

this Chinese opening to the sea and the larger world came to naught, indeed was deliberately reduced to naught ...

By 1500, anyone who built a ship of more than two masts was liable to the death penalty, and in 1525 coastal authorities were enjoined to destroy all oceangoing ships and to arrest their owners. Finally in 1551, it became a crime to go to sea on a multi-masted ship, even for trade ...

This deliberate introversion, a major turning point in Chinese history, could not have come at a worse time, for it not only disarmed them in the face of rising European power, but set them, complacent and stubborn, against the lessons and novelties that European travellers would soon be bringing.

Why? Why did China not make that little extra effort that would have taken it around the southern end of Africa and up into the Atlantic? Why, decades and even centuries after the arrival of European visitors in Chinese waters, were there no Chinese vessels in the harbors of Europe? (The first such vessel, a vehicle for diplomacy, visited London for the Great Exhibition of 1851) ...

To begin with, the Chinese lacked range, focus, and above all curiosity. They went to show themselves, not to see and learn; to bestow their presence, not to stay; to receive obeisance and tribute, not to buy. They were what they were and did not have to change. They had what they had and did not have to take or make. Unlike the Europeans they were not motivated by greed and passion. The Europeans had a specific target: the wealth of the Indies. They had to get around Africa; that was the point of the exercise. The Chinese did not have to. They could find what they wanted in the Indian Ocean, and what they wanted was so trivial that it was not an appetiser but a dessert...

The question remains: Suppose the Chinese had not given up on trade and exploration, suppose the Portuguese had arrived in the Indian Ocean to find these huge Chinese ships ruling the seas? Or even more, suppose the Chinese had not stopped somewhere around the Mozambique channel but had gone around the Cape into the Atlantic, thereby opening maritime links to West Africa and Europe? ...

On the surface, the Chinese were immeasurably stronger and richer. Who could stand up to them? Yet reality ran the other way. The Chinese had learnt the secret of gunpowder before the Europeans, but the Europeans had better guns and greater fire power, especially at a distance. The Chinese had bigger ships but the Europeans were better navigators. If we compare the two sides around 1400, the Chinese might have come out on top, at least in the Indian Ocean or South China Seas. But fifty years later, even in Asian waters, the Europeans would have run circles around the Chinese vessels ...

Isolationism became China. Round, complete, apparently serene, ineffably harmonious, the Celestial Empire purred along for hundreds of years more, impervious and imperturbable. But the world was passing it by.[13]

These two long quotes indicate the importance of openness, of curiosity, and of confidence—we need them all together. With just confidence, one doesn't learn. With just openness and curiosity, one learns but may not try to improve. The Portuguese voyages sought to learn; the Chinese, to be seen. The Portuguese wanted to trade and prosper by engaging with the world; the Chinese might allow the world to engage with them. The Portuguese had ambition and aspired to reach the top; the Chinese were already on top. But, as Landes says, 'the world was passing it by'.

In a magisterial introduction to Rabindranath Tagore's lectures on *Nationalism,* Ramachandra Guha points out how Tagore prompted Gandhi and Nehru to develop a nationalism for India that was

---

13 Landes, 92–98.

inclusive and open. He gives us the full version of a famous Mahatma Gandhi quote: 'I hope I am as great a believer in free air as the great poet. I do not want my house to be walled in on all sides and my windows to be stuffed. I want the cultures of all the lands to be blown about my house as freely as possible. But I refuse to be blown off my feet by any.'[14]

The message is that we should have the humility to learn from the best, to match them in what they do, and then have enough confidence in our own abilities to improve it and go further.

One of the reasons I love those Landes quotes is because they seem so different to the world we know now. Is this description of eager curiosity what we know of a European country? And is this lack of interest in engaging with the world really China?

Can Culture Change?

It would seem it can. Contrast contemporary China with its fifteenth-century naval expedition, summarised in Landes' sentences: 'To begin with, the Chinese lacked range, focus, and above all curiosity … They had what they had and did not have to take or make.' The Australian-American cartoonist Patrick Oliphant had a wonderful cartoon on the occasion of Ronald Reagan's visit to China in 1984. Reagan and Chinese premier Zhao Ziyang are toasting each other. Reagan: 'To peace, truth, justice, freedom, the pursuit of happiness, church, God, John Wayne, capitalism, victory over communism, prayer-in-the-schools, and the American way.' Zhao's reply: 'To your technology'. Chinese eagerness to soak up the best technology from the US, Europe, Japan and Taiwan hardly reflects a lack of curiosity.

The US has long seen itself as a land of opportunity. The Statue of Liberty is the 'mother of exiles', calling out 'Keep, ancient lands,

---

14   Mahatma Gandhi, quoted by Ramachandra Guha in his Introduction to Rabindranath Tagore's *Nationalism* (New Delhi: Penguin Random House, 2009), xxxi.

your storied pomp … Give me your tired, your poor, your huddled masses yearning to breathe free'. All this is not just rhetoric—'land of opportunity' is repeated again and again in the US, as a truism. But is it? Or is it still? Recent analyses show that privilege now counts for more in the US than it does in Europe. Those born into wealthier households are more likely to become wealthy themselves than in Europe. Education is less of an enabler in the US than in Europe, and even when it is, admissions to the best colleges also reflect privileged backgrounds more than they do in Europe. And all this shows in capital and inherited privilege leading to less social mobility than in those ancient lands of storied pomp.

Or take Germany. Contrast the racist outrages of Nazism and *Lebensraum* with Germany being the most welcoming country in Europe during the migrant crisis of 2015 and 2016. Over a million people applied for asylum and Angela Merkel, in a defining act of statesmanship, declared 'Wir schaffen das' (We can do this).

Or Britain, the nation that pioneered the industrial revolution in the eighteenth century, was derided by Napoleon as a 'nation of shopkeepers' in the nineteenth century, and then apparently lost its entrepreneurial spirit. The historian Martin Wiener wrote a book, *English Culture and the Decline of the Industrial Spirit,* where the title captured the change.[15]

So culture, it would seem, can change—with dramatic effect, for good and bad, on economic progress. But is it culture that changed— or leadership and institutions? It was the fifteenth-century Chinese Emperor, presumably supported by his elites, who represented the celestial kingdom that did not need the world. And remember Acemoglu and Robinson's discussion in *Why Nations Fail* from the previous chapter. China's disastrous political and economic policies under Mao kept it poor and killed millions. The change in leadership

---

15   Martin Wiener, *English Culture and the Decline of the Industrial Spirit, 1850–1980* (Cambridge: Cambridge University Press, 1981).

changed China. Deng Xiaoping transformed its economic policies. The dramatic change in incentives that resulted led to a flowering of entrepreneurship. Over time economic institutions have been built that have entrenched a new set of incentives for a dynamic economy.

Could the US' moving from a land of opportunity to one of greater entrenched privilege reflect not so much a change in culture, as an evolution of institutions? Does fundraising by American universities feed on legacy admissions, which combines with technical change that grows the returns to advanced education, which combines with laxer antitrust policy and industry concentration, and the whole combination entrenches privilege? Many of our institutions today are obviously better than the really horrible ones in the past. But continuing discrimination—whether of African-Americans or Dalits—can entrench privilege and limit upward mobility.

Hitler to Merkel reflects a different time and lessons of history, but it also surely reflects evil making way for good. Countries are lucky to have a Washington, Nehru, Adenauer, Mandela, Merkel or Ardern in the right place at the right time.

A culture of GDP growth: Dore describes how the Japanese government from the Meiji Restoration (1868) onwards fostered a succession of national goals. They ran roughly as follows[16]:

> 1870s: Keep Japan free of colonialism.
> 1890–1911: Revise the unequal treaties (that the Western powers had extracted).
> 1890s: Keep China from seizing control of Korea—this culminated in the Sino-Japanese War of 1895 and Formosa/Taiwan beoming a Japanese colony.

---

16   Ronald Dore, *Japanese Industrialisation and the Developing Countries: Model, Warning or Source of Healthy Doubts?* (Singapore: Institute of Southeast Asian Studies, 1971).

1900s: Keep Russia from seizing control of Korea—which culminated in the Russo-Japanese War of 1905 and Korea becoming a Japanese colony.

1930s: Total equality with the Great Powers—we know what that ended in.

These goals were presented as the shared objective of *all* the Japanese people, and were highly effective in galvanising action through a nationalist spirit. Nationalism often ends badly—for both the nation and its neighbours. So did this episode. 'Badly' meant defeat in war and occupation—for the Chinese in 1895, the Koreans in 1905, and for the Japanese themselves in 1945 following two nuclear bombings. Post World War II, things were more positive. Economic growth was the only way to glory, so the Japanese daily papers published a league table of GDP growth rates. Each time Japan overtook a country in per capita GDP (which is what matters), it hit the headlines. The target was glory and prestige, not economic growth in itself.

I read this description of Dore's in the mid-1990s, and was struck by the contrast with India. In 1994, our finance ministry estimated growth at 5.5 per cent. We discovered six months later that we had actually grown almost 1 per cent faster. The same happened again the following year. And the following year. And then, with some corrections in the national accounts, it seems that India grew at 7 to 7.5 per cent per year for three years running in the mid-1990s, the best we had ever achieved. This would have been headline news in any other country. We instead had a small article on the middle page of a financial newspaper—which said, accurately but unbelievably, 'Finance Ministry's estimate of growth wrong'. Economic growth was just not something we took pride in then. The Vajpayee government finally changed things with an official growth target of 8 per cent. Economic growth then moved centre stage, and we went to the other extreme. By 2014, a decade of sustained rapid economic growth meant we were beginning to take it as our birthright, not something to be worked at. Indian culture did not change, nor did our institutional fabric. But our leaders and policies did, with spectacular results. Even if we agree with Abhijit Banerjee and Esther Duflo's view (discussed in chapter 2) that the spurt in growth we saw in the 1990s and, especially, the 2000s, was only a result of 'misallocating less badly', we needed to work at finding more areas to keep misallocating less badly. And there are many—as we have seen through this book.

Continuing the story, the Modi government took pleasure in announcing that we were the fastest-growing large economy in the world in 2015 and 2016. This repeated assertion had good and bad undertones. The positive message was: 'We are a land of opportunity, we need your help in rising faster, come and invest here and we will prosper together.' The negative one was: 'We are a rising land. You need us more than we need you. Line up to invest here for your own good, and we will see what terms to let you in on.' If you think I am exaggerating, here's a personal experience. On a mission I led to a friendly rich country, the Indian head of mission there gave our visiting delegation an introductory briefing. This country needed us; we must carry ourselves accordingly. This country, we were told, was searching for growth opportunities, it needed India as a country to invest in. India, meanwhile, was the destination of choice and we should engage with this country on our terms (hints of the Landes China quote). I thought it eminently pointless to make a visit to attract investment where we were to convey that we did not need it, and approached it differently. We spoke instead of our great need to build out our infrastructure, education, R&D, and we would deeply appreciate firms from this country and its sovereign wealth funds helping us do so by investing in India. To the diplomat's great irritation, conveyed in strong language to a member of our delegation.

Demonetisation greatly damaged the Indian growth story. Between 2018 and 2020, every quarter saw successive falls in the growth rate, to

3 per cent in the quarter ended March. Correspondingly, the inspiring target set by the Modi government of a $5 trillion economy by 2024 suffered from not being backed up by a specific calculation. Even before Covid put paid to achieving it, getting there by 2024 required a 9 per cent rate of growth for four years—with little indication of how we would achieve that on the back of a rapidly slowing economy. The right goals can galvanise action, but they need credibility to be widely accepted.

Further up. Up, a little to the right and up – that's it! – And now let us set about achieving it!

I now worry we are making a virtue of the failure to achieve our goals. It started with some leading ministers saying 'What does it matter if we miss the 2024 target—we will still get to $5 trillion.' Yes, of course, but $5 trillion by 2024 is a GDP growth target; $5 trillion *eventually* is meaningless. And now, instead of a focus on growth, there is talk of well-being and self-reliance. This troubles me. We are too poor a country to accept modest growth rates. Growing at 8, 9, and 10+ per cent annually must be our mission for the next few decades, as a collective goal for all India. We have to start by making up for heavily negative growth during Covid to get back on the old growth trajectory. Joel Mokyr's recent book on why the modern economy originated in Europe is titled *A Culture of Growth*. Mokyr defines this culture as 'the fundamental belief that the human lot can be continuously improved by bettering our understanding of natural phenomena and regularities and the application of this understanding to production'.[17] We need to sustain our recent culture of growth too. But we also need to supplement it with the right policies and institutional framework of economic competence in the government, a subject we will return to in the last chapter.

The question 'can culture change?' is one I've wrestled with for some time. Like others, I conclude that it depends.

We start with culture. Leaders change—sometimes by chance, sometimes with systematic progress. Policies change—again, by chance and deliberation both. These changed policies sometimes get embedded in changed institutions, especially with good leaders who learn the lessons of history, and who value independent institutions. And over time, the culture—beliefs, practices and values—evolves. It may not be all at once, or completely, but the evolution can be fundamental. For good and for bad and back again to good. The number of qualifying words in this paragraph—'sometimes', 'chance', 'over time', 'evolves'—reflects the uncertainty inherent in this process

---

17 Joel Mokyr, *A Culture of Growth: The Origins of the Modern Economy* (Princeton, MA: Princeton University Press, 2016), xiii. Economists like to write like this.

of building a culture of development. But that makes it no less important.

Social Capital and Trust

Albert Hirschman's *Exit, Voice and Loyalty*, published fifty years ago, is considered one of the most influential books in the social sciences. It is also one of my five favourite books.[18] The book's subheading, *Responses to Decline in Firms, Organizations, and States*, tells you what it is about. A decrease in quality can be met either by the exit option (one stops buying the good, or pulls a child out from the school, or emigrates from the country) or the voice option. Voice comes in two forms, vertical voice (a direct complaint or protest) and horizontal voice ('the murmuring of the people'—in our time, 'murmuring' is a very quiet way of describing the chatter on WhatsApp groups). Horizontal voice is a precondition for vertical voice—the complaining and discussion among citizens precedes the actual complaint or protest to the authorities. Horizontal voice can also provide some security that there is wider backing for a direct complaint. Whether one chooses exit or voice depends on loyalty. If one is loyal to the organisation, instead of deserting it one would choose voice, and could even attempt to 'save' the organisation.

Changing perspective, let us say we are the government and wish that our institutions keep striving to perform better and improve. A vibrant institution is one where both voice and exit are used to drive improvement. Loyal citizens are encouraged to mutter and complain. If the state or institution hears them and responds, a protest may

---

18   In case loyal readers are keeping count, here are the five. Ramachandra Guha, *India after Gandhi;* David Landes, *The Wealth and Poverty of Nations;* and, Albert Hirschman, *Exit, Voice and Loyalty* are the three non-fiction ones. And then there's P.G. Wodehouse, *Leave it to Psmith* (I would have loved to choose a Jeeves book, but which one?), and Alan Bennett, *The Uncommon Reader.*

never be necessary. But if it misses the muttering, a protest can get its attention. If it then responds, we are still fine. If, instead, an authoritarian regime chooses to restrict voice by suppressing actual protests, and drowning out horizontal voices of dissent (by using social media trolls, for example), that makes decline more likely. Exit may then be the only option. If a state represses both voice and exit, then 'passivity, acquiescence, inaction, withdrawal, and resignation' hold sway. And instead of improving, the institution or state declines further.

If one seeks voice over exit as the signalling mechanism for quality, and if voice depends on loyalty, how do we foster more loyalty? Hirschman says 'the presence of trust ... will help to enlist the voice of the organisation's members in the tasks of recovery and reform.'[19] The OECD defines trust as 'a person's belief that another person or institution will act consistently with their expectations of positive behaviour'.[20] How do we build trust in each other and in our institutions? And do all groups trust institutions equally? This problem is not unique to India. The Black Lives Matter movement in the US is the culmination of years of mistrust within the black community about the impartiality of the police. Muslims have the same view about the police in India, and our current climate of communal polarisation only makes things worse. Building trust in institutions is a long haul, it happens step by step over years if not decades. Not only should people be equal before the law, but they should perceive that they are.

Trust makes a difference: Do we trust strangers? That question is at the heart of the concept of social capital, a term we first came across when we spoke of Moe Abramovitz's work in chapter 2. He argued that countries which caught up fast had high social capital. For Abramovitz, social capital included both formal education and trust.

---

19 Albert Hirschman, *Rival Views of Market Society and Other Recent Essays*, (New York, NY: Viking Penguin, 1986), 81.
20 OECD, 'Trust and Social Capital', in *For Good Measure* (Paris: OECD, 2018).

But the political scientist Robert Putnam is most associated with the concept. His first book on social capital in 1994, *Making Democracy Work*, compared northern and southern Italy. Putnam argued that northern Italy had greater civic involvement and economic prosperity because of its community organisations.[21] His most famous work was *Bowling Alone*, in 2000, where he showed that bowling leagues had declined in the US from the 1960s to the 1990s, while people were bowling more.[22] He used this as a proxy for the decline in community spirit in the country.

Putnam identifies two kinds of social capital, bonding capital (which bonds similar people together) and bridging capital (which bridges the gap between dissimilar groups). When both are strong, we end up with a high trust society, with many attendant benefits. What is important is that one must not strengthen at the expense of the other. Appealing to majoritarian instincts may strengthen bonding capital within a large group, but if it simultaneously weakens bridging capital it weakens social trust.

Levels of social trust will be inherently challenged by India's size and high diversity. We may need decades of fair, effective and efficient contract enforcement to build trust over time. That takes us back to our discussion in the previous chapter on the institutions of law enforcement—the police and judiciary. Both suffer from a deep lack of trust in India; when we improve their functioning for all Indians we will simultaneously build trust in society and wider government functioning.

Consider the benefits of trust—at a very small scale. I belong to a tiny community, the Parsis. Parsis have a reputation for being both fastidious and trustworthy, affecting everything from business to looking

---

21   Robert Putnam, *Making Democracy Work: Civic Traditions in Modern Italy* (Princeton, NJ: Princeton University Press, 1994).
22   Robert Putnam, *Bowling Alone: The Collapse and Revival of American Community*, (New York, NY: Simon & Schuster, 2000).

after the things we own. This is best typified by the highest premium someone selling a used car can claim—'single Parsi owner'.

We will return to trust in our discussion of entrepreneurship.

Trust and Covid: The year 2020 dramatically illustrated the power of trust. As Covid spread around the world, countries diverged enormously in the effectiveness of their response. Taiwan, South Korea, Japan, Singapore, Sri Lanka, New Zealand, Australia, Thailand, Germany and Norway responded effectively, with spread of infection and/or death rates well below those of their peers. After foisting the virus on the world, so did China. The US, Brazil, Peru, Mexico, the UK, Italy, Spain, Belgium and India did not.

As Francis Fukuyama pointed out: '... the factors responsible for successful pandemic responses have been state capacity, social trust, and leadership. Countries with all three – a competent state apparatus, a government that citizens trust and listen to, and effective leaders – have performed impressively, limiting the damage they have suffered. Countries with dysfunctional states, polarised societies, or poor leadership have done badly, leaving their citizens and economies exposed and vulnerable.'[23] The messages are clear: public health institutions matter. So does the quality of leadership. Polarising society might be politically expedient but it fundamentally damages trust in the state's motives and competence and undercuts its ability to act effectively. Decades of weak investment in public health, low social trust from a polarised society and compromised bureaucracy, and a political leadership that visibly risked public safety as it campaigned across the country, led to the disaster of India's second wave.

Dissent and noise as assets: The media plays an essential role in holding power accountable. But it also gives voice to people. A wise government would be one that encourages a free and independent

---

23 Francis Fukuyama, 'The Pandemic and Political Order: It Takes a State', *Foreign Affairs* (July/August 2020).

media, encourages dissenting opinion, picks up currents of discontent, and responds. An independent media would give voice to all groups, regardless of their affinity to the government. But the media is often not independent, either from choice and ideology or because it is dependent on advertising revenue from a friendly government. I was told the story of a leading Indian newspaper that suddenly found it was receiving no government advertising. When it asked why, it was told it was because it was excessively critical of government policy. The newspaper put together three thick dossiers of articles from the previous year, one with articles critical of government policy, one with articles positive of government policy, and one with articles critical of the previous government's policy. Each was about the same thickness. That is a tangible statement of independence; unfortunately, very few of our newspapers—and even fewer TV news channels and electronic media—can claim it.

An essential component of building a culture of development is to build social capital. That means building trust. In so diverse a society as India's, trust will have to be built step by step, with a government and institutions that must palpably represent the interests of all society, and especially its weakest members. We can use voice and dissent as a prompt to respond. Sometimes simply hearing people out patiently builds understanding. Understanding does not necessarily mean agreement, but it does mean respect.

A Culture of Entrepreneurship

In December 2003, I had the great pleasure of travelling around India for ten days with a visiting group from the US that included the great economist Gary Becker and his wife Guity Nashat.[24] One of the places we visited was Jaipur, and as every tourist does, we went to the Amber

---

24 The group included Gerhard and Regina Casper from Stanford, and Bob and Mairie Pritzker from Chicago. Those ten days were among the most educational, intellectually stimulating and enjoyable imaginable.

Fort. Gary and Guity, together with our other guests, rode an elephant up the hill to the gates of the fort. As we exited the fort an hour or so later, a man came up with some very nice photographs of Gary and Guity on the elephant, which Guity really liked. Gary bought two. Guity wanted more. Gary told our group he would demonstrate to us the law of diminishing marginal utility—the photographs would be useless to the photographer once we left. The price started at Rs 100 each, to which Gary said no. Rs 80—no; Rs 50—no (all the while getting closer to the car); Rs 40—no; Rs 30—no (now in the car); Rs 20—no, and he stopped. Gary said he'd get them for Rs 10 each, to which the photographer said no, and we left. The whole way down the hill, Gary got a lecture from Guity—on what possessed him to think that a photographer at the Amber Fort would operate according to the law of diminishing marginal utility. And what difference did the Rs 10 per photograph make?

Once you come down the hill from the Amber Fort and head back to Jaipur, there is a very pretty palace, the Jal Mahal, in the middle of a lake. We stopped to take a photograph. As we got out of the car, another man appeared—'Photographs, Sir?' The *same* photographs that Gary had not bought at the Amber Fort. Gary reached for them, 'Rs 20 is what I was offered up at the Fort'. 'No Sir, Rs 100 each.' 'Pay the man,' said Guity, which Gary did. For the rest of his life Gary told this story as an example of Indian entrepreneurship, with the subtext of how someone working in the informal sector seemed to understand incentives better than a Nobel laureate in economics. His point was that you did not need great education to be a great entrepreneur—some people just had it, and Indians clearly had it in abundance.

Many countries have traditions of entrepreneurship. When I started working on my Stanford dissertation on technical entrepreneurship in India, I needed to read much of the literature on entrepreneurship in various developing countries, and technical entrepreneurship in the US. Silicon Valley was, and is, clearly the model that the rest of the world sought to emulate in its technical entrepreneurship. Other countries have had varying experiences.

Taiwan had a few large primary producers and thousands of small firms—to begin with, firms exported directly from Taiwan, and then as wage levels rose and China opened up, through ventures they established on the Chinese mainland. Some of those firms are huge today—including the world's largest bicycle maker, Giant, and the world's largest contract manufacturer of electronics, Foxconn. A systematic programme in the 1980s to attract home highly educated Taiwanese in the US played a key role in establishing Taiwan as one of the world's leading suppliers of electronic hardware and semiconductors.[25] Entrepreneurship is said to be in the water in Taiwan, and China's manufacturing success owes it much.

In Japan and South Korea, the general sense was that the success of very large firms—the *chaebol* in Korea and the *keiretsu* in Japan—squeezed out entrepreneurs, including new technical entrepreneurs. Both countries systematically tried to foster entrepreneurs and technology-based start-ups in the late 1990s and 2000s. Japan would still seem to be struggling to make entrepreneurship part of the corporate culture, but South Korea has made substantial progress and today has a vibrant start-up ecosystem.

China is thoroughly confusing. Under Mao, private ownership was vilified, even outlawed. As China opened up, there was a flowering of enterprise. State-owned firms dominated for many years, but there were also thousands of foreign-owned enterprises. The great bulk of these were set up by firms based in Hong Kong, which served as a conduit for investment from Taiwan which was not officially allowed.

---

25 The largest semiconductor producer in the world, TSMC or Taiwan Semiconductor Manufacturing Corporation, was founded by Morris Chang in 1987. He was invited to move to Taiwan by the government after a thirty-year career at Texas Instruments and General Instruments in the US. He was first chairman of ITRI before founding TSMC.

For much of the 1990s and early 2000s, China attracted the second highest FDI (after the US) in the world, between $30 billion and $50 billion each year. Hong Kong accounted for over half of all this FDI into China. Most of this investment went into manufacturing, unlike India where the top five FDI sectors are services. In three years in the mid-1990s, China attracted $100 billion from 50,000 separate foreign investments.[26] While the mental construct is of big-ticket investments by Volkswagen or GE, the bulk of FDI into China was investment by Taiwanese and Hong Kong companies in small manufacturing plants with an average investment size of $2 million. China also had a unique organisational form—Town and Village Enterprises. These were officially owned by the local authorities, but were often run by the children of city officials, who over time seemed to end up as owners of the business—especially of the more successful ones. On a CII visit to China in the early 2000s to understand how it was so competitive, we kept asking the enterprises we visited as to who the owner was, a question that was always met with complete incomprehension. The Chinese tech giants—Alibaba, Baidu, Tencent and Huawei—either have close connections to the Communist Party or are threatened if they stray too far from what the state determines as desirable.

And finally to India. My story of Gary Becker and the photographer reflects centuries of entrepreneurial tradition. Harish Damodaran's fine book on entrepreneurship, *India's New Capitalists*, shows how Indian enterprise was dominated by traditional mercantile communities through the 1960s. He points out that the key prerequisite for trading across long distances was 'a mechanism for remitting large sums of money to remote corners. The facilitating financial instrument here was the hundi, a centuries-old Bania innovation akin to a bill of exchange.' The entire system worked on trust (remember the discussion earlier on social capital, particularly bonding capital), so trade was kept within

---

26 I owe this insight to Nick Hope, who spent many years in China as the local
    head of the World Bank, and later became a professor at Stanford University.

the community, and often within the extended family. Trade spread in proportion to the number of sons, brothers, cousins and nephews.[27] These traditional business communities spread far and wide. India exported entrepreneurs—controlling business in Nigeria, Kenya, Uganda and Fiji—and Indians were prominent among entrepreneurs in Spain, the UK (convenience stores) and the US (motels). In the nineteenth century, the Parsis ran a highly profitable trade (of, among other things, opium) with China, the Gujaratis with East Africa and the Middle and Near East, while the Chettiars of South India headed to South East Asia. In the inter-war period, the Chettiars essentially controlled business in Burma; there were 1,650 Chettiar firms in Burma in 1929, and in 1936 they held a quarter of the land in Burma's principal rice-growing districts. A visit to Chettinad even today is an unforgettable experience, the Chettiar palaces in a hundred villages around Karaikudi a unique part of our national heritage, a reminder of the power of entrepreneurship and community. (It could and should be the heart of a booming tourist industry.)

The Parsis were the first to move into manufacturing, starting the first textile mill owned by Indians in India in Bombay in 1854. Gujaratis soon followed in Ahmedabad. The Marwaris came much later, after World War I. But well past Independence, industry in India was controlled by the traditional trading communities, some of whom moved into manufacturing.

After Independence, things began to change, but slowly. Damodaran gives us two data points—in 1963, of India's 75 top industrial houses, just seven were Khatris (Thapar and Mahindra) or Brahmins (Martin Burn, Seshasayee, TVS, Amalgamations and the Kirloskars). 68 of the 75 were traditional mercantile communities— Gujarati Bania/Jains, non-Gujarati Bania/Marwari, Parsis, Sindhis, Chettiars and a couple others. After 1991, change speeded up. In

27   Daughters, sisters and nieces were unfortunately too rarely part of the picture.

2018, of the total 119 Indian billionaires in the Forbes list,[28] just over half (65) were from traditional mercantile castes. In the intervening years, there were several new entrants: 'The remaining 54 represent a mixed bag: 15 Brahmin,...12 Khatri/Arora, 5 Muslim, 4 Patidar, 3 Christian, 2 Jats, 2 Nadar', and one each of eleven other castes.[29] In my study of technical entrepreneurship in Pune in 1984, almost all of the technical entrepreneurs were from non-traditional mercantile backgrounds. Most were Brahmins and Marathas who had received a good technical education. Most complained that as they were from non-business families, they had to overcome substantial social pressure in their effort to venture out on their own.

In 2000, I wrote a paper for the annual Stanford conference on the Indian economy, where I compared the annual *Business India* listing of top firms in 1991 and 1999. The 1991 and 1983 listings showed little change; I cannot find the number now, but I think around 80 of the top 100 firms were the same in the two years. The 1999 listing showed great change from 1991: 48 of the 100 firms were new entrants. Whole new sectors were represented, such as pharmaceuticals, IT services, hotels and branded FMCG products. These new enterprises—such as Infosys, Wipro, NIIT, Dr Reddy's, Cipla, Dabur and Lupin—had replaced several older Marwari groups—the Modis (4 firms in the top 100 in 1991 to 0 in 1999), Mafatlals (4 to 0), Chhabrias (2 to 0), Birlas (12 to 9) and Thapars (4 to 1).[30] This churning of enterprise, the arrival of new industries like pharmaceuticals and software, entrepreneurs from non-traditional backgrounds, and a move away from commodity producers and licence permit entry is extremely

---

28 No connection!

29 Harish Damodaran, *India's New Capitalists: Caste, Business, and Industry in a Modern Nation* (New Delhi: Hachette, updated edition, 2018), xvii, 10–11, 51.

30 See Forbes, 'Doing business in India: What Has Liberalisation Changed?' in *Economic Policy Reforms and the Indian Economy*, edited by Anne Krueger (Chicago, IL: The University of Chicago Press), 2002.

healthy. Creative destruction, as the Austrian economist Schumpeter said, is what entrepreneurship is all about. (Damodaran, I should add, has a somewhat different take. He welcomes the entry of non-traditional entrepreneurs, but he attributes this significantly to the rise of regional political parties in the 1990s, and to new industrialists allied to those parties in Tamil Nadu, Andhra and Karnataka. Whatever the source, Indian entrepreneurship was becoming more widespread and less exclusive to a small number of communities.)

But there is a wider concern.

Damodaran's book is largely devoted to the period up to 2008, when he published the first edition. Writing an insightful foreword in 2018 for the second edition, he says, 'The defining development since then [2008]—more specifically, in the current decade—has been the destruction of capital alongside the drying up of the supply and growth of *new* entrepreneurs.' This is entirely consistent with what I found in 2015, when I did a quick update of the *Business India* Super 100 list. The 1999 list saw half the entrepreneurs change from 1991. The 2015 list showed much less change in the sixteen years from 1999, than in the eight years that led up to it. Indeed, the 2015 list shows re-entry of some firms that were on the list in 1991, dropped off in 1999, and then returned. Commodity businesses seem to play a bigger role, as do more service firms. For some reason, the entry of new entrepreneurs slowed down in the 2000s, which has persisted to the present day. The Indian market seemed to become less welcoming to entrepreneurship at precisely the time it was growing fastest. Why?

One of the classic economic papers of the twentieth century is Anne Krueger's 'Political Economy of the Rent-seeking Society'.[31] Government restrictions upon economic activity give rise to rents. These restrictions can include limits on entry (no foreign investment in multi-brand retail), protection (tariffs on steel, say, that push Indian prices up), or licences to operate (as was common across sectors before

---

31   Anne Krueger, 'Political Economy of the Rent-seeking Society,' *American Economic Review* (June 1974).

1991, and continues for sectors like telecom, mining and airlines). People then compete to capture those rents using legal (bidding processes, lobbying for higher tariffs) and illegal (bribes, favours from connections) means. Was there a fall in rent-seeking from 1991 to the early 2000s, and a return since? Rent-seeking thrives on political connections; this favours incumbents and deters new entrants. Is that what has been happening from 2004 to the present day? Add to that the increase in bureaucratic power and discretion since 2017. The last page of Kelkar and Shah's book has two sentences of great power: 'The private sector is fearful of the arbitrary power wielded by officials, and does not speak up. There is no voice, but there is an exit in the form of reduced investment.'[32] One form of this 'reduced investment' is reduced entrepreneurship.

Cultural Attractiveness: Using Our Soft Power

I began this book with a description of the international Family Business Summit in Udaipur. The ease with which Austrians, Japanese and Brazilians on their first visit to India adopted sherwanis and saris, danced to Bollywood songs, and fed on a variety of kebabs and dals is a statement of soft power. Great opportunity lies in India's soft power. Bollywood songs illustrate Indian culture at its most inclusive. The instruments, rhythm and tunes draw in the best of every culture, and produce something uniquely Indian.

As Guha points out, in 1980 India crossed the US as the world's largest film producer. The gap has only widened since: 'Filmgoing in India was now unarguably the most popular form of entertainment ever devised. In 1997, the fiftieth year of Independence, it was estimated that the daily cinema audience in India was 12 million—more than the population of many member-states of the United Nations.'[33]

---

32 Vijay Kelkar and Ajay Shah, *In Service of the Republic: The Art and Science of Economic Policy* (New Delhi: Penguin Random House, 2019), 388.
33 Ramachandra Guha, *India After Gandhi: The History of the World's Largest Democracy* (New Delhi, Picador Macmillan India, first edition, 2007), 722.

Bollywood has long been among our most successful exports. As we have opened Forbes Marshall offices in places as far-flung as Cairo, Jakarta, Ho Chi Minh and Lagos, my colleagues tell me that the most popular local films are often from Bollywood. I can think of any number of journeys in taxis from Seoul to Tehran to Malta where the driver, after examining me carefully in the rear-view mirror and discovering I'm from India, will say 'Shah Rukh Khan' (assuming that I must know him). Vikram Seth's first book, *From Heaven Lake,* is an autobiographical account of his hike across central China and Tibet.[34] He describes his arrival in a pre-reform Turfan, a hundred miles from Urumqi in north-western China. Turfan is even today no metropolis; in 1981 much less so. Out on a walk one evening, he comes across a musical troupe that is performing songs, with different members from the audience volunteering to sing:

> It is now my turn to sing. There is no real choice. It will have to be the theme song from *Awara (The Wanderer),* a sentimental Indian movie from the 1950s that is astonishingly popular in China. It comes as a shock to me sometimes to hear it hummed on the streets of Nanjing— to be transported without warning back to both India and childhood. No sooner have I begun than I find that the musicians have struck up the accompaniment behind me: they know the tune better than I do. The tubby man with the twirling moustaches is singing along with me, in Hindi at that.

To connect with locals in 1981 by singing a Raj Kapoor song from the 1950s—which everyone in this remote part of China seems to know: talk about soft power.

The chapter it is from, 'A People's Entertainments', was regrettably omitted from the otherwise even more magnificent second edition.

34   Vikram Seth, *From Heaven Lake: Travels through Sinkiang and Tibet* (New Delhi: Penguin Random House, 1983), 13–14.

Contrast China. As Martin Wolf says, 'people respect China, but they do not like it'.[35] Guha calls China 'a superpower without a soul' in a 2018 article. The strap for his article says, 'The rise and consolidation of British global hegemony in the 19th century, and of American global hegemony in the 20th century, were made (slightly) more palatable by the culture of the superpower, by the literature, art, music, film, and sport brought with it.'[36]

The same applies to sport. Cricket is the quintessential English game—except that it isn't. Football is by far England's most popular sport.[37] Hockey is the Indian national game—except that cricket is much more popular. When I was growing up, some leading Indian players would spend part of the year playing English County cricket. Today, I do not hear of English County cricket (I assume it does still exist). Instead, the best players in the world are today part of various teams in the Indian Premier League, an annual entertainment that make up the sport's richest matches.

Both cricket and Bollywood, as Guha points out, are as successful as they are because they build on India's pluralism. Both are truly representative of the Indian nation, drawing on every community and every region without discrimination. Gary Becker showed years ago that the baseball teams in the US that first stopped discriminating against black players were so successful that in one or two years all teams stopped discriminating. If you don't discriminate, you win.

I can go on and on. A shop called Varana, in London's most up-market shopping area (it is just off Bond Street), sells beautiful clothes, all made of the finest cashmere, silk and linen, and all designed and made in India. The clothes have a uniquely universal aesthetic—

35 Martin Wolf, 'The fading light of liberal democracy,' *Financial Times*, 22 December 2020.

36 Ramachandra Guha, 'A superpower without a soul: In search of Chinese culture', *The Wire,* 12 June 2018.

37 Fishing is supposed to be more popular. But only the English would consider an activity where you stand silently in the rain, holding a pole, for hours at on end, with no result, a sport.

they are neither Western nor Eastern, in a way that only India can make natural. In the same way, the British national dish is said to be chicken tikka masala. And an Indian company, Tata, is Britain's largest manufacturer. No one is threatened by any of this, and no government has felt it necessary to have the Canadians arrest the daughter of the founder.[38]

This is India's opportunity. Indian culture—our music, film, sport, dance, dress, food—appears to have an inherent attractiveness to being adopted by countries all round the world. This gives us an influence and soft power that we can use much more. It is this great strength, too, that we put at risk when we behave at home in a manner that is intolerant, parochial and non-inclusive. Instead of whining about 'unfair' criticism and bridling at an 'unconscionable interference in India's internal affairs', we should be proud of being held to a higher standard.

Conclusions: Building a Will to Develop Out of Our Cultural Leadership

The last issue of *The Economist* for 2020 had an article on the farm protests in Delhi, which ended with the words, 'India's rulers would be wise to learn its lessons: in such a diverse and noisy country, you cannot make one rule for all, and you cannot make rules at all without first winning people to your cause.'[39] Our heterogeneity limits the scope for government intervention. There is less opportunity for the government to follow policies of detailed decision-making. Its choices of technology, or foreign investors, or location will be met by accusations of favouritism, corruption and crony capitalism. Instead, we must rely on broader rules and incentives, available to all. We need

---

38 Sorry! (The reference, of course, is to the daughter of the founder of the Chinese company Huawei, arrested in Vancouver on the US' prompting.)

39 *The Economist*, 'A lonely furrow: India's government is undermining its own reforms', 16 December 2020.

discussion and debate as we build a consensus around policies, and we must get alignment by persuasion, not diktat. So how does one then harness our culture for development?

We must start with the right aspiration for growth: double-digit growth, year on year, for decades. That is in the interest of all Indians. Policies must present it as so, and work to make it so. We have come a long way in seeing rapid economic growth as crucial to our development, a perception we must sustain in spite of our current difficulties. Our growth target should be an expression of our will to develop, stemming from a sense of backwardness, of our poor relative standing, and clarity on how much we have to achieve. This sense of backwardness must be shared by all people. Leaders must speak the facts of our current position and aspire to catch up. Catching up will come from the humility that enables us to learn from the best, but enough cultural confidence to then improve on this best. We must foster trust above all. Especially trust in institutions that must be seen as equally fair in their treatment of all. Equality before the law has to be felt by all in India—every community, state, gender, nationality and ideology. As our size and diversity limits our natural social capital, we need better and better contract enforcement to build trust step by step. This trust must be built in both directions— by citizens of the government, and by the government of its people. It must show in our making laws and regulations that assume honesty, not dishonesty.

No one, least of all in India, expects the government to be perfect. But an honest statement of its competence and where it needs to build it—in public health at the current time, for instance—could help. What we do not need is the rhetoric and hubris of tall claims, which keeps us from learning. And during the deep crisis of the second wave of Covid, we certainly expected the government to coordinate the supply of oxygen and vaccines, not the optics of 'positivity' and denouncing negative international coverage. Here is Laxman, yet again:

Of course, socialism is applicable to us also. But we promised it to the people and we must give it to them first!

Hypocrisy destroys trust; authenticity builds it.

Trust, also, in our entrepreneurs, who must be respected for creating wealth. There will be some who are greedy and indolent, but we must draw a line between behaviour we do not like that is legal, and behaviour that is illegal and must be punished. Business must repay this trust—in word and deed a point I will return to in the last chapter.

Finally, we should recognise the enormous strength that is India's soft power. On a CII visit to the US a few years ago, we had a stormy meeting with the United States Trade Representative (USTR). India had just blocked progress on a key WTO agreement. What came across in the meeting was that the USTR, Mike Froman, seemed to be in equal measure as irritated with India's stand as he was interested in India's progress. We have an abundance of international goodwill, something I have experienced on every CII visit to countries around the world. Indian business must build on this goodwill, investing much more strongly in local operations overseas.

India at its best cannot be matched. To end this chapter, here are three favourite moments of the last few years. In 2017, as CII president, I gave a talk at the National Defence College in Delhi. This institute brings in 100 younger leaders from our armed forces, the IAS, and a few younger members of the armed forces of friendly countries, including the UK, Bhutan, Nepal, Bangladesh, the US and Australia. The freewheeling spirit of intellectual exchange left me impressed and inspired. A few months later, Rakesh Mohan's book, *India Transformed*, was released at a function in Delhi. The book was launched jointly by Dr Manmohan Singh and Arun Jaitley. Manmohan Singh did not speak, but Arun Jaitley gave a speech of such warmth and grace, acknowledging not only Rakesh Mohan's exceptional contribution to the reform process, but the leadership of Manmohan Singh, and his incredible legacy in creating a better future for India. Such acts are acts of statesmanship; they build countries. And in January 2020, protests against the Citizenship Amendment Act (CAA) rocked Delhi. The same month my niece and I were at the Jaipur Literature Festival. CAA saw the Indian government at its worst, passing a terrible law using a brute majority, stifling debate, deterring and delaying constitutional questions being taken up by the Supreme Court, and using the Delhi Police to harass peaceful protesters. My niece and I went to Jaipur depressed. A few days at JLF was invigorating. We attended session upon session that were demonstrations in free speech and critical thought. And the audience, the 400,000 who make JLF the world's largest literary festival, consisted overwhelmingly of young people, especially college students. They had done their homework, had read the books closely, and asked perceptive and specific questions of the many authors wandering around. They renewed our hope. We would be in safe hands if the young attendees at JLF could come to represent India's future.

11

Politics: Authentic, Open, Democratic, Listening

The frustrating thing about India is that whatever you can rightly say about it, the opposite is also true.

—Joan Robinson to her student Amartya Sen

With the growth of nationalism, man has become the greatest menace to man.

—Rabindranath Tagore

It is easier to preach passionately to a country that it should adopt some vast, revolutionary ideology and centralise and simplify and subordinate everything to a single goal or a single man or a single party. It is not difficult to call for a return to the past, to tell man to turn their backs on foreign devils, to live solely on one's own resources, proud, independent, unconcerned. India has heard such voices. Tagore understood this, paid tribute to it, and resisted it.

—Isaiah Berlin

I don't make jokes. I just watch the government and report the facts.

—Will Rogers

Most children revere their parents. I'm no exception, but mine gave me constant cause. My view of the proper relationship between government and business was formed by conversations at the dinner table while growing up. Listening to my parents talk in the 1970s about some new policy folly, and its impact on our business, formed a lasting impression.[1] My brother and I inherited two deeply held principles. That we should never enter a field of business where success depended on the government (whether through connections or permits) to be successful. And that we should never do anything that kept us from sleeping well at night. The end result was that we liked government at a distance, never inviting anyone from the government to visit us at work or hosting ministers or bureaucrats at home. We did not wish to oblige, nor wish to be obliged. As we got more involved in CII, especially at the national level, it was a new experience to interact with the government at close quarters. We were always bemused by our fellow industrialists who seemed to live for that five-minute conversation with a minister on the sidelines of some function.

As I said in the first chapter, being president of CII gives one the opportunity of seeing government up close. I was impressed by the intelligence, commitment and hard work of many of our past and current ministers and senior bureaucrats. I was depressed by how unprepared, unmindful of international best practice, diverted by optics over content, and petty some of these same great minds were. I kept a daily journal through my year as president, trying to capture not only what I did, but what I thought noteworthy, and how it made me feel. This chapter draws on those experiences, as I try to connect the dots of the politics and political economy we need. In so doing, I will return to the principles that provide the foundation for leadership that I mentioned in chapter 1. This is the *how* of leadership. Principles of inclusiveness, openness, and a strong and independent private sector are critical. And I spend much of this chapter on a variety of practices and norms that provide cultural-leadership and require a liberal intellect. I return to my theme throughout this book that

---

1   My father ran the company. My mother ran finance.

while there is much for India to learn, improve and change, we have a unique foundation of culture and norms of behaviour on which we can build leadership.

The How of Leadership

Designing policy for inclusiveness: Inclusive growth has been the official policy of both the previous and present governments. How do we achieve it? The previous government put in place MGNREGA,[2] a rural employment programme. The present government has provided direct benefit transfers to over a hundred million farmers. But these are support programmes; they are not policies of inclusion. Inclusion requires a much more institutional approach, as we saw in chapter 9. Education and health are the primary tools for social inclusion. That is why industry should be concerned with educational outcomes. Putting people to work in productive jobs spreads wealth around, and provides the consumption power to drive economic growth. That requires a focus on labour-intensive manufacturing and tourism, sectors that can put millions to work. It is this that should attract the focus of policy. Developing 'sunrise' sectors like artificial intelligence and robotics can be left to the private sector.

An inclusive approach to institutions must extend across government. Intellectual property laws that provide as much weight to disclosure and diffusion as to protecting the inventor would be more inclusive. Implementing competition laws to prevent market dominance in key sectors favour both the consumer and innovation. A frequent comment is that we need a few firms to become our national champions, and policy should favour such firms. I do not

---

2   The Mahatma Gandhi National Rural Employment Guarantee Act, MGNREGA, assures 100 days of paid unskilled work to every adult in rural India. It was passed by the UPA government in 2005, and extends to every district in the country. Narendra Modi criticised the scheme while in the Opposition and in the 2014 election campaign, but has supported it and expanded it in office.

agree. The *chaebol* in South Korea acted in close concert with the government, and became huge. At one point, I believe the four largest *chaebol* (Samsung, LG, Daewoo and Hyundai) had a combined sales turnover that exceeded national GDP.[3] Our needs are different. India needs a thousand multinationals, spanning many industries, operating around the world. Our model should not be South Korea but Germany, with its thousands of *Mittelstand* companies. Any policy that depends for its success on the government picking winners is bad policy. In our bad old days of industrial licensing, there was an official policy against bigness. But only large firms were able to develop the connections in Delhi, installing 'liaison officers' or 'government-relations departments', to get those licences. This kept new entrants out, and became an extractive policy. This is also the problem with the current Production-linked Incentive scheme we discussed in chapter 4. By granting incentives to individual firms we benefit a few. If our commerce and industry minister instead focused his energy on the ease of doing business, he would benefit all industry—PLI is a policy of extraction; EODB, a policy of inclusion.

Openness to trade: We discussed trade policy and our international stance at length in chapter 4. Protection benefits producers (and when it is primary producers it harms other industries) and harms consumers. It is a tax on consumers, who are much more numerous than producers, but in a much more dispersed way. The Indian consumer pays more for her air conditioner because of the 30 per cent tariff on import of a complete unit. She pays more for a range of goods because steel carries a tariff of 12.5 per cent, which makes the entire engineering industry less competitive.[4] Openness to trade, then, is a policy of inclusion.

---

3   If you're wondering how that's possible, it is because GDP measures value added and not sales, and firm turnover includes what is contributed by overseas subsidiaries. The comparison is still instructive.

4   A friend in the pump business in Coimbatore messaged me in January 2021, attaching a news item reporting record steel company profits, with

I attended a Board of Trade meeting chaired by the commerce minister on my first day as president of CII. Of thirty different industry associations represented, CII was the sole industry voice that argued in favour of an outward-looking stance. Even within CII, the loudest voices are often those asking for protection. The meetings we convened with different industry groups during the final RCEP negotiations were dominated by voices wanting protection of the Indian market. But when we took a poll at a CII meeting of the country's leading industrialists, 57 per cent present felt it was a mistake to drop out of RCEP, while 27 per cent supported the government's decision. This says to me that the loudest voices may not be the most numerous. We hear those who are inward-looking and seek protection. It is those who are quietly and happily doing business around the world that we must see as our future. Our trade policy must suit their needs.

This is not new. The so-called Bombay Club of industrialists of the early 1990s argued vociferously against the opening up of the economy. At the pre-budget meetings that Manmohan Singh called from 1992 to 1996, each industrialist would begin his (no hers were present then) comments by congratulating the finance minister. Most would specifically compliment him on liberalisation, including opening up on trade. This was good for everyone, they said, but an exception of course needed to be made for their own sector. The honourable exceptions were Ratan Tata, Keshub Mahindra and whoever was that year's president of CII. We hear some of those same voices calling for protection today. What is new is that the government is listening to them—and protecting industry.

Openness to migration: I have long held the view that all people should have the right to live and work wherever they choose. I will not try to make the case for migration here, but simply point the reader to the second chapter in Abhijit Banerjee and Esther Duflo's *Good*

---

the comment, 'All our pump raw material costs have become so high! Pump prices have skyrocketed. Customers in export markets are not ready to pay.'

Economics for Hard Times. They make the economic case for migration (internal and international), and suggest how we can address the concerns of both the migrants and the locals affected by the migration.

The best and the brightest made their way to Britain in the nineteenth century, just as they did to the US in the twentieth. There is little indication that this is happening with China in the twenty-first century. India, for the reasons of culture we discussed in the previous chapter and as we will see again later, has a much better chance.

The late 1980s saw a major change in policy towards those of Indian origin residing overseas. They were finally made welcome. The Rajiv Gandhi government invited Indians living abroad to participate in India's development, much as the overseas Chinese had done.[5] The Vajpayee government then introduced a Persons of Indian Origin card that amounted to a permanent visa. From 2005 onwards, the Manmohan Singh government provided that any person of Indian origin was eligible for an Overseas Citizen of India card,[6] which gives the holder the permanent right to visit, live and work freely in India. There are an estimated 32 million persons of Indian origin (defined as having at least one Indian parent, grandparent, or great-grandparent) residing overseas. There are 6 million OCI holders. India's diaspora is also the world's largest, at 18 million, who remitted $79 billion home in 2019, the world's highest, and over 3 per cent of our GDP.

We are, unfortunately, reversing some of these sensible policies of the past. In March 2021, the government issued new rules for OCIs. Overseas Citizens of India will henceforth be treated more as foreigners than citizens. OCIs now need special permission to 'undertake research and to undertake any missionary or Tabligh or mountaineering or journalistic activities'. This is a step back to a

---

5   Hong Kong and Taiwan accounted for over half of Direct Foreign Investment into China in the 1990s and early 2000s. See the previous chapter.

6   India does not permit dual citizenship. OCI was a way of finessing the issue, without calling for a constitutional amendment.

more parochial time. Laxman captured the implications best in the 1970s:

Next time if someone asks, just say, 'I want to be a doctor when I grow up'. No need to add, 'I want to be a doctor and emigrate'!

Several of the names that have featured in this book are persons of Indian origin living overseas. Amartya Sen, Abhijit Banerjee, Raghuram Rajan, Arvind Panagariya, Arvind Subramanian, Jagdish Bhagwati, Kaushik Basu, Devesh Kapur and Milan Vaishnav have either played key policy roles in India, or done exceptional academic work on India. We must encourage all comers.

When I became president of CII in April 2016, Raghuram Rajan was still RBI Governor. Rajan is not only an outstanding monetary economist, but a deep-thinking public intellectual. His speeches on everything from tolerance to our economic growth performance irritated the government. At a time when we were proudly proclaiming India as the world's fastest-growing large economy, he quoted the fifteenth-century Dutch philosopher Erasmus, 'In the land of the blind, the one-eyed man is King.' This was accurate. India had overtaken China not because we had grown faster but because China had grown slower. But this was raining on a parade. Rather than deal with the comment at face value, the reaction took a personal tone. One of our ministers raised questions over his connection with India; a noisy MP from the ruling party asked whether he was adequately 'committed'. A leading industrialist that I ran into at Dubai airport argued that Rajan 'did not understand India'. And the Press Trust of India correspondent in, of all places, Washington, DC, asked me if I didn't think that Raghuram Rajan was less fit to be Governor because he had a Green Card. The question irritated me, so I asked him if he himself had a Green Card as he had been in Washington so long (he had), and if he felt this made him a less effective PTI correspondent.[7]

Post Rajan's announcement that he would not seek a second term, I needed to do a series of interviews. The press wanted to know what impact it would have on India's standing in the world to have lost one of the world's leading monetary experts as the leader of our central bank. I was clear it would have no implication on our standing in the world. But it could impact our ability to attract the best and the brightest NRIs to come to India, and we needed to make up for losing Rajan by getting a few brilliant NRIs to return to assignments in the government. But after a welcome hiatus—when our government seemed open to outside input—we seem to have returned to being inward-looking. I am

---

7   We got zero coverage from the interview.

particularly nostalgic for the outstanding economists this government had in its first term—Arvind Panagariya, Arvind Subramanian and Raghuram Rajan. The importance of having world-class economists in government is critical to sound policymaking. It is not enough to provide advice from outside government; they must be *in* government, both giving advice and working out how to make the advice happen. Arvind Panagariya's *Free Trade,* discussed in chapter 4, is dedicated to Jagdish Bhagwati, who famously remarked of the RSS under the previous NDA government in 1998, 'Who are your economists? If these guys are economists, then I am a Bharat Natyam dancer.' Modi-II has done a poor job of employing world-leading economists. To paraphrase Oscar Wilde, to lose one great economist is a misfortune. To lose three is carelessness.

A Strong, Open, Inclusive and Independent Private Sector

All four qualifiers are important. 'Strong' reflects the ability to be successful in the long run. 'Independent' is vis-à-vis the government. 'Inclusive' operates at two levels—firms must set out, as I argued in chapter 3, to directly contribute to including as many of our 1.4 billion population in growth. But inclusive, also, in entrepreneurship. We are the world's most diverse country. This diversity needs to reflect, too, in our entrepreneurs. As we saw in our discussion of entrepreneurship, the dominance of traditional business communities has waned since Independence, but we need to go much further. We need many more successful entrepreneurs who are women, Muslims, Dalits. *Defying the Odds: The Rise of Dalit Entrepreneurs* tells us the stories of twenty such successes. India, the authors say, 'has until now eschewed the transformational possibilities of entrepreneurship as a tool of social empowerment'. Their book is about 'those few who, through a combination of grit, ambition, drive and hustle—and some luck— have managed to pull themselves up ... inspirational stories that are hopefully also aspirational for the millions of young Dalits ... who are trying to make something of their lives'.[8]

'Open' also operates at two levels—Indian industry must be open to the world, in exports, investment and imports. But open, also, in ease of entry for new entrepreneurs. We need much more churn in our top firms with new industrial sectors and new firms replacing the old. A good political economy would assume a strong, independent, inclusive and open private sector.

Raghuram Rajan's book, *The Third Pillar,* is an argument for strengthening the community in addition to the two other pillars (state and market). His comments on the Indian private sector are telling:

> India also has a private sector that is still dependent on the state, which makes it a feeble constraint on it. So India has the paradox of having an ineffective but only moderately limited state. India's challenge in the years to come is not its democracy ... but the need to strengthen both state capacity and private-sector independence ... unlike the United States, where a still-independent private sector criticises government policy, including on social and political issues that are not directly related to their business, the Indian private sector—the market pillar—largely applauds all government policy. A determined government, despite being ineffective in most areas that benefit the public, can still cow the private sector and the press with threats, or bribe them with credit or government contracts ... If India is to bury the spectre of authoritarianism and cronyism, if Indian democracy is to be better informed and a stronger check on the state and corruption, India needs a more competitive, and thereby independent, private sector with higher public status. It needs many

---

8   Devesh Kapur, D. Shyam Babu, and Chandra Bhan Prasad, *Defying the Odds: The Rise of Dalit Entrepreneurs* (New Delhi: Vintage Books/Random House India, 2014), xvi.

more small and medium enterprises to grow and flourish, providing competition to the established business houses.[9]

The Confederation of Indian Industry as a development institution: In 2008, when Chandrajit Banerjee became Director General of CII, he told me that CII should not be seen as just an industry association, but as a development institution. When I first heard that at the time, my reaction was 'I'm not sure that's right. We're not the Government of India.' By the end of a year as president of CII, I was no longer so sure. The DG of CII runs it; those of us who serve in the presidium for three years come and go. Some office-bearers get hooked by the opportunity to contribute to wider development and continue being active in CII, even if it is only to play the classic past-president role of exercising authority without responsibility. Others finish their time in office and vanish. Chandrajit needs to deal with them all. Watch him on the dais at a CII programme (Zoom is much less entertaining, as he can switch his camera off): one can see him passing notes to the president of what to say or who to call on, while giving side instructions to a staff member on some other issue, rearranging the dais while the programme is under way and various ministers drop out, exceed their time or delay their arrival, all the while drafting a message on his phone. I've often said that if there was a Nobel Prize for multitasking, he would get it every year.

CII's range of activities is huge. CII does not just advocate policy but helps the government formulate and implement it. Eleven Centres of Excellence and several special divisions offer services in environmental sustainability, competitiveness, quality, logistics and start-ups. The membership, spread across sixty-six zones in all of India's states, enables companies to network with each other. During the Covid crisis, the CII secretariat, supported by some key members,

---

9   Raghuram Rajan, *The Third Pillar: How Markets and the State Leave the Community Behind* (New Delhi: HarperCollins India, 2019), 273–74.

worked to advocate a clear policy-agenda for economic recovery, and also helped put together a supply-chain for the essential medical supplies we lacked—PPEs, ventilators, masks, hand sanitisers, oxygen, drugs. Organising meals for migrant workers stuck in various metros across the country went together with helping industry address the fallout from an uncoordinated and haphazard implementation of the lockdown by the Centre and states, and an equally messy restart.

But what does CII as a development institution stand for? As discussed in chapter 4, on trade policy, CII stands *in general* for openness and free markets.[10] CII defines an Indian firm as one which operates in and manufactures in India, regardless of whether it is foreign or Indian owned. And industry should not seek incentives and concessions, as our firms do not want concessions, they want an easy business environment.

As we went around the country talking to CII members, we tried to follow two additional principles: that a CII office-bearer speaks first for India, then for Indian industry, then for CII—and never for our own firm. I also added that India does not mean the Indian government. This distinction is important. CII's credibility as an institution depends on having an independent, strong voice. CII's views may coincide with those of the government—but they may also not. On GST, CII has argued consistently for fewer rates, no exemptions, scrapping the NAA, and implementing the electronic payments linkage system. CII seeks to provide an independent view based on principles. At times, this independent view may be different from official policy; it might even be contrary to it. It is still important for us as a country, for CII's credibility as a development institution, to articulate this independent view in a forthright manner. I believe it is possible to be positive, independent, forthright and polite all at the same time. The country greatly needs the voice of strong and independent private-sector institutions.

---

10   I stress 'in general'. Too many CII members want protection and intervention, but openness and free markets is broadly the stance of CII as an institution.

The government relies on industry institutions such as CII to help in formulating policy and organising domestic and international events. A wise government would also rely on them to help implement policy—driving an ease of doing business programme, for example, and coordinating the nitty-gritty work of making change happen across Union, state and local governments.

Criticism and the private sector: Our government has varied in its response to criticism. Some have been oblivious to it; others jump on every word. In the aftermath of demonetisation, I participated in an interview on its impact on growth. I made the comment that with a revival of agricultural growth to 6 per cent (with a good monsoon after two drought years) and the Seventh Pay Commission award also taking effect,[11] the previous year's 7.9 per cent GDP growth should have risen to over 9 per cent. But growth had slipped to 7 per cent. I concluded that demonetisation had cost the country 2 per cent of GDP. That same evening an irate minister called to complain about what I had said. (No matter that the finance minister, in an early statement on demonetisation, had said it probably had an impact of 2 per cent too!) The minister asked how the government could work in partnership with CII when its president criticised government policy. The story went on and on for a week or two, but I found it quite a dispiriting experience. Why did what I said, correct or wrong, bother the government so much?

Consider two other instances. In early 2015, Deepak Parekh of HDFC made the comment that 'After nine months, there is a little bit of impatience creeping in as to why no changes are happening and why this is taking so long having effect on the ground.' A few months

---

11 The Pay Commission is periodically set up by the Union government to recommend changes in salaries of its employees. In calculating GDP, government output is measured by how much it spends. So each time government employees get a pay rise, GDP rises too.

earlier, he had said, 'Uncertainty hurts and, therefore, it should go. It is time the government started taking decisions.'[12] In December 2019, Rahul Bajaj, chairman of the Bajaj Group, made the comment to Home Minister Amit Shah, Finance Minister Nirmala Sitharaman and Commerce and Industry Minister Piyush Goyal at an awards function that 'During UPA [the previous government], we could abuse anyone. You are doing good work, but if we want to openly criticise you, there is no confidence you will appreciate that. I may be wrong but everyone feels that.'[13] These comments made the headlines across the media, with our talk shows organising their usual shouting matches several evenings running. An industrialist criticising the government should not make the headlines. That must be a basic feature of an independent private sector.

In CII, we always say that we do not see any merit in criticising in public. We would rather offer constructive criticism in private. I agree with that approach—public criticism fosters defensiveness more than receptiveness. My experience, though, is that we very rarely (and that too only with highly selected ministers) offer criticism in private too. I will make an assertion. I know *no* industrialist today who thinks this government is open to criticism. And it is not only industrialists. One of our leading economists, returning from a pre-budget meeting led by the Prime Minister in January 2021, said people were not giving bad news to the government. The current environment, he said, was such that the truth was not being told. And he included himself in the absence of truth-telling. This is too bad. If senior government officials do not know how things actually are, how will they fashion the right policies?

My experience with criticism has occasionally been more positive. My monthly column in *Business Standard* has tried to be as independent and forthright, as it is positive and polite (well, I think it is polite!). I

---

12 *Business Standard*, 'Deepak Parekh sharply revises up rating of Modi government', 30 August 2016.

13 *Business Standard,* 'Without fear or favour', 1 January 2020.

wrote several columns making the case for RCEP, and criticising our decision to drop out in 2019. The day after one of these columns appeared, I met a minister in Delhi on a completely separate matter. He started by complimenting me on my column. He liked the column, he said, and had wanted to phone me to say so, but had held off because he was 'a loyal member of the government'. Our government is not a monolith. At any point in time, there will be views circulating that differ from the prevailing official line. Those views may well be the kind of reform that's needed. By speaking out, we strengthen the hand of these reformers within the government.

For industry to operate without fear, it must also operate without favour. We cannot speak truth to power if we plead for favours and special privileges. For too many years, Indian industry has looked to the government for help—for protection from imports, for tax relief to help boost demand, for concessions and incentives to boost investment, for a word put in with a bank to renew a loan, and (in the bad old days of the 1970s) a licence to manufacture a particular product. It is time to shed this culture of supplication, of deference, of vassaldom. It is little better if deference is bought by import tariffs and incentives such as PLI instead of by fear. We must deal with the government as equals, praising where praise is due, but criticising when criticism is called for. We must stop asking the government for things. Let the government respond by trusting industry to do right. And let industry repay that trust. Industry and government must be as tough, demanding and unforgiving of each other as they are mutually respectful.

The final word from Laxman in the 1970s, which could have been drawn yesterday:

I think you should forgive him, sir. He says he had honestly no intention of hurting your feelings when he called you a crazy old buffoon!

The How of Leadership: Cultural Leadership and Liberal Intellect

My favourite cartoonist Laxman was simultaneously comic and tragic. Comic, in the brilliance and accuracy with which he caught a particular moment in history. Tragic, in the brilliance and accuracy with which he depicted waste of opportunity and the unnecessary poverty that resulted. One of his favourite themes was hypocrisy. The 1970s were his heyday as they gave him so much opportunity.

Hypocrisy and authenticity: I recall an occasion in my year as president, when CII hosted two Prime Ministers. (I provide no clues to enable you to guess which.) The schedule was for them to spend fifteen minutes with each other (they were meeting for the first time) in an informal discussion before we all went out on to the stage. After a brief greeting, they spent the entire time just staring ahead of them, not saying a word to each other, while I hung around in the background wondering if I should attempt to entertain them. Fifteen minutes up, we went out on to the stage. They were laughing and chatting, reaching out to each other's chairs. Instead of me, they now had a real audience—three thousand people and dozens of cameras. I do not need my leaders to be superhuman or saints (much as they might try to look the part). I suppose politics is partly theatre, but I'd rather seek out professional actors for my entertainment.

Two more examples, concerning alcohol. Indian politicians are petrified of being photographed holding a glass of alcohol in their hand. At a state banquet in an unnameable capital, I was fortunate to still be president designate. This enabled me to sit at the second table; the president had to be at table one with the chief minister. We were all served with good alcohol. No alcohol at table one, though the chief minister was known to like a drink as much as my predecessor and me. At another programme, the opening dinner was held in a spectacular setting. Here, I was at table one and the waiters were bringing us drinks at the table. We all had an excellent whisky—except the Governor of the state and a Member of Parliament, both of whom were sitting with us and seemed to look distinctly thirsty. At some point, well before dinner was served, the waiter brought the Governor a bowl of soup, with ice cubes floating in it. Which he started to drink with his soup spoon with some relish. The MP asked for the same soup—the waiter started to explain in a low voice, and the MP sent him away with the clear instruction 'I want THAT soup'.

I agree. Liquor, night clubs, good food, travel facilities, etc. will help tourist traffic, but what guarantee is there that our own people will not start enjoying them?

Authenticity is to me a hugely underrated value. Treating citizens as adults, telling them how things really stand, reminding people that politicians are as frail in their morality as other human beings, not pretending that the government has a cure for everything, admitting mistakes—these, to me, are as much a mark of statesmanship as putting country before party and the advocacy of unpopular, but right, reform. I have little time for the minister who tells you in person what he really thinks, and then gets on a public stage and says the opposite. And I actively distrust an industrialist who recites one-on-one what a disaster the government has been, and then on the dais praises it in the tones of the hallelujah chorus. Soon after a budget (a very average affair),[14] a prominent industrialist in a closed-door session referred to the finance minister as the greatest in India's history, and the budget as the best in living memory. The most surprised expression in the room was, you guessed it, the finance minister's. We are not respected when we act this way. After all, do our ministers really like it when we go and see them and waste their time telling them how wonderful they are? I genuinely believe that our ministers want to do their best for the country. We can help them with ideas, honest feedback, and, yes, criticism. We do not help them by being poodles.

The alternative to treating citizens as adults is to see them as poodles, sheep or, worse, a pack of wolves to be set loose. This is what Donald Trump did when he encouraged his supporters to march on the Capitol in January 2021. And this is what the great writer George Orwell is describing when he says: '[...], because in his own joyless mind he feels it with exceptional strength, knows that human beings *don't* only want comfort, safety, short working-hours, hygiene, birth-control, and, in general, common sense; they also, at least intermittently, want struggle and self-sacrifice, not to mention drums, flags and loyalty-parades.' Sound familiar? The missing first word in the Orwell quote is 'Hitler', and the quote is from Orwell's 1940 review of *Mein Kampf*.[15]

Broad shoulders: To continue in the same vein, our government often reacts to things that they should ignore. In early 2016, The Jawaharlal Nehru University Students Union president Kanhaiya Kumar gave a speech on campus attacking the RSS.[16] He was arrested and charged with sedition. For days there were protests and talk shows

---

14 Sometime in the last ten years!
15 George Orwell, 'Review of *Mein Kampf*', in *The New English Weekly*, 21 March 1940. One of the great statements of liberalism.
16 The Rashtriya Swayamsevak Sangh, or RSS, is a right-wing, Hindu-nationalist volunteer organisation. The BJP is its political wing, though there is no formal relationship.

arguing for and against. At a meeting with one of our most pragmatic and effective ministers, we were ushered into his room while he was on the phone discussing the issue with another minister. At the end of our meeting, I asked if he would mind me making an unsolicited comment—which was that the government would have been best off ignoring Kanhaiya Kumar's speech. It would never have been reported in every paper, and I for one would never have read it or heard of him if the government had not reacted so strongly to it and made it such a big issue. The government had made him into a hero. The minister indulged me as I said this, and then just said, 'I agree with you.' Kanhaiya Kumar is now a member of the Opposition.

The current government may have made prickliness into a fine art, but it does not have a monopoly on it. A few years ago, the wit of a minister in the previous government, Shashi Tharoor, regularly got him into trouble. During the global financial crisis in 2009, ministers were expected to no longer travel business class. Asked by a journalist if he would travel cattle class when he next went to Kerala, Shashi Tharoor tweeted: 'Absolutely, in cattle class out of solidarity with all our holy cows.' Another hoo-hah, with statements from the Congress spokesperson, and embarrassed comparisons with Sonia Gandhi who had travelled economy. (So?) And our TV media, who clearly have nothing better to do, running the usual talk shows and treating as a profound statement of government perspective what was at most a witty quip.

But we also do better. Every year, there are two training programmes in Delhi for India's heads of missions from around the world. The CII president usually interacts with them. I found the session enormously stimulating—a free and frank discussion on India, Indian industry, our prospects, and the role of our diplomatic corps in our prospects. It helped that the session was chaired by our then foreign secretary, and now minister for external affairs, S. Jaishankar.

I always found interacting with Finance Minister Arun Jaitley a complete pleasure. You could count on his speech to provide insight and content almost regardless of the programme. His speech, and occasionally that of a chief minister (Andhra Pradesh and Madhya Pradesh), was the one thing worth listening to in the three to four hours of an otherwise interminable inaugural function of state investment summits. (These were the one thing I swore I would never attend again as soon as my year as president was over.) At a programme in Mumbai on Bond Markets in BRICs,[17] I made the comment in my speech that as CII president I found myself occasionally talking about subjects I knew nothing about—this being a case in point, so I would absolutely follow my briefing notes. When I sat down, Arun Jaitley leaned over and told me that only lawyers and politicians could talk about any subject at all—and he was both.

Norms of behaviour: We spoke in chapter 9 of the norms of behaviour that make institutions. Here are three more instances, two of protocol, one of substance.

One of the things the CII president does is to attend banquets at Rashtrapati Bhavan for visiting dignitaries. The protocol at these grand affairs always impressed me. The President is our head of state, and he and the Vice President outrank everyone else, including the Prime Minister. At banquets for a visiting head of state, the guests line up before the two Presidents enter. The Vice President is first in line, then the Prime Minister, then the past Prime Minister (in this case Manmohan Singh), then the foreign minister, then lesser ministers, and so on down. Before the President enters, the guests are all circulating and chatting. Watching Narendra Modi, Manmohan Singh and Sushma Swaraj chatting informally was a view of Indian democracy at its civil best. It is, unfortunately, too rare in public.

Consider another experience. At the biannual CII Agro Tech show in Chandigarh, in 2016, CII was privileged to have our President, Pranab Mukherjee, and Israel's President, Reuven Rivlin, as the joint chief guests. Since our President was there, so too were the two Governors of

---

17 BRICS refers to the association comprising the five major emerging economies: Brazil, Russia, India, China and South Africa.

Haryana and Punjab as we were in their shared capital. Israeli security is, depending on your perspective, either the best or the worst in the world. They think it is the best, and needs to be, given Israel's security concerns. I think it is the worst, in sheer obnoxious bullying of anyone it comes up against. But Israeli security had not counted on the security of Rashtrapati Bhavan. Before the two Presidents arrived, we were entertained by a quarrel between Israeli security, wanting to protect its President by being around him, and Rashtrapati Bhavan security, which had a list of people allowed to be present in the room with our President—which included all of us, but did not include Israeli security. So they were shooed off. Watching our security get the better of Israeli security that afternoon in Chandigarh was highly satisfying!

The sequence of arrival at Agro Tech and the cars they used could have been choreographed for amusement. The President of Israel showed up in an old-model Mercedes and then came our President accompanied by one of the Governors in a white Ambassador. The Ambassador is a high car, and Pranab Mukherjee was short, so a small footstool had to be deployed. The final arrival (he was late) was the other Governor, who arrived in a brand-new Mercedes, and was greeted by us all including our President—to the Governor's great discomfiture as it so violated protocol to be received by the first citizen instead of vice versa. The speeches, too, said something. The President of Israel spoke informally with warmth and humour about how much he was enjoying his visit to India, and how Israel had achieved food security. This prompted Pranab Mukherjee to discard his prepared speech that he had been carefully going through, marking up passages with a pen. He gave the file back to his aide, and also spoke extempore. He spoke with equal warmth, of India's own story of food security going back to the 1960s and American food aid, the green Revolution, our challenges with water shortages (especially in Punjab), and how welcome Israel's involvement would be.

Events of this kind display norms of civilised behaviour between Prime Ministers from different parties and Presidents from different countries. But there were others.

Every year, each region of CII holds its own annual meeting where it invites senior ministers and bureaucrats based in that area. The night before the inaugural, the ministers from two states dropped out, and the deputy chief minister of another, representing an opposition party, dropped in. A senior government secretary was on his way to the inaugural that morning when he read his notes and saw who was on the programme. He called, very upset, saying he could not possibly appear on the same platform with this government, and dropped out—at five minutes' notice. Now our bureaucrats are supposed to be apolitical—they are there to serve the interests of Union and states—*all* states. My sense was that an informal message had gone to the bureaucracy that this political party should be avoided as dealing with them gave the party credibility. Democracies need to constantly remind themselves that the Opposition is not the enemy.[18]

'Too Much Democracy'

While growing up, a frequent topic of conversation at the family dinner table was why our development record in India lagged. My mother generally felt that we had too much democracy. My father, brother and I felt we had too little.[19] I would argue that if you could promise me a Lee Kuan Yew, I'd consider (only consider) a benevolent dictatorship. But the chances are much greater that we would instead get a Donald Trump (I'm updating the argument to the present day—please pick your own favourite contemporary tyrant). And if we did, we needed the right to get rid of him at the end of a few years.

I was reminded of this old dinner-table argument by our headlines in December 2020 of the CEO of NITI Aayog doing us a disservice by saying we had 'too much democracy'. Amitabh Kant had to write an

---

18   India is obviously not alone in this need. Populists everywhere need reminding of this fact. It was shocking to me that Donald Trump actually seemed to favour the Russians over Hilary Clinton—and his Republican supporters thought that acceptable.

19   My mother generally outnumbered the three of us and won all arguments.

article in the *Indian Express*,[20] protesting at having his remarks taken out of context and applied to situations he had not discussed. But he repeated his assertion that when it comes to reform, we are 'too much of a democracy to mirror a China model'. He implied that China can move faster than India. Many think the same. Are they right?

Our discussion in chapter 9 of *Why Nations Fail* distinguished between inclusive and extractive economic and political institutions. My starting point, here, is a review of the book by Arvind Subramanian, which he summarised in a single picture.[21]

Figure 11.1: 'Why Nations Fail' in a Single Picture

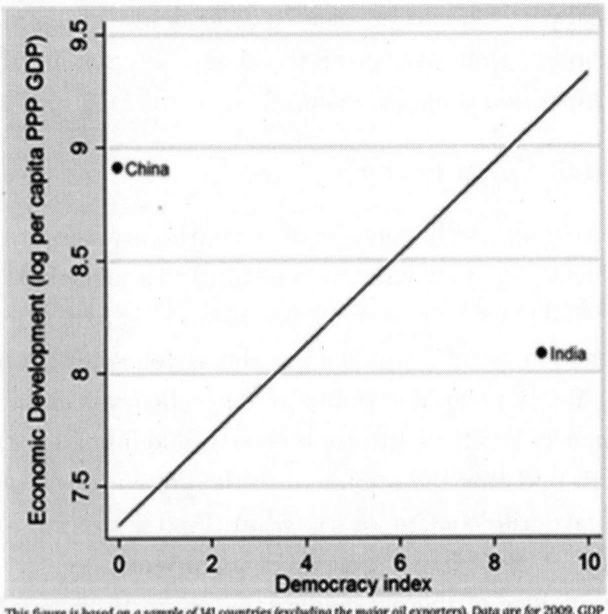

This figure is based on a sample of 141 countries (excluding the major oil exporters). Data are for 2009. GDP per capita data are from the Penn World Tables (version 7), and data for the democracy index are from the Polity IV database.

Source: Arvind Subramanian, 'Review of *Why Nations Fail*'.

---

20 *Indian Express*, 'Democracy is the lifeblood of India: A rebuttal by Amitabh Kant', 11 December 2020.

21 Arvind Subramanian, 'Why nations fail: And why India and China don't fit the story', *American Interest*, 1 February 2013.

Figure 11.1 shows that 'India (which is way below the line) is too economically underdeveloped given the quality of its political institutions, and China (which is well above the line) is too rich given its lack of democratic institutions'. Subramanian continues, that were we to revisit the book in the future: 'India in 20 years would have to slide into authoritarian chaos and become the equivalent of countries such as Venezuela today politically, or it would have to boom to become the equivalent of countries such as China in terms of standard of living. Conversely, China would either have to become a near-Jeffersonian democracy or suffer a dramatic collapse in output (that is, post negative growth).' He ends with the line, 'The inability of Acemoglu and Robinson to explain the development trajectories of these two large countries is not a fault of their rich and excellent book but of the unusual, uncooperative reality of Chinese and Indian history.' Acemoglu and Robinson responded to Subramanian's 'thoughtful review' by stressing that their theory argues that 'the link is between inclusive economic institutions and sustained economic growth'. And they stand by their theory that 'inclusive economic institutions can only survive in the long run if they are supported by inclusive political institutions'.[22]

Much would seem to depend on the definition of short run and long run.[23] Fifty years may be a short run relative to the great sweep of world history, but it is quite long for most people. This debate on democracy and growth is an old one. The general view would seem to be that once a country crosses a per capita GDP of around $8,000, sooner or later a transition to democracy takes place. The *Journal of Democracy* has had several issues discussing different societies that have either made the transition, such as South Korea, Taiwan, Chile and Argentina in the 1990s, or failed to, such as much of the Arab world.

---

22 Daron Acemoglu and James Robinson, 'China, India and All That', *Why Nations Fail* (Blog), 2 November 2012.

23 As Keynes memorably put it, 'in the long run we are all dead'.

Harry Rowen, a close friend and mentor at Stanford, was very specific. In 1996, he predicted that China would become a partial democracy by 2015.[24] In 2007, with 'China [having] remained deep in Not Free territory', he reaffirmed his prediction for China becoming a full democracy by 2025. Harry, who passed away in 2015, a month after celebrating his ninetieth birthday, did not reckon with Xi Jinping.[25] China, today, would not only still be 'deep in Not Free territory' but has reversed some of the improvements in civil liberties that its citizens saw in the pre-Xi era.[26] So can China continue to grow rapidly while becoming increasingly repressive politically? Acemoglu and Robinson say that it cannot achieve a per capita GDP matching Germany or the US, or even Portugal or Spain, with its current extractive political institutions. China seems bent on proving otherwise, and has been using its response to Covid to argue that its system is more effective at delivering safety and prosperity in general.

Harry was a frequent visitor to both China and India. His career reflects the kind of open system that is the US. He was a highly respected professor of strategy at the Stanford Business School, but had several spells in government—as director of the Bureau of the Budget, chairman of the National Intelligence Council, and assistant secretary of defence. He was also president of the RAND Corporation for many years. Harry was a consummate master of strategy—as an academic, and in his policy work. He had the ability to combine mastery of theory (the hallmark of a fine academic) with an ability to seize the moment (the hallmark of a fine practitioner) with sheer insight (the hallmark of a fine mind). I remember three stories he told me. In 1961, the US air force had recently deployed high resolution, high altitude surveillance photography. In his late thirties, Harry was in a briefing with President Kennedy at the White House, poring over

---

24 See Henry Rowen: 'The Short March: China's Road to Democracy', *National Interest* (September 1996) and 'When Will the Chinese People be Free? *Journal of Democracy* (July 2007).

25 India didn't, either!

26 See Cai Xia, 'The Party that Failed', *Foreign Affairs* (January–February 2021).

photographs taken 40,000 feet over Cuba. They were trying to figure out why the Soviet Union seemed to be building grain silos in Cuba—a country not known for its grain. 'Maybe it's to house missiles,' Harry said, to the President's great irritation. 'Check it out,' was the response; the rest, as they say, was history—the history we call the Cuban Missile Crisis. In government again thirty years later, as assistant secretary of defence under George Bush, Sr, in the run-up to the Gulf War, the discussion was around getting support and involvement from allies—Saudi Arabia, Germany, Japan. Harry suggested the allies be asked to help pay for the war. The US ended up making a profit on the Gulf War—the contributions from other countries outweighed the cost.

And there was a failure. As assistant secretary of defence, Harry was tasked with some shuttle diplomacy between India and Pakistan around 1990. He offered India equipment to automatically monitor incursions over the Line of Control—the new surveillance technology could pick up crossings by single individuals. India refused the offer, because we were concerned that the US would then also know what we were doing along the border. Harry and his wife Beverly were perfect hosts at their house near the Stanford campus. (Beverly was an incredible cook. Twenty years on, I can still taste a veal stew, made with wine, with a cheese soufflé floating on top—made from a recipe she had seen a few days earlier in a magazine.) In their last years, they moved to a new retirement home run by Hyatt on the Stanford campus. It had just started, and Hyatt were concerned that their brand should not be confused with retirement homes so they pulled the residents together to suggest a better name. Harry's suggestion, The Last Resort, was pure genius, but Hyatt went for a much weaker *Vi*.

Harry's ability to move back and forth between public and private life is a feature of the American system that greatly strengthens it. George Shultz, who died at 100 as I was writing a draft of this chapter, exemplified it.

But back to democracy—and India. India gave all adults the right to vote at independence regardless of income, education, gender, caste and religion. We take this for granted today, but it was unique then. Every forecast at the time predicted that a united India would not survive. Ramachandra Guha's magisterial *India After Gandhi* tells the story of how we not only survived as a democracy, but survived *because* we are a democracy. For the rest of the world, the transition to becoming a democracy would be when they crossed $8,000 in per capita GDP. We were a democracy when, emerging from colonial rule in 1947 as one of the poorest countries in the world, our per capita GDP was $150.[27]

Arvind Subramanian presented his two alternatives for India's future—of authoritarian chaos or a China-style boom—as a false dichotomy. Our experience in the eight years since he wrote his review says we have become somewhat more authoritarian and seen average growth fall significantly (from 8 per cent to 5 per cent) compared to the previous eight years. India generally manages to prove and disprove most theories, often at the same time.[28] Far from strong government helping drive good economics in India, the opposite seems to be true. The 1990s saw the decline of Congress's dominance in Indian politics, with minority or coalition governments ruling India from 1989 to 2014. Since 2014, the BJP has increased its hold on Indian politics, enjoying a dominance held before 1989 by Congress. Political scientists have argued that the absence of a strong majority government created space in Indian politics, with power fragmented between dozens of regional parties.[29] Weak and coalition governments have to be more inclusive for them to survive—inclusive of other political parties by definition, but also of the views that these parties represent. Power

---

27 In current dollars.

28 As one of the quotes I love to repeat from the economist Joan Robinson, says: 'The frustrating thing about India is that whatever you can rightly say about it, the opposite is also true.'

29 See, for example, Devesh Kapur, Pratap Bhanu Mehta and Milan Vaishnav's introduction to *Rethinking Public Institutions in India* (New Delhi: Oxford University Press, 2017). Also, Madhav Khosla and Milan Vaishnav, 'The Three Faces of the Indian State', *Journal of Democracy* 32, no. 1 (January 2021).

gets spread around, even if venality and vote-bank politics also spread around. In the absence of dominant political power, some constitutional institutions had gained renewed authority—the ECI, the Presidency, the Rajya Sabha, the Comptroller and Auditor General, and the autonomy of states. The two decades from 1992 to 2012 was the period when we enjoyed our most rapid growth ever. Since 2012, growth has consistently under performed, as it did before 1991. Those same institutions have seen their autonomy and power wane too. The absence of a dominant political party may have created space not only for more inclusive politics, but also more inclusive economics.

All analysts agree that democracy is much more than a periodic free and fair election. The rule of law and equality before it for all, laws that themselves must comply with a constitution that separates powers and limits its concentration in a ruling party, and independent institutions with public servants who do their job without regard to their political loyalties are even more important. We saw this play out in the US with Donald Trump, with institutions such as the media, courts (including the justices he appointed), election officials from the Republican Party, and, in the final analysis, the Senate and Vice President doing their jobs in spite of the President's bullying and pressure. The Capitol in Washington, DC has one of my favourite inscriptions above its entrance: 'We shall build no temple but the Capitol and consult no oracle but the Constitution.' Together with secularism and the separation of church and state, the message is that it is the constitution, and not the people, that the government and every public servant is accountable to.

Countries constantly need to search for a balance between 'what the people want' and relying on others to decide what's good for them. The extremes are wrong in my view. Going by what the majority want is not always right. For example, the majority in many countries wanted capital punishment to continue, but lawmakers in the UK, for example, voted to end it. Much progressive change happens 'against the will of the people'. Indeed, the essence of liberty in any civilised society is to protect the rights of the minority against the will of the majority.[30] The people have the right to turn out one government in favour of another, but they do end up relying on government doing what it deems best for them. In short, I believe in a fudge: a fuzzy combination of democracy (the people know best) and paternalism (someone else knows better), where the mix varies by issue, over time, and one has to keep working at it because one never gets it completely right. Leaders must be accountable to their constitution and people, but the people must rely on leaders to take them forward. Our ability as a country to compromise, to blend and balance the seemingly irreconcilable, enables us to navigate this fudge best. We will never get it completely right, but we can get it better than anyone else. We have to keep working at it, constantly raising our politicians' standards of education and understanding, which means raising it for the people who elect them. This is why we must have many great universities of our own that would produce thousands of intellectuals educated in the humanities and social sciences to progress our own liberal intellect.

At one end of the scale is Singapore, where the People's Action Party has ruled since 1959. The party simply knows better, it knows it knows better, and the people, apparently, also know it knows better. Singapore is organised, clean, and went, as Lee Kuan Yew's book says, *From Third World to First* in one generation. Its government can take great credit for its transformation, and continued success. When we have visited Singapore on CII visits and done the rounds of the government, it is head and shoulders more capable and competent than those we encounter on visits to any other country. Every minister we meet is completely aligned with the others, every minister is fully briefed and has better notes from our last visit than we do, and in the fifteen minutes that it takes to get from anywhere to anywhere in Singapore, the next minister you meet will be briefed on the meeting you just completed. The whole place smells of competence, judgement and governance.

---

30 John Stuart Mill's *On Liberty* is the classic statement. It narrowly missed being in my list of five favourite books.

As my comment at the start of this section indicates, I think very highly of Lee Kuan Yew. So I was thrilled some years ago at a dinner at Stanford to be seated next to him. A new course on the history of modern Singapore was being taught at Stanford that term, and the professor had the students begin by reading Plato's *Republic*. His theory was that Lee Kuan Yew had read Plato at Cambridge and fashioned Singapore in the image of his republic. I thought it a great opportunity to check that theory out first-hand, so asked Lee Kuan Yew if it was true. He shrugged. 'Theories are for professors,' he said. 'My theory was very simple. I tried something. If it worked, I kept it. If it didn't, I changed it.' As a statement of pragmatism, that comes near perfection. Lee Kuan Yew didn't leave things to chance, of course. Singapore invested strongly in educating its talent—including many ministers and bureaucrats—at the best universities overseas, and in building great universities at home. He ensured that government salaries were benchmarked against the best paid in the private sector, and that performance was constantly reviewed and assessed. Together with paying ministers and bureaucrats amongst the highest salaries in the world, ministers got no further perquisites.[31] They had no official cars, for instance. Lee Kuan Yew himself drove a Toyota, so while his ministers could afford any car of their choice, they naturally could not drive a car superior to that of the founder of the country.

As an alternative, consider the UK. On a CII visit, a group of MPs hosted us to dinner at a restaurant across the street from the House of Commons. They did so because Parliament was in session then, and a bill was being debated which would require frequent votes on various

---

31   The salary of the Prime Minister of Singapore was reduced by 35 per cent in 2011—at US$ 1.7 million annually, it is still the highest *official* salary of any political leader in the world. The President of the US has a salary of US$ 400,000 and the Prime Minister of India US$ 50,000. Those last two are official salaries—other than this they get housing, transport, travel, and a variety of other perks. The Singapore PM's salary may seem high, but once you add in everything else it is not, and it has the advantage of being completely transparent.

amendments. A bell, called a division bell, would be rung, and that gave MPs eight minutes to get to their places and vote. The division bell rang three times while we were at dinner. Each time the group of MPs, placed between the CII delegation, would leap up, disappear for about fifteen minutes, and then return and continue with the discussion and meal with us. I'd read in the papers that morning that the house was debating the education reform bill. This interested me, so I asked the MP next to me what the bill was about. 'It's about education,' he said. 'What about education?' 'Education reform.' 'Yes, what reform of education?' 'Ah, there you have me,' he said 'Let me check.' He asked around the table. Of the eight or so MPs at the table with us, not one knew what the bill was about—the bill they had just gone and voted on three times. Somehow I just cannot imagine a similar scenario in Singapore.

Excuse me, I am the deputy minister in the ministry of what, please?

Patience, gentlemen, patience! We have announced our policy only a few days ago – give us some time to understand it!

As a result, I was more disappointed than surprised by Brexit. The original sin was David Cameron's when he committed to holding the referendum on whether the UK should remain in the EU. He did it to get the anti-Europeans in his *own* party off his back. It was a huge mistake, for both Cameron and the UK. The referendum unleashed the populism of Nigel Farrage and Boris Johnson. When we had met both Conservative and Labour members of parliament the year before the Brexit vote, they were very confident the referendum would fail. In the end, left to Parliament, the UK would have stayed in; left to the people who were influenced by populists and false information, they voted to leave.

So is paternalism better? Is rule by those who 'know better' better? My discussion of Singapore and the UK would seem to say so, but this is dangerous territory. The Brexit campaign was not helped by the patronising approach of the 'remainers' who irritated many voters by claiming to simply know better. Surely the optimum solution is one where the MPs do indeed vote and determine what policies happen, that they vote freely and not according to the dictates of their party, that the norms of the system say they must be fully briefed and involved in what they're voting on, and that they constantly engage with voters, explaining their position with logic and data. Wishful thinking? Perhaps.

Pictures on the wall: One of the things I did when wandering around ministers' offices while CII president was to note the photographs they had on their walls. The norm was two—a photograph each of the President and Prime Minister. Those who departed from that norm were noteworthy. President Pranab Mukherjee was of course from the Congress, though he went out of his way as President to be above politics in both statements and actions. Some ministers in the BJP government had only photographs of the Prime Minister, and their second picture was of Mahatma Gandhi, or Sardar Patel (more of a Congressman than Gandhi ever was, but that's not a fact the BJP likes to acknowledge). Some went well beyond. One chief minister had, I noted, an abundance of pictures—President Mukherjee, the Prime Minister, Swami Vivekananda, Mohan Bhagwat (the chief of the RSS) and Deen Dayal Upadhyaya (one of the heroes of the RSS and leader of the Bharatiya Jana Sangh, the party that foreshadowed the BJP).

There seemed to be a need to pick your photographs to show your loyalty. There is a famous story of Atal Bihari Vajpayee, as foreign minister, getting Nehru's portrait restored in South Block—a display of statesmanship that is quite rare these days.

One should not read too much into photographs on display. A senior bureaucrat in the Ministry of Science and Technology had a fine photograph of the scientist Vikram Sarabhai just above his desk. A colleague of mine admired it. The bureaucrat clearly did not know whose photograph he had shared his office with for years.

Gandhiji; Sir ...

I have myself two wonderful sketches by R.K. Laxman, of Manmohan Singh and T.N. Seshan. To me they symbolise India's movement in the right direction—of economic reform and institutional strength. Together, they represent India's promise.

Criticism is patriotism. So is humility: I hope two things come across in this book. I believe we are a country of tremendous strength and potential. But there's a but. We are a country of tremendous *potential*. Realising this potential is what this book has been about. That means starting with where we are, being clear of where we have to go, and then learning from the best wherever it is available to get there. Two attributes are essential as we learn to lead. I have always believed in the importance of criticism. I would much rather focus on improvement, on what we must and can do better, than on what we are already doing well. I have always approached our own company in this self-critical manner. In the same way, I am more critical of India than of any other country. I am critical of anything I really care about. Criticism is at the heart of Hirschman's voice.[32] A country concerned about its success would be receptive to more voices of dissent. Yes, one would always prefer those voices to be constructive and positive, as I aspire to be, but we have to be open to hearing everyone. We must constantly seek a better solution, more educated polity, and more statesmanlike politician. Dissent is the foundation of improvement.

A Laxman cartoon from 2003 did the WhatsApp rounds again in February 2021.

What's the matter with these people? I give them all the good news ... The Sensex is soaring, and we've won against Australia. But he's still grumbling & complaining

© R.K. Laxman

---

32 See chapter 10 for a discussion of Albert Hirschman's *Exit, Voice and Loyalty*.

In the same way, I believe it much more important to err on the side of humility than hubris. If we think that we've done it all, or are doing it all, what's there to learn? If we keep reciting that we're the world's fastest-growing country, are administering vaccines faster than anyone, and have the world's biggest this and best that, what's there to improve? We must constantly remind ourselves that we are among the world's poorest one-third of countries, of our abysmal record in child nutrition and stunting which has got worse since 2014, of the fact that Bangladesh overtook us in per capita GDP in 2020, that China is five times richer than we are, and that four months into our vaccination programme we had fully vaccinated under 3 per cent of our population. We have a long way to go before we can claim victory. We have to learn how to lead, and humility makes for being better learners. For now, let's restrict our triumphalism to beating Australia at the Gabba.[33]

---

33 The Gabba is a famous cricket stadium in Brisbane. The home side was not supposed to lose there—until January 2021 when India pulled off an improbable victory.

Epilogue
Restoring India's Potential

So here they are, the chapters ready,
And, half against my will, I'm free
Of this warm enterprise, this heady
Labor that has exhausted me
Through thirteen months, swift and delightful,
Incited by my friends' insightful
Paring and prodding and appeal ...

The Golden Gate, Vikram Seth
(with my thanks)

L et's now put it all together. This book has been about leadership in the three spheres of economy, institutions and culture. Each chapter has talked about the *what* of leadership. What should the government, industry and people do to lead?

Economic leadership starts with setting the right growth aspiration: ours must be to grow at 8–10 per cent for the next thirty years. As we saw in chapters 2 and 3, GDP growth per capita is a productivity question. Putting more people to work and giving them more capital to work with are the obvious drivers of growth. This is why increasing our labour force participation rate, especially our female labour force participation rate, is such an obvious win. But it is not an easy win. Both Hindus and Muslims have seen women withdraw from the public sphere, damaging both women's rights and the economy. Moving people from lower-productivity occupations, such as agriculture, to higher-productivity occupations, such as manufacturing and modern services, is the biggest driver of growth as any country develops. When millions of migrant workers return from higher-wage jobs in cities to underemployment in their villages, this reduces GDP. Conversely, investing in human capital through skilling and education increases lifetime earnings, and adds substantially to GDP. The returns to primary education can be enormous—upwards of 20 per cent in poorer countries. Multiplied across our huge population, the gains can be dramatic. The returns to secondary education are also substantial—with good schooling providing the essential foundation for the efficient manufacturing of the East Asian miracle. The returns to higher education are more tenuous, but it is essential to the success of individual organisations.

No country has grown rapidly over long periods without trade playing a major role. Our own experience since 1991 shows its power. Exports and imports are two sides of the same coin; protection makes exports more expensive. As I said in chapter 4, it is the choice we make in Indian industry that matters. Are we confident of being competitive enough to compete with the world on its terms? As the economy opened up post 1991, exports and imports boomed, industry thrived, and for a while, corporate India saw the world as its market, investing, and acquiring companies on every continent. Several Indian firms still see it in those terms—it is they that must set the direction for our trade policy more generally.

The residual in GDP growth calculations is technical change. Our skill and capital-intensive industrial structure demands, as chapters 5 and 6 argued, that we invest strongly in technology and design. We need to address both the 'supply' and the 'demand' for technical change. The demand comes from the discipline of the market—the threat of being left behind drives firms to invest in technology and R&D. This requires competition, not just a lot of it, but high-quality competition, firms that compete on features and customer benefits more than price. The supply comes from firms investing in technology. We must grow in-house R&D spending by a factor of five to match the world average as a per cent of GDP. Firms must learn how to do so productively. The lower cost of good engineers in India means that we can, over time, outclass any firm worldwide if we match them in R&D spending.

Our **institutions** of higher education and public research must support this aspiration to build world-leading technical capacity. This requires addressing institutional issues, but it especially requires shifting public funding of research from autonomous government laboratories to our higher education system and industry (chapters 7 and 8). Both research and teaching would benefit. Our higher education system has demonstrated its ability to respond to demand—opening, as we saw earlier, 4.4 new colleges each day in the last twenty years.[1] The critical change needed is for the state to get its role right. To develop a specific technology—in defence or atomic energy or space—government should fund the development in industry instead of doing R&D in its own autonomous laboratories. More broadly, the state must grow its funding of research in the higher education system, increase support for the humanities and social sciences, guarantee a student loan system that covers all students, and provide a strong accreditation

---

1   Devesh Kapur's wonderful statistic. *Financial Times*, 'Covid piles pressure on India to embrace online degrees', 6 January 2021.

system across all institutions. It should stop setting fees, sanctioning seat numbers, determining which colleges can offer what degrees, and influencing admissions and recruitment practices. Its role must move, especially, from defining input to assessing output.

I have long wrestled with the role of the state. In the US, I believe a more effective state is needed to provide infrastructure and substantially improved governance, even if it then ends up being larger. In India, I used to believe that we did not need better government, we needed less government; that less government *was* better government. I've moved progressively to the view that the Indian state should do fewer things, but do them better. Covid has said to all countries that the state has an important role to play. The abdication of responsibility by the last US President in handling Covid and the initial fumbling of the UK Prime Minister contrast with the quick response and effectiveness of the Chancellor of Germany, Presidents of Taiwan and South Korea, and Prime Ministers of New Zealand, Australia and Singapore. Countries have paid the price in widely different mortality rates. But India needs a special state. As Covid showed, we responded very promptly in March 2020, but the initial implementation was so erratic and uncoordinated that we badly hurt the economy without halting the spread of infection. Things settled down after the first three months of bumbling and bullying. Instead of learning from that, our state demonstrated dismaying incompetence in the second wave. In January 2021, the Prime Minister addressed the World Economic Forum and extolled India's success in the fight against Covid. In February, the BJP complimented the Prime Minister on successfully defeating Covid. The government started to believe its own hubris. The hubris trumped the facts: the health minister issued a statement in mid-March claiming victory as cases were rising rapidly. And then went in for terrible signalling, with election rallies and religious festivals of hundreds of thousands of maskless attendees. All notable for the presence of senior political leaders and the absence of Covid protocols. The ensuing disaster gave India worldwide press coverage that undid three decades of improving image at a stroke.

We can do better. Our federal system of Union and states, with governments that are nothing if not representative of their polities, and vibrant society and private sector says that when we work together we can do a lot better. The Union can provide funding and be a central repository of best practice, states can experiment with different models of behaviour against a unified set of metrics provided by the Union government, the private sector can be relied upon to help with implementation, and our NGOs can help with last-mile delivery and hold both government and private sector to account. If we need a different state, Indian society—the culture we discussed in the last chapter, our huge number of active and committed NGOs in every field, and enough good industrial citizens—says we can have it.

On visits to Hanoi and Jakarta, we met industry associations and the government. The senior members of the government we met just seemed to be more articulate, worldly and capable than their industry. I was struck by the contrast with India.

This need to correct the areas where the state underplays its role and withdraw from those areas where it overplays it is a theme I have discussed often in this book, and as a topic in itself in chapter 9. The state must recognise that it has limited capacity and that this capacity must be reserved for those things that only it can do. The rest must be left to civil society, the private sector and independent institutions. The state may set up institutions but must then leave them to get on with their jobs without interference, even tolerating some obstruction. The selection, governance and funding structures of institutions should ensure this independence. That is how our noisy democracy will progress. Progress can become leadership if we can build out those key principles we discussed in the last chapter of inclusiveness, openness, a strong and independent private sector, and the liberal intellect that leads to practices and norms for cultural leadership.

As chapter 10 said, India's **culture** is the foundation of its promise. People like us and want us to succeed. I have personally experienced this from a variety of sources around the world: the former Prime Minister of Singapore, the United States Trade Representative, the Iranian foreign minister, the Indonesian trade minister and the Myanmarese Senior Counsellor. All conveyed a message that India was a welcome investor, that they wanted India to succeed, even as they wanted specific things—our trade policy, say—fixed. We have huge international goodwill we can and must build on.

Why do they like us? However frustrating our noisy democracy, when we operate in a democratic manner, we foster trust. However much foreign firms complain about the capriciousness of Indian tax officials, it is a pretty perfect defence that most Indian firms experience their cussedness with more than equal regularity. China cannot claim that. Our diversity means that whatever an individual foreigner likes, she will find somewhere in India. Diversity of food, yes, but also diversity of belief. If you believe in argument, we are champions.[2] If you believe in law and order, we can point to many of our leaders willing to trample on civil rights in the interest of order. If you believe in dissent, read some of our great public intellectuals and columnists, many quoted in this book. Some years back, I dropped some family friends from the UK at the station in Pune to catch a midnight train to Bengaluru. As we threaded our way through the station, with hundreds of people sleeping on the platforms, my friend Richard had a blissful smile on his face. 'There's so much life here,' he said. 'Yes, too much,' I replied. Thinking about it, I wouldn't have it any other way. Here is Ken Juster speaking in January 2021, his last week in India as the US Ambassador: 'India is the most fascinating country in the world. It's many countries rolled-up in one. There's a tremendous vibrancy and energy in India … I truly do understand the strength of the people-to-people relationship because I felt it every

---

2   The correct answer to the question 'How many Parsis does it take to have an argument?' is 'One'. We use a mirror.

day. There's a special feeling in India when you're interacting with the people.'[3]

I deeply believe our diversity is a strength. By including the capabilities of our exceptional diversity, it becomes the source of our massive potential. The importance of policies of inclusion has been a theme running through this book—in chapters 2 (focus industrial policy on areas which help *all* of Indian industry, instead of trying to pick winners), 3 (social inclusion for growth), 4 (favouring consumer over producer interests), 5 (widespread innovation across Indian industry), 6 (design, so the average Indian's life is better), 7 (merit must determine access to high quality higher education), 9 (designing institutions to include), and 10 (developing a shared culture of development and growth). If we celebrate and harness the diverse strands that make up India, we'd be in wonderful shape.[4] It is this that we put at great risk when we try to homogenise. Yes, those 'others' may not vote for me, but so long as they add to our GDP, employ thousands of Indians, and enrich our culture, I must respect and protect them even if I don't agree with them. I find thoroughly dispiriting attempts to somehow involve anything of significance in a majoritarian project that excludes those we don't agree with. It weakens us greatly.

To repeat, our culture is the foundation of our promise and diversity is at the core of our culture.

Our promise comes from things we have *now,* things unique to us that cannot be learnt or bought. No one else can match these. But, as our Japanese visitor (in the story I began this book with) discovered, there are also many things to fix. This book has been largely about what we must fix—in economic policy for productive employment (chapters 2 and 3), in trade policy (chapter 4), in innovation and research policy (chapters 5, 6 and 8), in education policy (chapter 7). I have expectations of more sensible policy in all these areas.

---

3   Interviewed by the *Indian Express*, 8 January 2021.
4   My niece Riah has been a brilliant reader and critic of various drafts of this book. Some of these words are hers, commenting on various chapters.

But my expectations of what Indian industry must do are higher. Indian industry must invest in inclusive growth (chapter 3), see an open trade policy as the heart of being competitive (chapter 4), and invest in innovation and design (chapters 5 and 6) to build proprietary capabilities. Both government and industry have much to fix in policy and practice, as we learn to lead.

Ultimately, it is the combination of government and industry, acting in synchronisation with our culture, that can build leadership. When government tries to do too much, we struggle. When it plays its role in a limited and unambitious but effective way, the private sector can be empowered and motivated to act.[5] We must make it easy to do good, without messing around with FCRA laws because some study criticised the government, or changing the OCI rules and making millions of NRIs feel unwelcome because some journalist with a foreign passport attacked the government. We should expect industry to help in delivering outcomes in primary school education, in vaccinating whole districts against Covid and in skilling the wider population. We should trust industry and NGOs to do good. Remove the culpability from the CSR law, let NGOs and trusts freely access foreign funds and ensure that for anyone to be arrested criminal wrongdoing must be first proven in a court of law. When government distrusts and tries to control and punish, we struggle.

Finally, in the last chapter (11), I dealt with the *how* of leadership. I argue for a policy stance that is inclusive, open (to trade and migration) and that fosters entrepreneurship in an independent and

---

5   The Satyam saga showed how a quick, effective and very limited state intervention could be highly successful. Our third largest IT firm went bust suddenly in 2009, when its chairman admitted to falsifying the accounts of $2 billion. The Manmohan Singh government stepped in and used powers so rare few knew they existed to replace the entire company board with members drawn entirely from the private sector, all with legendary reputations. In two days. The new board steadied the company, and in three months sold it to the Mahindras, saving all the jobs involved and with Satyam the reputation of the Indian IT industry.

strong private sector. Rely on institutions like CII to fill the space left by the state. Finally, I argue for building cultural leadership around a liberal intellectual vision. This means operating in a manner that is authentic, relaxed about criticism, and with norms of behaviour that live up to a rich cultural heritage. It means relying on democracy and constitutional propriety. And learning, constantly, to be better informed and more independent and involved in decision-making—whether as a member of Parliament or a citizen. Some of those features are personal preferences; some are essential to a constitutional democracy. Between them, they add up to a liberal polity that the world can look up to.

To illustrate both promise and struggle, consider the country's top challenge, of controlling Covid. Our only way out is vaccination. We need to vaccinate 850 million adults to control Covid. We began well. The government established the right protocols of health and front-line workers, then those most vulnerable, then wider groups. We approved vaccines in early January 2021. Then we tried to control. Initially only government hospitals were permitted to vaccinate, then limited to larger private hospitals. All—hospitals and vaccinees—had to use the same rather clunky and unreliable app. And hospitals had maximum numbers of vaccinations they could do daily—300, say, when they had the capacity for 1,000, and without the freedom to go beyond those registered for the vaccine that day. We have since kept responding and improving. We eventually do the right and sensible thing, but why must we seek out every alternative before we get there? Keep in mind that our task is to vaccinate eight to ten million people a day. We need to do each day for many months what Singapore and Israel must do in total.

Our fumbled vaccination programme is a direct reflection of deep state incompetence. Four months on, as the second wave hit, we had covered just 10 per cent of our population with at least one dose, and 3 per cent with both. We could have prevented the depth of the second wave that ravaged India. We must do much better. We cannot afford the delay from missteps and tinkering. We have the world's largest vaccine manufacturers in India—but did not place adequate orders with them. Serum Institute, Bharat Biotech, Dr Reddy's Laboratories, Biological-E, Zydus, Genova Pharmaceuticals, Wockhardt—these are only some of the Indian firms with the capability of each providing vaccines by the hundreds of million. We have a wider private sector that offered to take on the job of vaccinating entire towns and their surrounding areas. Thousands of NGOs can ensure no one is left out. As we tackle our health crisis, we will simultaneously redeem confidence in our potential. Let's get on with it as India, not as the Indian government.

This book has been part description of how things are, part prescription of what we must do, part a personal story of how I came to believe what I do, and the mentors and experiences that influenced these beliefs. In my public writing, I have always tried to be positive and polite, while being forthright and independent. I believe that is not only a right but a duty. To return to my discussion of Albert Hirschman's *Exit, Voice and Loyalty* (chapter 10): when one sees things we believe to be wrong, it is voice that says we are loyal and care. The alternative to voice is exit, in the form of reduced entrepreneurship, reduced investment or even emigration. Dissent is patriotism.

I have another Albert Hirschman favourite. In a short essay, 'Having Opinions', he argued for the importance of forming one's own opinion.[6] He saw this to be an essential element in the quality of life. Hirschman argued that too often our opinions come as a package from those sources we identify with—a political or religious leader, or a particular ideology. I have always been suspicious of packaged '-isms'. As the many I have quoted in this book make clear, I respect common sense more than grand theory, and pragmatism and compromise over ideological

---

6   Albert Hirschman, 'Having Opinions—One of the Elements of Well-Being?' *American Economic Review* (May 1989).

commitment. I admire nuance and qualification, experimentation and learning, humility and fallibility. There is a burden of proof on the great and the good to show they really are great and good. Those with wisdom, to me, draw on this same learning, experimentation, humility and fallibility. But one of my deepest and longest held opinions is in India's potential. I am at my most frustrated and angry when I see us squandering our potential, such as in the second wave of Covid. I am at my most hopeful when we redeem ourselves by surprising the world in some area—a surprise win for a better government in one election and loss of a worse government in another, the sudden rediscovery of spine in our higher courts or some other institution, the eradication of polio, or mounting a remarkable vaccination effort to cover most of our 1.4 billion people in a few months.

India's potential to lead stems from the things we have which others find difficult to match—our diverse culture, a young and aspirational population, parents willing to make sacrifices to educate their children at great cost, a breadth and depth of institutions, and a diverse and entrepreneurial private sector. The things we have to fix can be learnt from best practice elsewhere. My construct in this book has been to set our sights high for India. Others also have. But too often, our prescriptions for India seem to demand a government that is suddenly wise, capable and effective in translating policy into implementation. We must start with the state we have and expect only that it takes on fewer things and so does them better. Instead of expecting the state to be enterprising in fixing problems itself, let us seek policies that unleash the enterprise that fixes the problems. Sometimes this means just stepping out of the way to 'misallocate less badly'. Achieving our potential means a minimal but wise economic policy that relies on private enterprise and NGOs for implementation. Private enterprise itself must be open to the world at home and invest overseas. Firms must invest, too, in innovation, education and research. It means institutional progress, where independence and competence is built step by step, and the combination of institutions sets the rules under which we all operate. And it means, especially, the moral leadership that builds off our culture, drawing together and unifying in a spirit of tolerance and compromise.

Let's stop struggling to lead and deliver on our promise.

Glossary of Abbreviations

AGM	Annual General Meeting
ASEAN	Association of Southeast Asian Nations
ASER	Annual State of Education Report
ASI	Annual Survey of Industries
CBI	Central Bureau of Investigation
CCI	Competition Commission of India
CII	Confederation of Indian Industry
CMIE	Centre for Monitoring the Indian Economy
CSIR	Council of Scientific and Industrial Research
CSR	Corporate Social Responsibility
CTIER	Centre for Technology Innovation and Economic Research
DFI	Direct Foreign Investment (interchangeable with FDI)
DPIIT	Department for Promotion of Industry and Internal Trade
DRDO	Defence Research and Development Organisation

341

DST	Department of Science and Technology
ECI	Election Commission of India
EPRI	Electric Power Research Institute, Palo Alto, California
ESIC	Employees' State Insurance Corporation
FBN	Family Business Network International
FCRA	Foreign Contribution Regulation Act
FDI	Foreign Direct Investment
FTA	Free Trade Agreement
GST	Goods and Services Tax
IAF	Indian Air Force
IAS	Indian Administrative Service
IATA	International Air Transport Association
ICAR	Indian Council of Agricultural Research
IDC	India Design Council
IIM	Indian Institute of Management
IMF	International Monetary Fund
IISc	Indian Institute of Science
IIT	Indian Institute of Technology
ITRI	Industrial Technology Research Institute, Taiwan
JLF	Jaipur Literature Festival
Lok Sabha	The Lower House of Parliament
MLA	Member of Legislative Assembly
MP	Member of Parliament
MRTP	Monopolies and Restrictive Trade Practices
NAA	National Anti-profiteering Authority (for GST)
NCAER	National Council of Applied Economic Research
NCL	National Chemical Laboratory
NDA	National Democratic Alliance
NEP	National Education Policy
NGO	Non-Government Organisation
NID	National Institute of Design
NPA	Non-Performing Asset
NRI	Non-Resident Indian

NSDC	National Skills Development Corporation
OCI	Overseas Citizen of India
OECD	Organisation of Economic Cooperation and Development, Paris
PIO	Person of Indian Origin
PLI	Production-linked Incentive
PMO	Prime Minister's Office
PPE	Personal Protective Equipment, kits
Rajya Sabha	The Upper House of Parliament
RCEP	Regional Comprehensive Economic Partnership
RSS	Rashtriya Swayamsevak Sangh
UPA	United Progressive Alliance
WHO	World Health Organization
WIPO	World Intellectual Property Organization
WTO	World Trade Organization

Indian Monetary Units

Rs 1 lakh = Rs 1,00,000 (as of mid-2021, around $1,400)

Rs 1 crore = Rs 100 lakh, or Rs 10 million ($140,000)

Rs 1 lakh crore = Rs 1 trillion ($14 billion)

Acknowledgements

Usha Laxman, for licensing the rights to reproduce several wonderful cartoons by the great R.K. Laxman.

Arvind Subramanian, for permission for Figure 11.1, reproduced from his book review, 'Why nations fail: And why India and China don't fit the story', *American Interest,* (1 February 2013).

Vikram Seth, for the reproduction of lines from his 'Dedication' to *The Golden Gate* (New York: Random House, 1986).

Nishith Prakash, for permission for Table 3.3, Effects of English language skills on wage rates. Adapted from Table 5 from Mehtabul Azam, Aimee Chin and Nishith Prakash, 'Does it pay to speak English in India?', *Ideas for India* (20 September 2013).

T.N. Ninan, for his permission to reproduce Table 12.2 from *The Turn of the Tortoise,* as Table 2.2.

CTIER, especially Janak Nabar and Madhurjya Deka, and for permission to use tables from the *CTIER Handbook 2021: Technology and Innovation in India* (Pune: CTIER, 2021).

Chhaya Gogate at Forbes Marshall, for her meticulous and painstaking work on this book.

Acknowledgements

Select Bibliography

This is not an academic book. I list only those books that I have found particularly beneficial to my understanding of the world. They include many favourites. The text (in chapters 9 and 10) has my five favourite books. The first list here that I think everyone should read is a wider set. (Any complete list of favourite books would include a lot of fiction, but that would take me so far afield that I did not dare try to get it past the publisher.) I have chosen to include only a few papers, particularly those that I (and others) regard as the definitive statements on their subject.

Books and articles I think everyone should read

Adams, James L. *Good Products, Bad Products: Essential Elements to Achieving Superior Quality*. New Delhi: Tata McGraw Hill, 2012.

Banerjee, Abhijit, and Esther Duflo. *Good Economics for Hard Times: Better Answers to Our Biggest Problems*. New Delhi: Juggernaut Books, 2019.

Becker, Gary S. 'The Economic Way of Looking at Life'. Nobel Prize Lecture, Oslo, 13 October 1992.

Casper, Gerhard. *The Winds of Freedom: Addressing Challenges to the University.* New Haven, CT: Yale University Press, 2014.

Coyle, Diane. *GDP: A Brief but Affectionate History.* Princeton, NJ, and Oxford: Princeton University Press, 2014.

Dore, Ronald. *Shinohata: Portrait of a Japanese Village.* New York: Pantheon Books, 1978.

Guha, Ramachandra. *India After Gandhi: The History of the World's Largest Democracy.* New Delhi: Pan Macmillan (Picador), 2007, and Pan Macmillan India (second edition) 2017.

———— 'Introduction'. In *Nationalism*, by Rabindranath Tagore. New Delhi: Penguin Random House, 2009.

Hirschman, Albert. *Exit, Voice and Loyalty: Responses to Decline in Firms, Organizations, and States.* Cambridge, MA: Harvard University Press, 1970.

————. 'Having Opinions: One of the Elements of Well-Being?' *American Economic Review* 79, no. 2 (May 1989).

Landes, David. *The Wealth and Poverty of Nations: Why Some Are So Rich and Some so Poor.* New York, NY: Norton, 1998.

Maddison, Angus. *The World Economy—Volume 1: A Millennial Perspective.* Paris: OECD Publishing, 2001.

————. *Volume 2: Historical Statistics.* Paris: OECD Publishing, 2003.

Mill, John Stuart. *On Liberty.* London: John W. Parker and Son, 1859.

Seth, Vikram. *From Heaven Lake: Travels through Sinkiang and Tibet.* Delhi: Penguin Random House, 1983.

Singh, Manmohan. 'Budget 1991–92'. Speech, Minister of Finance. New Delhi: Government of India, 24 July 1991.

General Economics and Management; Economic History

Abramovitz, Moses. 'Resource and Output Trends in the United States Since 1870'. *American Economic Review* 46, no. 2 (1956): 5–23.

Adams, James L. *The Building of an Engineer: Making, Thinking and Teaching.* Stanford, NJ: Ad Hoc Press, 2011.

———. *Conceptual Blockbusting.* New York, NY: Basic Books, fifth edition, 2019.

Ashton, T.S. *The Industrial Revolution, 1760–1830.* Oxford: Oxford University Press, 1948.

March, James C. 'Exploration and Exploitation in Organizational Learning', *Organization Science* 2, no.1 (1991): 71–87.

Gerschenkron, Alexander. *Economic Backwardness in Historical Perspective.* Cambridge, MA: Belknap Press, 1962.

Landes, David. *The Unbound Prometheus: Technological Change and Industrial Development in Western Europe from 1750 to the Present.* Cambridge: Cambridge University Press, second edition, 2003.

Mokyr, Joel. *The Lever of Riches: Technological Creativity and Economic Progress.* Oxford: Oxford University Press, 1992.

———. *A Culture of Growth: The Origins of the Modern Economy.* Princeton, NJ: Princeton University Press, 2016.

Noll, Roger, editor. *Challenges to Research Universities.* Washington, DC: Brookings, 1986.

Panagariya, Arvind. *Free Trade and Prosperity: How Openness Helps Developing Countries Grow Richer and Combat Poverty.* New Delhi: Oxford University Press, 2019.

Rajan, Raghuram. *The Third Pillar: How Markets and the State Leave the Community Behind.* New Delhi: HarperCollins India, 2019.

Rodrik, Dani. *Straight Talk on Trade: Ideas for a Sane World Economy.* Princeton, NJ: Princeton University Press, 2018.

Solow, Robert M. 'A Contribution to the Theory of Economic Growth', *Quarterly Journal of Economics* 70, no. 1 (1956): 65–94. https://doi.org/10.2307/1884513

Wade, Robert. *Governing the Market: Economic Theory and the Role of Government in East Asian Industrialization.* Princeton, NJ: Princeton University Press, 1990.

The Indian Economy

Bhagwati, Jagdish, and Arvind Panagariya. *Why Growth Matters: How Economic Growth in India Reduced Poverty and the Lessons for Other Developing Countries.* New York, NY: Public Affairs, 2013.

Bhagwati, Jagdish. *India in Transition: Freeing the Economy.* Oxford: Clarendon Press, 1993.

Desai, Ashok V., editor. *Technology Absorption in Indian Industry.* New Delhi: Wiley Eastern, 1988.

———. *The Price of Onions.* New Delhi: Penguin, 1999.

Kelkar, Vijay and, Ajay Shah. *In Service of the Republic: The Art and Science of Economic Policy.* New Delhi: Penguin Random House, 2019.

Kochhar, Kalpana, Utsav Kumar, Raghuram Rajan, Arvind Subramanian, and Ioannis Tokatlidis. 'India's Pattern of Development: What Happened, What Follows?' Working Paper WP/06/22. Washington, DC: International Monetary Fund, 2006.

Mohan, Rakesh, editor. *India Transformed: 25 Years of Economic Reform.* New Delhi: Penguin Random House, 2017.

Ninan, T.N. *The Turn of the Tortoise: The Challenge and Promise of India's Future.* New Delhi: Penguin Random House India, 2016.

Panagariya, Arvind. *India Unlimited: Reclaiming the Lost Glory.* New Delhi: HarperCollins India, 2020.

Economics of Technology and Innovation

CTIER. *Handbook of Technology and Innovation in India,* 2019 and 2021. Pune: CTIER, 2019 and 2021.

Cirera, Xavier, and William F. Maloney. *The Innovation Paradox: Developing Country Capabilities and the Unrealized Promise of Technological Catch-Up.* Washington, DC: World Bank, 2017.

de Solla Price, Derek J. *Little Science, Big Science.* New York, NY: Columbia University Press, 1963.

Forbes, Naushad, and David Wield. *From Followers to Leaders: Managing Technology and Innovation in Newly Industrializing Countries.* London: Routledge, 2002.

Fransman, Martin, and Kenneth King, editors. *Technological Capability in the Third World.* London: Palgrave Macmillan, 1984.

Hall, Bronwyn, and Nathan Rosenberg, editors. *Handbook of the Economics of Innovation.* Volumes 1 and 2. Oxford: North-Holland, 2010.

Hobday, Michael. *Innovation in East Asia.* Aldershot: Edward Elgar, 1995.

Kealey, Terence. *The Economic Laws of Scientific Research.* London: Macmillan, 1996.

Kim, Linsu. *Imitation to Innovation: The Dynamics of Korea's Technological Learning.* Cambridge, MA: Harvard Business School Press, 1997.

Kim, Linsu, and Richard Nelson, editors. *Technology, Learning & Innovation: Experiences of Newly Industrializing Economies.* Cambridge: Cambridge University Press, 2000.

Kline, Stephen Jay. 'Research, Invention, Innovation and Production: Models and Reality'. Report INN-1C, Department of Mechanical Engineering. Stanford, NJ: Stanford University, 1987.

———. 'Models of Innovation and Their Policy Consequences', Report INN-4, Department of Mechanical Engineering. Stanford, NJ: Stanford University, 1989.

Lall, Sanjaya. *Building Industrial Competitiveness in Developing Countries.* Paris: OECD Development Centre, 1990.

Landau, Ralph, Timothy Taylor, and Gavin Wright, editors. *The Mosaic of Economic Growth.* Stanford, NJ: Stanford University Press, 1996.

Landau, Ralph, and Nathan Rosenberg, editors. *The Positive Sum Strategy: Harnessing Technology for Economic Growth.* Washington, DC: National Academies Press, 1986.

Nelson, Richard, editor. *National Innovation Systems: A Comparative Analysis.* Oxford: Oxford University Press, 1993.

————. *The Sources of Economic Growth*. Cambridge, MA: Harvard University Press, 1996.

————. *Technology, Institutions and Economic Growth*. Cambridge, MA: Harvard University Press, 2005.

Odagiri, Hirayuki, and Akira Goto. *Technology and Industrial Development in Japan: Building Capabilities by Learning, Innovation and Public Policy*. Oxford: Clarendon Press, 1996.

Rhee, Yung Wun, Larry Westphal, and Gary Pursell. *Korean Industrial Competence: Where it Came From*. Washington, DC: World Bank, 1981.

Rosenberg, Nathan. *Perspectives on Technology*. Cambridge: Cambridge University Press, 1976.

————. *Inside the Black Box: Technology and Economics*. Cambridge: Cambridge University Press, 1982.

————. *Exploring the Black Box: Technology, Economics and History*. Cambridge: Cambridge University Press, 1994.

Rosenbloom, Richard, and William Spencer, editors. *Engines of Innovation: U.S. Industrial Research at the End of an Era*. Boston, MA: Harvard Business School Press, 1996.

Rush, Howard, Michael Hobday, John Bessant, Erik Arnold, and Robin Murray. *Technology Institutes: Strategies for Best Practice*. London: International Thomson Business Press, 1996.

Vincenti, Walter. *What Engineers Know and How They Know It*. Baltimore: Johns Hopkins University Press, 1991.

Papers on the 'Economics of Innovation' I have Found Helpful

Arrow, Kenneth. 'Economic Welfare and the Allocation of Resources for Invention'. In *The Rate and Direction of Inventive Activity*, edited by Richard Nelson. Princeton, NJ: Princeton University Press, 1962.

David, Paul. 'From Market Magic to Calypso Science Policy: a review of Terence Kealey's *The Economic Laws of Scientific Research'*. *Research Policy*, no. 26 (1997): 229–55.

Desai, Ashok V. 'The Origin and Direction of Industrial R&D in India'. *Research Policy*, no. 9 (1980): 74–96.

Forbes, Naushad. 'Higher Education, Scientific Research and Industry: Reflections on Priorities for India'. Speech, 4th Annual Conference on India's Economic Reforms. Stanford, CA: Stanford Center for International Development, 2003.

Klevorick, Alvin, Richard Levin, Richard Nelson, and Sidney Winter. 'On the Sources and Significance of Interindustry Differences in Technological Opportunities'. *Research Policy*, no. 24 (1995): 185–205.

Kline, Stephen Jay, and Nathan Rosenberg. 'An Overview of Innovation'. In *The Positive Sum Strategy: Harnessing Technology for Economic Growth*, edited by Ralph Landau and Nathan Rosenberg. Washington, DC: National Academies Press, 1986.

Nelson, Richard. 'The Simple Economics of Basic Scientific Research'. *Journal of Political Economy*, no. 67 (1959): 297–306.

———. 'The Role of Firms in Technical Advance'. In *Technology and Enterprise in a Historical Perspective*, edited by Giovanni Dosi, R. Giannetti, and P. Toninelli. Oxford: Clarendon Press, 1992.

Pavitt, Keith, 'The Social Shaping of the National Science Base'. *Research Policy*, no. 27 (1998): 793–805.

———. 'Public policies to Support Basic Research: What Can the Rest of the World Learn from US Theory and Practice? (And What They should Not Learn)'. *Industrial and Corporate Change*, no.10 (2001): 761–79.

History, Culture, Institutions

Acemoglu, Daron, and James Robinson. *Why Nations Fail: The Origins of Power, Prosperity and Poverty*. New York, NY: Crown Books, 2012.

————. *The Narrow Corridor: States, Societies and the Fate of Liberty.* London: Penguin Random House, 2019.

Agarwal, Pawan. *Indian Higher Education.* New Delhi: Sage, 2009.

Chandra, Pankaj. *Building Universities that Matter: Where are Indian Universities Going Wrong?* New Delhi: Orient Blackswan, 2018.

Damodaran, Harish. *India's New Capitalists: Caste, Business, and Industry in a Modern Nation.* New Delhi: Hachette, updated edition, 2018.

Dore, Ronald. *Japanese Industrialisation and the Developing Countries: Model, Warning or Source of Healthy Doubts?* Singapore: Institute of Southeast Asian Studies, 1971.

————. *British Factory, Japanese Factory.* London: George Allen and Unwin, 1973.

————. *Taking Japan Seriously: A Confucian Perspective on Economic Issues.* Stanford, CA: Stanford University Press, 1987.

————. 'Reflections on Culture and Social Change'. In *Manufacturing Miracles,* edited by Gary Gereffi and Don Wyman. Princeton, NJ: Princeton University Press, 1990.

————. *Cantankerous Essays: Musings of a Disillusioned Japanophile.* Folkestone: Renaissance Books, 2015.

Hirschman, Albert. *Essays in Trespassing: Economics to Politics and Beyond.* Cambridge, MA: Cambridge University Press, 1981.

————. *Rival Views of Market Society.* New York, NY: Viking Penguin, 1986.

————. *A Propensity to Self-Subversion.* Cambridge, MA: Harvard University Press, 1995.

Kapur, Devesh, Pratap Bhanu Mehta, and Milan Vaishnav, editors. *Rethinking Public Institutions in India.* New Delhi: Oxford University Press, 2017.

Kapur, Devesh, and Pratap Bhanu Mehta, editors. *Navigating the Labyrinth: Perspectives on India's Higher Education.* Hyderabad: Orient Blackswan, 2017.

Kapur, Devesh, D. Shyam Babu, and Chandra Bhan Prasad. *Defying the Odds: The Rise of Dalit Entrepreneurs*. New Delhi: Vintage Books/Random House India, 2014.

Khosla, Madhav, and Milan Vaishnav. 'The Three Faces of the Indian State'. *Journal of Democracy* 32, no. 1 (January 2021).

Pritchett, Lant. 'Is India a Flailing State? Detours on the Four Lane Highway to Modernization'. Faculty Working Papers RWP09-013. Cambridge, MA: Harvard Kennedy School, May 2009.

Tagore, Rabindranath. *Nationalism*. With an Introduction by Ramachandra Guha. New Delhi: Penguin Random House, 2009.

Wiener, Martin. *English Culture and the Decline of the Industrial Spirit, 1850–1980*. Cambridge: Cambridge University Press, 1981.

Useful Data Sources

CTIER. *Handbook of Technology and Innovation in India, 2019 and 2021*. Pune: CTIER, 2019 and 2021.

National Science Foundation. *Science and Engineering Indicators*. Washington, DC: National Science Foundation, 2020.

OECD. *Main Science and Technology Indicators 2020*.

OECD. *Education at a Glance 2020*.

European Union. *The 2020 EU Industrial R&D Investment Scoreboard*.

UNESCO. *Statistical Yearbook*.

World Bank. *World Development Indicators*.

List of Tables and Figures

Tables

Figures

Index

359

About the Author

Dr Naushad Forbes is co-chairman of Forbes Marshall, India's leading steam engineering and control instrumentation firm. Forbes Marshall has consistently ranked amongst India's Great Places to Work. He is also chairman of Ananta Aspen Centre and Centre for Technology, Innovation and Economic Research (CTIER).

Naushad received his bachelor's, master's and Ph.D. degrees from Stanford University, where he also taught an occasional course for twenty years. He has written widely on innovation in developing countries and higher education in India, including a book, *From Followers to Leaders*, co-authored with David Wield. He writes a monthly column for *Business Standard*.

He is on the board of several educational institutions and public companies. Naushad has long been an active member of the Confederation of Indian Industry (CII) and was president of CII for 2016–17.